The Peace
of
Christmas Eve

The Peace
of
Christmas Eve

⇒⟫ ⟪⇐

FRED L. ENGELMAN

New York
Harcourt, Brace & World, Inc.

E
358
E5

44734

Library of Congress Catalog Card Number: 62-10495
Printed in the United States of America

To Joyce

Preface by Carl Carmer

It augurs well for the future of the writing of history in America that so young and so gifted a writer as Fred Engelman has chosen history as his subject and has applied to it the skills and inspirations of an artist. It is encouraging, moreover, that Mr. Engelman recognized in the subject matter of his first book material deserving of his creative interpretations and his rhythmic and well-worded sentences.

It is obvious in *The Peace of Christmas Eve* that its author has taken as a matter of course Professor Edward Hallet Carr's recent remark that "the belief in a hard core of historical facts existing objectively and independently of the interpretation of the historian is a preposterous fallacy." Mr. Engelman regards such facts as he has found relevant much as a sculptor regards the stone from which he will chisel a work of art. This does not mean that he has not done the wearying day-by-day digging of the scholar. It indicates, rather, that at the beginning of his career as a writer of history he is aware that the readers of history, both laymen and students, insist that "scholarship" as the term is now understood is not enough. There are undoubtedly in America scholars with a special aptitude for discovery and communication of facts whose abilities do not include a talent for communicating them in effective English.

While other better-known and more experienced historians have been arguing, as does Samuel Eliot Morison, that "history is almost as much a creative art as the novel" or claiming, as does C. V. Wedgwood, that "the novelist's material is the same as that of the historian," Mr. Engelman has seen in the historic situation at Ghent a conflict involving characters of such fascinating qualities that his book takes on, without the use of artful and imaginative fiction, the semblance of it.

He understands the shadings and subtleties that exist in the minds of the representatives of the United States and Great Britain and selects from authentic sources such materials as will reveal them most successfully.

He has respectfully gone beyond "scientific history," as Mr. Morison chose to designate works that are recommended as scholarly, in an effort to achieve literary excellence. He has chosen as his goal a recountal of the facts involved in the accomplishing of a treaty to end a war which could not be regarded as generally popular in either of the two nations concerned. As the negotiations progressed, the negotiators did also. There was a development of situation and a development of character, both attributes regarded as essential in most definitions of the novel. Out of both came a peace hardly more satisfactory to the peoples of Britain and the United States than the conflict had been. The English diplomats are pictured by the author as about what might be expected. They run true to form. But there was an unseen and composite character which developed mightily in this novel history which is a true history that reads like a novel. Born of the relationship of the heterogeneous American representatives to each other and to their more homogeneous English counterparts emerged the beginning of an image which has since grown into a definable concept of the United States of America.

The disagreement between the historian as scientist and the historian as artist has not, of course, been resolved. It may never be. Still, some historians will believe that books containing the accumulation of documented facts, books complying with the disciplines of Ph.D. theses, are more important to the body of American history than any poet's interpretations published in highly readable books. The scientists continue to use such words as solid, sound, authentic, admirably annotated, and the critics who look for literary merit reply with imaginative, perceptive, sensitive, intuitive, and the like. It is probably true that both groups are sincere and both are prejudiced. It has occurred to some readers, however, and the number of these has grown of late to vast proportions, that with hard work and understanding the writer of history may come to deserve *all* these admiring adjectives. It is not unfair, in a world which demands increasing responsibilities in other fields, to insist that the historian combine the science and the art of his subject into a triumphant whole. This, I believe, Fred Engelman has done successfully. May his breed increase.

Foreword

In the more than four years since work on *The Peace of Christmas Eve* was begun, many persons have assisted me in the preparation and writing of it. Certainly more than are mentioned in the following paragraphs are deserving of thanks. I can only trust that all who have given help and encouragement will somehow realize how appreciative I am for what they have done, and I hope that this book, so much the product of their generosity and knowledge, will not disappoint their expectations.

To three gentlemen, especially, do I owe gratitude: to Samuel Eliot Morison, the distinguished historian of Harvard and the United States Navy, who first assured me that I could write history and should publish what I wrote; to Dr. F. A. Kertess, my good friend, patron, and counselor; and to Carl Carmer, whose example, advice, and friendship have created a pleasant debt that can never be repaid.

I am indebted also to a number of libraries and librarians and wish to thank them for permission to quote from manuscript collections in their possession: the William L. Clements Library, University of Michigan, and particularly the Director of that library, Howard H. Peckham, who brought the very significant Henry Goulburn Papers to my attention; the John Hay Library, Brown University, and Norma Kacen, Assistant, Special Collections; David C. Mearns, Chief of the Manuscript Division of the Library of Congress; the New-York Historical Society and the assistance of Wilmer R. Leach, that library's Curator of Manuscripts; and the National Archives.

To the New York Public Library, however, more than any other, I owe thanks, perhaps even rent. Dr. Gerald McDonald, Chief of the American History and Genealogy Division, Robert W. Hill, Keeper of Manuscripts, Ralph Smith, Wilson G. Duprey, Betty Roth, Shirley L. Spranger, Paul R. Hugen, and Jean McNiece, among others of its staff, have been unfailingly helpful, patient, and kind; and Leon Weidman, who has suffered the project virtually since its inception, has given of his service and sympathy far beyond the call of even the most dedicated librarian.

And I express sincere thanks, too, to those who have helped so much in the editing and final preparation of the book—especially James R. Jacobs and Edith Goldstein.

Lastly, though I abhor possible implications of togetherness, I must confess that there might be no book at all, certainly none at this time, if it were not for my mother and my wife. The former is the cheapest, best, and most devoted and flattering typist I know. I offer inadequate thanks to the latter in the dedication of this book.

Fred L. Engelman

Hastings-on-Hudson, New York
December, 1961

Contents

Illustrations
(between pages 176 and 177)

March of the British army to Washington. (*Inset*) The Battle of Blandensburg.
E. D. Ingraham. *A Sketch of the Events Which Preceded the Capture of Washington, by the British*. Philadelphia, 1849. (*Inset*) John S. Williams. *History of the Invasion and Capture of Washington*. New York, 1857.

Plan of the Siege of Plattsburg and Capture of the British Fleet on Lake Champlain.
"Select British Documents of the Canadian War of 1812." Ed. William Wood. *The Publications of the Champlain Society*. Toronto, 1926. Map from Dominion Archives of Canada.

Macdonough's Victory on Lake Champlain.
Phelps Stokes Collection, New York Public Library.

The Signing of the Treaty of Ghent, 1814.
National Collection of Fine Arts, Smithsonian Institution.

Bruin become Mediator or Negociation for Peace.
Print Room, New York Public Library.

The Hartford Convention or Leap No Leap.
Print Room, New York Public Library.

PART ONE

War and Mediation

The Wages of War
and the Promise of Mediation

A chilling breeze filled the sails of the *Neptune* as she bore southeast, away from the Orkney Islands toward the Skagerrak. To the east the gray Norwegian coast was an abrupt palisade against the spread of the cold blue waters of the North Sea. The morning sky was spotlessly clear. The day, June 18, 1813, was the fortieth day of the *Neptune's* voyage, the first anniversary of the American declaration of war against Great Britain.

The three-hundred-ton vessel carried twenty-three crew members and eleven passengers. On this bright Friday, everyone who did not have to remain below huddled in sheltered but sunny corners of the deck or sought warmth and exercise by pacing its perimeter. It was one of the few pleasant days of the journey, and as rare as the day was Albert Gallatin's appearance above deck. His face was sallow, more so than usual, and from underneath a black and tangled but receding mass of hair his dark eyes struggled to adjust to sunlight. This long-nosed Genevan, Secretary of the Treasury of the United States, was one of President James Madison's key advisers and one of the two principal members of the *Neptune's* passenger list.

For more than eleven years Gallatin had guided the financial affairs of the administrations of Jefferson and Madison. He was privy to the government's most intimate and far-reaching decisions. Some thought that he was the genius of Madison's cabinet. To a few he was an evil genius. But whatever the character of his political brilliance, he was a patient and devoted counselor. He had tried, with some success, to build a stable economic foundation at a time his country was caught in the political eddies of a world at war. With less success, he had

expressed doubts concerning a national policy of economic retaliation—without the sinews of military strength—against the
world's two great warring powers, France and Great Britain. He
had felt little sympathy for Jefferson's embargo. He had watched
Madison's weapon of nonintercourse drain the coffers of the
Treasury. A moral man and a wise one, he had neither wanted
war nor thought his country prepared to fight, but after years
of Congressional drift and dissent and the paucity of administrative leadership he could see no other course but to lend his
tacit assent to hostilities. The results had been a harvest of
military fiascos and impoverishment of the national government;
so that when Emperor Alexander I of Russia had offered to
mediate between Britain and the United States and President
Madison had happily seized the opportunity, Gallatin had with
alacrity volunteered his services. Now he and James A. Bayard,
Federalist Senator from Delaware, were Ministers Plenipotentiary and Extraordinary of the United States, on their way to
St. Petersburg to seek peace.

For nearly six weeks they had been without news of the war
at home or of Napoleon's fate on the Continent. On Sunday,
May 9, at New Castle, Delaware, Gallatin's and Bayard's families
had wished them bon voyage, and at three that afternoon the
Neptune had slipped her cables and eased into the Delaware.
The wind being light, it was not until Tuesday morning that the
ship passed between the Capes and headed into an Atlantic
sunrise and the path of the vigilant British navy. Bayard, an
early riser, was still digesting his breakfast when the British
thirty-eight-gun warship Spartan parted from the pack of block-
aders, pulled abreast, and demanded the Neptune's papers. The
incident, occurring within sight of the American shore, left no
doubt as to which belligerent controlled American waters.

Neither breeze nor British ship ruffled the calm of that afternoon, and it was not until Tuesday evening that the Neptune
made any forward progress. By nightfall, though, the stillness
had given way to a surly gale that plunged the protesting ship
into the boiling waters of the Atlantic. It was but a taste of things
to come. With a persistence suggesting that nature was in British
employ, one tempest followed another. Saturday morning, Bayard
ventured timidly through the bulkhead onto the pitching deck.
"The sky was dark, the waves ran mountain high, the wind roared

thro the ropes of the ship," and to Bayard, who had never been out of the country, "the sight was awful and sublime."

For weeks the storms continued. During most of that time only Bayard and young John Payne Todd, secretary to Gallatin and son of Dolly Madison's first marriage, possessed wills and stomachs strong enough to get them out of the gloom of the cabins. In the infrequent placid interludes, Bayard and Gallatin, taking one another's measure, discussed the war and their instructions from Secretary of State Monroe. The two ministers had known each other but distantly for a decade. Bayard had voted against the war. His political life had been spent in opposition to the Republican party which had raised Gallatin to its inner circle. Fearing he might be intended as scapegoat, the handsome Senator from Delaware suffered grave doubts about the mission on which he was embarking. He tried to gain Gallatin's confidence, but the latter, tight-lipped in any case, was now governed by the violent and unrelenting distress in his vitals. The *Neptune* was nearly three weeks at sea when Bayard, in disgust, confided to his diary that Gallatin "has scarcely ever recovered his spirits and gaiety after one gale, before he was deprived of them by another. This is the more unfortunate as he stands in need of the whole stock with which nature has supplied to render him tolerable company."

In time even Bayard's more adventurous spirits were stifled by the turbulent weather. After he was nearly flushed from the deck he stuck closer to his cabin, but he could not sleep and it was too cold to read or write with any comfort. The monotony was oppressive. The only break came early one morning in late May when the *Neptune* was hailed by the United States brig *Ida*, beating its way westward to Boston. The *Ida* waited while the *Neptune*'s passengers hastily wrote letters to their families. To the homesick Bayard, overwhelmed with affection for his wife and children some 1,300 miles away, it was a moment of pardon from a prison afloat in brine and harboring insufferable companions.

Life took on more cheer as the ship neared the Scottish coast, and the weather and men's dispositions improved. The barren hills of the Orkney Islands were a refreshing novelty, and throughout Friday and Saturday, June 18 and 19, a bright sun played on the crevices of the Norwegian fiords to port. When

Gallatin and Bayard came on deck on Sunday morning they found the *Neptune* safely anchored in the channel that led to Gothenburg, Sweden.

While the *Neptune* sat in quarantine, waiting for Swedish officials to grant clearance, the ministers and their secretaries were rowed ashore to scamper about the naked rocks, like children on a school holiday. The next morning they set out by boat and then by horse and carriage on the ten-mile trip to town. At four in the afternoon their carriages rumbled through the ancient stone gate of Gothenburg, down to the broad, canal-riven main street, under the lindens, and past the East India warehouses, the cathedral, the market square, the Governor's mansion. The market reminded Bayard of Dover, Delaware, and he marveled at the women flaying their wash on rafts in the canal. At the inn at the far end of the street the party came to a halt. The ministers were quickly embraced by Mr. Fosdick, a native of Boston and acting United States consul.

After six weeks aboard ship the reluctant sailors rejoiced at the prospect of a night in a structure that neither tilted nor trembled, and their hearts were warmed by the sight of a fellow countryman. With Fosdick and other Americans of Gothenburg who could be gathered on short notice the envoys spent an evening of reunion exchanging news, dissecting rumors in search of some morsel of truth. The resident Americans, some of them for years strangers to their homeland, were restless with questions on the war and chances for peace. As well as they could, Gallatin and Bayard answered their queries.

Probably none of the Americans at the dinner table in Gothenburg asked why war had been declared. The causes of hostilities were as old as some of the men who sat there sawing the resistant beef and prodding the lobsters. In any event, all Americans, wherever they lived, thought they knew why war had broken out or were equally sure that no just man could ever give a reasonable explanation. Gallatin was one who believed he knew why, although he was also aware that the story was not entirely flattering to the administrations which he had so long served. Bayard was certain that the war could have been avoided. Both men ardently desired peace, but neither felt well-assured that peace would come soon or in accordance with their instructions.

In the year since war had been declared the American nation had been sobered by a series of military calamities that surpassed the dire expectations of her foremost pessimists. Not every American in June, 1812, had been filled with confidence, but most thought that Britain, harassed by the evil and apparently invincible Napoleon, would be reasonable in the face of the dreadful possibilities of losing North American trade and real estate. Impressment—the obnoxious English practice of removing her native-born and occasionally American-born seamen from American ships and ports—would cease. Illegal blockades, an excuse for high-seas piracy, would no longer be imposed. American trade never again would be regulated, taxed, or destroyed by British Orders in Council. Payment would be demanded for scores of illegal seizures of men and goods and ships. And, as a crowning glory, the United States would be enlarged by the addition of Canada and both the Floridas, the latter the possessions of Spain, Britain's ally, including the later state of Florida and a strip of Gulf Coast that extended to the Mississippi.

Since President Washington's second administration the youthful American Republic had been battered by the violence released by the convulsions of the French Revolution and its aftermath—by the far-reaching effects of the death struggle between Britain and France, Europe's titans and the only powers that could and did threaten disaster to a transatlantic neutral. Washington declared neutrality, sought agreements with both belligerents, and finally, in Jay's Treaty, bowed to British preponderance, saving his fragile nation from premature dissolution. John Adams, his successor, preserved the tenuous truce with England and, despite much provocation, staved off a break with France. As the nineteenth century opened, the United States, though enduring her first "cold war," was largely intact and officially at peace.

The task of continuing the peace passed to an agrarian philosopher to whom pacifism was almost a religion. At first, President Thomas Jefferson's burden was lightened by a temporary lowering of the European fever, but old sores festered and in 1813 Europe's Napoleonic infection was once more virulent. Great Britain knew that against Napoleon's mastery of the Continent she must maintain her control of the seas or perish.

"Boney will get you" was not just an idle threat to recalcitrant children. Boney might. And successive English cabinets, hoping to starve France and simultaneously fill English mouths and pockets, issued a series of Orders in Council, the net effect of which was to mock neutral trade—mostly American—and make it an adjunct to the British merchant marine. Bonaparte, who thought that neutrality during wartime was a fiction, answered with his Berlin and Milan decrees, closing Continental ports to ships that had seen British goods or British harbors. This dual challenge produced a gamblers' heaven. To American merchants the choice lay between letting their ships rot in their berths or taking the chance of making substantial profits before almost certain seizure and condemnation. Their decision need hardly be stated. In 1801, a year of relative peace, American exports exceeded $94,000,000; in 1803, when France and England announced the rules of the game, the sum had diminished to slightly less than $56,000,000; by 1804 the merchants were learning, and their outward-bound ships carried nearly $78,000,000 worth of goods; more than $95,000,000 in 1805; and a high of $108,000,-000 in 1807. That neutrality no longer existed and profits meant prostitution mattered little to those who reaped the harvest. This was not, however, the reaction of the Federal Government.

To Jefferson war was neither a means nor an end, but on the other hand, he could not allow American pride and integrity to be surrendered by acts of international piracy. His answer was to meet economic coercion by commercial restrictions of his own. Britain appeared to be the prime malefactor, and Jefferson's means of punishment was the Nonimportation Act, calling for self-denial of British manufactures, which went into effect in December, 1807. Long before Gandhi, Jefferson discovered the sometimes dubious rewards of passive resistance.

The flaw in his scheme lay in his obvious inability to take stronger measures. The yearling democracy that was the United States had never possessed a "big stick," and Jefferson took Adams's slender whip and whittled it down to a twig. The army would hardly have terrorized a tribe of passive Indians. The navy, consisting of a handful of frigates and a collection of unseaworthy gunboats, presented the awesome specter of a flotilla of bathtub toys. The British soon had an opportunity to express their disdain.

Shortly after seven on a June morning in 1807, before the application of the Nonimportation Act, the U.S.S. *Chesapeake,* nominally a forty-gun frigate, unfolded her canvas to a sturdy breeze and pointed her prow toward the Atlantic. Her decks were strewn with lumber and cables and gun parts. Her novice crew had scarcely had an opportunity to test-fire her weapons, some of which were not even securely fastened to the deck. Her captain, Commodore James Barron, had not been three weeks with his crew. But America was at peace on a peaceful day, and the distance of the *Chesapeake's* destination, the Mediterranean, offered ample time to set things in order.

By nine o'clock she had cleared Norfolk harbor and was cutting a wake through Lynnhaven Bay, past a squadron of British warships. The squadron, enjoying American hospitality, was lying in wait for passing Frenchmen. One of the squadron, the fifty-gun *Leopard,* cut loose from the others and took a path parallel to that of the *Chesapeake.* The British movements, which could be clearly observed from the deck of the American ship, created no anxiety. The sight of British men-of-war in American waters was as common as the knowledge that nearly every day one of them cruised off the Capes in search of enemy stragglers.

At noon, with the *Chesapeake* now a mile or two off Cape Henry, her officers sat down to a hearty dinner. A mile to the northeast the *Leopard* was still in view. In midafternoon the American vessel tacked shoreward to meet the pilot boat; the Britisher adjusted her movements accordingly. Her pilot dismissed, the *Chesapeake* headed into open sea, and by three thirty both she and the *Leopard,* still following a parallel course, were about ten miles from land. At that moment the *Leopard* came around. With the wind at her tail she bore down on the *Chesapeake.*

When the *Leopard* pulled alongside, her captain called across that he had dispatches to send over. Barron granted permission for a boat to be sent, and in a few minutes a British lieutenant, dispatches in hand, stood in Barron's cabin. Under a covering note from Captain Humphrey of the *Leopard* was an order from British Admiral Berkeley, listing certain British ships and deserters from them, some of whom were presumed to be aboard the *Chesapeake.* The men were to be searched for and surrendered.

Barron knew that he had deserters from one of the British ships anchored in Lynnhaven Bay, but, as far as he was aware, his crew contained none of the men listed by Berkeley. He said so to the English officer and repeated the same denial in a hastily penned note to Humphrey, adding, "I am also instructed never to permit the crew of any ship that I command to be mustered by any other but their own officers. It is my disposition to preserve harmony, and I hope this answer to your despatch will prove satisfactory."

It did not. Even while Barron conferred with the British lieutenant, the *Chesapeake's* officers grew suspicious of actions aboard the *Leopard.* When Barron was informed of them he ordered his men to go quietly to their stations. His order came too late; under the best of conditions the *Chesapeake* would have needed a half hour to prepare for battle, and conditions were far from the best. Humphrey, after his officer had returned, shouted across that Barron's answer would not do, that he must search the *Chesapeake's* crew. Barron, stalling desperately for time, called back that he could not understand what Humphrey had said. The British captain repeated his message. Once more, Barron pretended he could not hear. The British answer was prompt and could have been heard even by the deaf. A shot boomed across the *Chesapeake's* bow; a minute later another followed, and the *Chesapeake's* crew fell into a frenzy of preparation. But their time had run out—the *Leopard,* not two hundred feet away, burst out in vivid orange blotches, and the *Chesapeake* shuddered under the impact. The American crew, several of them spurting blood, could do no more than reply with angry curses through anguished tears. Again the *Leopard* spat out all the lead it could. And fifteen minutes after the first broadside came a third, crumpling men's bodies, leaving woodwork and rigging in splinters and tatters. Three men lay dead; eighteen, including Commodore Barron, were wounded. Barron gave the only order now possible. The American flag slid down its pole, and, as the flag collapsed in a heap on the deck, the one gun the *Chesapeake* was able to fire spoke its lonely report of defeat. Humphrey impressed four men and, satisfied that his duty was done, refused Barron's offer of the surrender of his ship. Late that night, the *Chesapeake,* the varnish of the blood on her decks shining in the moonlight, limped back to Norfolk.

The news of the *Chesapeake*'s humbling, like a tongue of bitter flame, seared the country. Politicians cut chunks of air with flailing arms. Mass meetings were held in cities and towns and wilderness clearings. Men oiled their guns and arranged for others to take care of their farms or businesses. Not for ten years had Americans been so anxious to fight.

The fever of retaliation spread even to Jefferson. He ordered British warships out of American ports and waters and sent for all American warships to return home posthaste. Governors received his call to muster their militia. The American ship *Revenge* sailed swiftly to England, bearing a demand that that government disavow its despicable act and end impressment once and for all. But no one, especially the English, took Jefferson's threats seriously. Like an evangelist mesmerized by the big sign in his tent, Jefferson could not for long consider actions that transgressed against peace. He would not fight, and a month after the fateful incident no one any longer expected him to.

The sharp edge of the *Chesapeake* affair was dulled and obscured by an eroding river of diplomatic verbiage. No adequate compensation was ever received from the British. Perhaps none, except that which pride and power could exact, was possible. In 1812, weeks before a confused and divided United States declared war, Great Britain paid token indemnities and of the four men who had been seized restored the two still living. But this gesture of restitution was too late and too little.

An act of violence was a phenomenon to which Jefferson could not adjust—any more than a gentleman can feel at ease when caught in the midst of a barroom scuffle. To impressment, to arbitrary and changing definitions of contraband, to illegal seizures of ships and goods, to the British Orders in Council, to Napoleon's answering decrees, to all assaults on and distortions of free ships and free goods and free men Jefferson decreed what he thought was the only, the certain act of retaliation: embargo. The means, as he conceived it, of bringing a wily and willful Napoleon to his knees, of humbling the outrageous and arrogant John Bull, was to close American harbors and keep American ships at home. Jefferson hoped, by ordering an absolute cessation of American participation in international trade, to starve the two principal combatants and perhaps all Europe.

It cannot be said that Congress or Jefferson's cabinet greeted his plan of an embargo with enthusiasm but, bereft of ideas of their own, the majority of the members acceded to it. Gallatin, to whose sorry lot fell the task of enforcement, was incredulous. Nevertheless, he did his utmost to see that the Act was obeyed, and in the process gained the undying hatred of many. To the opposition Federalists this measure, which seemed to them insane, was proof, if proof were needed, that Jefferson and his henchmen were in the employ of the French Empire. The embargo, which went into effect just before Christmas, 1807, seemed to New England, the beehive of Federalism, little short of an act of civil war by the rest of the Union. It struck the area from Portland, Maine, to New York City with the impact of a sudden noxious fog.

France, one of the two primary objects of America's self-blockade, was but little moved by it. What trade the French enjoyed outside the Continent was a mere seepage through the oceanic dike thrown up by the British navy. The trickle became a drop. Napoleon was apparently merely amused by the act. He confiscated all American ships, those already at sea and those which escaped, that ventured into French ports—in order, he said, to help Jefferson enforce his laws.

The punishment inflicted upon the British Empire was greater, especially upon her Caribbean islands, and had the embargo been continued for some years it might have had the results Jefferson anticipated. But the suffering from this questionable measure was greatest in the country that sponsored it. Seaports for a time became ghost towns, except where armed mobs made their own laws. United States Treasury funds, which depended heavily on customs collections, shrank to insignificance. Men swarmed the streets looking for employment. Prices rose fantastically. Worse, perhaps, than all of this was the inducement to accept crime and rebellion as natural conditions. Beaches where terns and gulls had known solitude became bustling quays for pirated goods. A thriving coastal trade developed among ships which wandered for days and weeks from their pretended courses. Along the Canadian border, alive with illicit activity, Americans spilled one another's blood. Men either cheated or they forswore the sea and took up manufacturing. Even this latter pursuit, the only positive result of the embargo, was a mockery to Jefferson.

The man who could never quite accept commercial pursuits as
suitable or completely honest, the champion of the landed com-
moner, unwittingly provided the impetus for the growth of
American industry.

For all countries, save Britain and France, the embargo was
repealed on March 1, 1809, three days before Jefferson wearily
passed on the office of the Presidency to his Secretary of State, a
quiet, fragile, prematurely wizened little man who possessed a
dry sense of humor, a dislike for campaigning, and an inquisitive
and penetrating intelligence. James Madison, known to his de-
tractors as "Little Jemmy," was one of the Fathers of his country.
The Constitution, the Virginia Plan which was one of the major
components of that notable document, and the Bill of Rights
owed much of their existence to this scholarly Virginia planter.
With Hamilton and John Jay, he had also authored the Federalist Papers, those remarkable pamphlets of political wisdom that
had so influenced a weak and divided country to adopt a Federal Government.

"Among the numerous advantages promised by a well-con-
structed Union," he had written in Federalist Paper No. 10 in
the *New York Packet,* November 23, 1787, "none deserves to be
more accurately developed than its tendency to break and control the violence of faction. The friend of popular governments
never finds himself so much alarmed for their character and
fate, as when he contemplates their propensity to this dangerous
vice." In his eight years as President, Madison was to know the
awful evils of "this dangerous vice" more than had any of his
predecessors. It was to be under his own aegis (he being partly
to blame) that the Federal Union which he had helped to create
waged its first war and suffered its first real threat of secession.

If political experience, as Americans have frequently been led
to believe, is a major qualification for the nation's highest office,
James Madison possessed an abundance of riches. Since the
age of twenty-five, when he was just four years out of Princeton,
he had served in nearly every colonial, confederate, state, and
federal office to which Virginia could elect or appoint him.
Throughout Washington's administrations the dignified, affable
Madison sat in the House of Representatives, first as a leading
Federalist and later, when he became appalled at Alexander

Hamilton's ambitions, as one of the growing tribe of Thomas Jefferson's disciples. When John Adams succeeded Washington, Madison voluntarily retired to Montpelier to farm, read, and snipe at the new President.

Madison's retreat from the active political scene was only temporary, and ended in 1801, when he became Jefferson's first and only Secretary of State. Not only did Madison bring a breadth of knowledge and some stability to Jefferson's chaotic and eccentric conduct of foreign affairs, but to Washington, a muddy, uncivilized backwoods capital, he brought his vivacious and charming wife Dolly. The thin, stunted philosopher with a face creased like a prune and the gay and buxom widow of a Philadelphia lawyer made an incongruous but happy pair. Furthermore, they brought a touch of sophisticated manners to a city crude in facilities and an administration lacking in grace. Since Jefferson was a widower, Dolly was therefore her nation's first lady, a title she kept for sixteen years. No other first lady, moreover, was to suffer such a combination of indignities as having to flee before an enemy through the woods, of seeing her official residence in ashes, or of eventually inadvertently lending her name to a brand of ice cream.

Dolly was an asset to her husband and to the hub of the American government, but she had neither the talents nor the power to improve the course of foreign relations. This responsibility was primarily her husband's; his inaugural address, which he delivered almost inaudibly, standing pale and trembling before the assembled Houses of Congress, indicated his sense of the weight of the burden he had assumed. "Assuring myself that under every vicissitude the determined spirit and united councils of the nation will be safeguards to its honor and essential interests," he said on that March day to a perplexed and abused nation, "I repair to the post assigned to me, with no other discouragement than what springs from my own inadequacy to its higher duties." It was hardly a message of confidence, and from the rest of his speech it was clear that his armory of international weapons offered nothing new. He was a man of reason and reasonableness in a world that seldom cogitated and long ago had set aside the rules of polite society.

Although the embargo was no longer more than an incident in a history lesson, the strategy of economic coercion lingered like a mother-in-law in residence. By the Nonintercourse Law, which replaced or, more accurately, revised, Jefferson's self-blockade, American ports were opened and her ships were once again free to trade with all countries that were not under British or French control. It was hoped that this measure would prove to be an effective agent for pitting one belligerent against the other. Instead, it stimulated American merchants and the French and British governments to conspire in a furtive and politically unhealthy game. The rules engendered by greed and the British navy decided what ports were or were not under French or English control, and American trade, abused though it was by both warring powers, flourished once more.

Again, of course, vessels, materials, and men were sequestered by Napoleonic or British whim or decree, and as long as gains exceeded losses, ships, goods, and men were expendable, and honor and liberty were subservient to profit. Such at least was the rationale for the behavior of many who lived in or near Atlantic ports. As one traveled south or west into predominantly Republican areas, however, adjustment to international larceny was less readily accepted, and Madison was aware that his own future, and that of his party and his country, depended on some action that would assert the rights and privileges of America. Dreading war almost as much as Jefferson and committed, through want of a greater revelation, to Jefferson's policy of commercial sanctions, Madison sought frantically for some sort of diplomatic coup. The mirage of one, at least, was not long in coming.

The illusion manifested itself in the person and sympathies of David Erskine, British minister to the United States and husband of an American wife. Erskine's zeal for Anglo-American accord, almost as intense as Madison's, induced him to suppress part of his instructions and alter much of the remainder. Thanks to the congruity of aims and some curious negotiations between Erskine, Madison, and Robert Smith, the bumbling Secretary of State, the new President, not more than a month after his induction into office, was able to announce what became known as the Erskine agreement. The three negotiators were happily intoxicated with the belief that the effects of the American Nonintercourse Law on Great Britain, and that of the British Orders in Council on the United States, would vanish simultaneously.

The date for this miraculous occurrence was set for June 10, 1809.

In the early hours of that June day hundreds of American ships hoisted their sails and, like fish released from a hatchery, scooted into the Atlantic. Hundreds more followed soon after. It was but a matter of weeks before English docks were cluttered with American goods—produce that served as a restorative from the emaciating inroads of nonimportation, embargo, and nonintercourse. Ordinary Englishmen were relieved. The President of the United States was jubilant. He had, with one stroke, it seemed, put an end to futile commercial warfare, obliterated its effects, and restored amity between the United States and its parent country.

Even the hostile Federalists condescended to praise Madison's astounding feat, but, unknown to Americans, the beautiful vision had in fact been doomed to destruction more than two weeks before the burdened American vessels had been released from their home ports. News of Erskine's agreement reached the British government late in May; Erskine was immediately repudiated and recalled, and as American ships tacked merrily up the Thames the British press reached a point of hysteria in its denunciation of Erskine for disobeying his instructions and of Madison for complicity in a dishonorable bargain. To the supercilious George Canning, British Minister for Foreign Affairs, the agreement and America's hasty publication of it confirmed his impression of the feeble cunning that permeated American politics. "The premature publication of the correspondence by the American government so effectually precluded any middle course of explanation and accommodation," noted Canning with his customary sarcasm, "that it is hardly possible to suppose that it must not have been resorted to in a great measure with that view." Canning lacked the charity to recognize either honest zeal or simple gullibility. Devious and therefore suspect himself, he suspected all others.

That America would eventually if tardily go to war was certain from the day, July 21, 1809, that Madison's administration received word of the British disavowal of the arrangement with Erskine. Madison the hero became Madison the bungler and the fraud. The Federalist press, which had momentarily praised the President, accepted Canning's version of the affair and indulged in rude abuse. Madison's own Republican party wondered at this Executive its votes had wrought and promptly resumed its customary internal wrangling.

By autumn, international relations had returned to their usual state of disarray. Napoleon was busily enacting new decrees and seizing American ships. Great Britain was firmly enforcing her Orders in Council. And in the United States nonintercourse was again the law of the land, and the friendly, sympathetic David Erskine had been replaced by Francis James Jackson, a proper English snob with an inflammable temper, who thought that Madison was a "rather mean-looking little man" and was soon to describe the administration as "a mob." It was obvious that Canning and many others in England despised their former colonies and little expected them to fight.

Nevertheless, at the end of 1809 the United States was still more than two years from war—largely because it knew not how to get out of or into one. Congress met that winter and strengthened the generalization that America's principal legislative body has always been a stage for low comedy. Men introduced bills only to vote against them. The Senate waged war on the House. Republicans did their utmost to ruin other Republicans and their measures and to discredit their own administration. The Federalists gave every indication they had been appointed by George III. It was not until May 1, 1810, only hours away from adjournment and the automatic expiration of the Nonintercourse Law, that a weary, irritated Congress passed Macon's Bill No. 2, for the most part because it had to pass something before its members could go home.

Macon's Bill No. 2, oddly enough named for a member of the House who had not written, supported, or favored it, was a curious hodgepodge of compromise and desperation and not quite what anyone had intended. It reopened trade with both France and Great Britain and stated that if before March 3, 1811, one of them should remove or greatly revise its restrictions against American commerce, and the other not do likewise within three months, the United States would restore the nonintercourse rule against the noncomplying power. It was assumed, of course, that if one nation so allowed itself to be blackmailed the other would soon be compelled to follow suit. But it was also generally realized that nonintercourse would be an insufficient weapon against whichever power might not co-operate. In short, Macon's Bill No. 2 clearly paved the road to war.

Napoleon, furiously engaged as he was in fighting most of Europe at once, nevertheless appreciated the niceties of extortion, as should one who had long been a master of the art, and he could always afford time to enjoy the erratic creations of the American government. He had relatively little to lose if America should join the coalition against him; for, as matters stood, so-called neutral American trade was governed by British edict and the British navy, and open hostilities could not do much to worsen the situation.

Both Napoleon and his subordinates held or confiscated American ships and goods as their moods and opportunities dictated. This infuriated Americans and their government, but it was not likely to cause war with France unless war with England, apparently the greater malefactor, occurred simultaneously. Ship seizures evoked only repetitious and ineffectual complaints from the American government and minuscule profits. Napoleon could expect greater advantages from an irrevocable break between England and the United States. Macon's Bill No. 2 was honed to perfection to fulfill Napoleon's desire for a stratagem to this end.

Napoleon withheld his trump until he had played his other tricks, but on August 5, 1810, his Foreign Minister handed a letter to John Armstrong, American minister to France. The note stated that "the decrees of Berlin and Milan are revoked, and that after the 1st of November they will cease to have effect; it being understood that, in consequence of this declaration, the English shall revoke their orders in council, and renounce the new principles of blockade . . . or that the United States . . . shall cause their rights to be respected by the English." Although Napoleon secretly ordered the sale of sequestered American ships on the same day and although there was not a particle of evidence to suggest French withdrawal of their decrees, Armstrong accepted and transmitted the letter without comment.

That fall, shortly after the United States had learned of Napoleon's apparent compliance with Macon's Bill No. 2, George III, King of England, passed irretrievably beyond the borders of sanity. Madison, as if in imitation, accepted Bonaparte's dubious statement as a promise of compliance and on

November 2, 1810, issued a proclamation threatening the restoration of nonintercourse against Great Britain if she did not repeal her Orders in Council within three months. Madison wanted desperately to believe that American commercial restrictions had finally worked, and, perversely, refused to acknowledge that no real change had occurred in the Napoleonic scheme of things. In March, 1811, nonintercourse was once more enforced against the English, and British-American relations disintegrated accordingly.

Mad as its sovereign was, the English government had not surrendered to hallucinations prompted by Napoleon. In time, even Madison was forced to adopt the argument that while France had not altered her edicts in practice she had done so in principle. This spurious reasoning was not very convincing to fellow Americans; to the British it was preposterous. Furthermore, it smacked of alliance with France and desertion of Britain at a time when she was fighting the world's battle against a monster. There were Englishmen who would admit that impressment and commercial restrictions were not always applied judiciously, but the measures themselves were imperative if England were to win the Napoleonic death struggle. Certainly Great Britain was not to be overthrown by a former group of colonies that the British very reluctantly and only occasionally regarded as an independent government.

The British replaced their irascible minister, Francis James Jackson, with a more amiable one, but they deliberately gave the new man no latitude to enter into serious negotiations, and the year 1811 dragged out its miserable and unpromising course. In November a new Congress met. Nearly half the membership of the House had been replaced by young men from the West and South—men who promptly took control of that body, elected Henry Clay as Speaker, and incessantly demanded war. In April, 1812, a new ninety-day embargo went into effect, obviously a prelude to sterner measures. In late May, Madison held long meetings with his cabinet, and on June 1 he called on Congress to declare war. Three days later the House strongly supported his request by a vote of 79 to 49. The Senate, with a greater proportion of Federalists in its membership, spent more than two weeks in bitter debate and finally resolved for war by a vote of 19 to 13. On June 18, 1812, James Madison proclaimed war against

Great Britain because of that nation's impressment of American seamen, her violation of the American three-mile limit of sovereignty, her paper blockades, and her Orders in Council. Madison did not know that two days before his fateful announcement Lord Castlereagh, Canning's replacement as British Foreign Secretary, had told a sober House of Commons that the Orders in Council were to be revoked so far as they affected the United States. England had suffered a bitter winter of starvation and defeat, and Bonaparte, the scourge of mankind, especially of Englishmen, was on the verge of invading Russia and perhaps of making Europe and part of Asia forever French. Castlereagh hoped that the suspension of the Orders would mollify the American clamor for hostilities and allow Britain to gain time and strength. But his move came after the fact. America made her declaration on the 18th; the Orders were canceled on the 23rd; Napoleon thundered into Russia on the 26th. The world, from the Mississippi to the Niemen, became maddened and belligerent.

Ostensibly, Americans took up arms for freedom of the seas, but, after the Orders in Council had been suspended, impressment remained as the only important maritime matter to be resolved. It seemed strange, however, that impressment should be almost the sole professed reason for bloodshed in 1812, when in 1807, the year of the humbling of the *Chesapeake,* it had caused bitterness but not battle. It seemed stranger still if one considered the vote for war. Federalist New England, home of most of the ships that were seized and most of the men who were impressed, cast an almost unanimous vote in the negative. Most of the opposition to the war, in fact, was centered in districts that lined the seaboard. The call to conflict came from the "war hawks" of the South and West, the young men who had fired the Twelfth Congress into a fighting frenzy, "pepperpot politicians" who for the most part had never seen the ocean and whose firsthand knowledge of vessels was largely restricted to ferryboats and canoes. Not softened by profits made from international piracy and human loss and degradation, they genuinely itched to punish Britain and restore American pride. They became apoplectic at the thought of American men and ships and goods being expended for peace and pieces of silver.

But Napoleon, too, was guilty of impressment, and in the preceding five years he had destroyed more American shipping than had England. Yet an act of war against France failed by a vote of 18 to 14 in the Senate, for the Southerners and the Westerners who cast the bulk of the votes for hostilities against Great Britain wanted to drive the Indians from the Northwest, wanted to annex East and West Florida—possessions of a crumbling Spain who was Britain's ally—and wanted above all to incorporate Canada into the Union. The demands for free men and free ships were not idle exhortations, but the burning quest that set men to fighting was the desire for land and more land. In Congress during the months preceding the war one word—Canada—was heard again and again and again.

Madison was not immune to the lust for territory, but his reasons for deciding on war were not so blatant as were those of the members of the national legislature. To the President the acquisition of land was not the purpose of the war; addition of territory was only a natural concomitant of efforts that were necessary to win rights from Great Britain. War was the only national policy that was left; everything else had been tried and found wanting. War came as naturally and as inexplicably as night. But Madison was sure it would be a brief war. England would be shocked into a state of reason. The United States would find unity in a common cause. America would grow more powerful in the ranks of nations, and her boundaries, if Britain did not sue quickly for peace, would soon stretch from the Caribbean to the Arctic.

A great and sudden surge into Canada was not a unanimous American expectation, for the Northeastern part of the country was adamant about and sometimes violent in its defiance of the war, and New England throughout refused men and money to her own national government, while supplying a largess of materials to the enemy. But in the rest of the nation the vision of an easy conquest amounted to a mania. Henry Clay boasted that but a handful of Kentuckians would have to walk into Canada to accomplish the deed, and even Thomas Jefferson momentarily lost his head and echoed the sentiment.

The Americans, however, tended to exert more energy in declaring than in preparing for war. Congress did call for increased enlistments in the army, but the legislators disbanded before

voting money for the army or for any other war purposes, neg-
lecting the feeble navy altogether. For the great crusade against
the remaining British possession in North America the United
States had a pitiable army led by incompetent generals, an insignificant navy, a doddering Secretary of War who had been a
surgeon in the Revolutionary War, and a President who thought
he could inspire a martial spirit by marching through the War
and Navy Departments in a little round hat with an enormous
cockade.

From such seeds of inspired preparation came a quick and
angry harvest, the nature of which should not have been unexpected. Even before war had been declared troops were as-
sembling in Ohio for the parade northward. On July 12 they were
crossing the Detroit River into Upper Canada, the peninsula that
noses from Lake Ontario into Lakes Erie and Huron. Victory
seemed certain, and Americans grasped at every particle of news
or rumor that filtered back through the Northwest wilderness.
In early August, however, General William Hull, the would-be
conqueror, was pleading for reinforcements, and on the morning
of August 16 he was sitting in his tent within the ramparts of
Fort Detroit, dazed and nearly incoherent, absently shoving wads
of tobacco into his mouth, so that "the spittle colored with to-
bacco-juice ran from his mouth on his neckcloth, beard, cravat,
and vest." A few hours later, the unbelieving and unopposed
British took the entire American force into their custody.

Throughout 1812 one assault on Canada followed another,
each reaching new heights of absurdity and impotence. Disillusionment spread through the land. Men still talked of the next
campaign with a desperate hope, but the gasconade of easy triumph was buried in hundreds of graves across the frontier. Madison's administration continued to nourish dreams of American
fulfillment, but began as well to consider welcoming an overture
of peace. Obstinacy on both sides withered several attempts at
armistice that came before the chills of repeated defeat. It was
not until the Emperor of Russia, his country suffering from the
lack of American goods, cast himself in the role of mediator, that
the desire for peace exceeded the appetite for the elusive fruits
of war. The Czar was America's friend; he believed in neutral
rights; he also had influence with England, his ally. Madison
promptly accepted the Russian's offer and to the commission for

peace named John Quincy Adams, minister to Russia, Bayard, and Gallatin.

· · ·

As he rose from his bed at the inn in Gothenburg, Albert Gallatin was absorbed in the problems of the mission he headed, and later that morning he wrote to Baring Brothers & Company, the British banking house that served American interests before and during the war. War is never a gentle occupation, but in the age before the weapons and the mentality of total destruction it allowed for some amenities. American relations with the Barings were strained but not entirely disrupted, and Gallatin, after detailing the purpose of his, Bayard's, and Adams's mission, instructed the banking house to pay the mission's salaries and expenses. He was aware that the contents of his letter would reach the leaders of the British government, and if that government had not yet committed itself to mediation Gallatin was hopeful that his statement might help to force the issue.

While Gallatin penned careful words to Alexander Baring, Bayard dickered with the landlord. Shortly after noon the two envoys rounded up their younger colleagues from the limited haunts of the provincial city, and by night were back on the *Neptune*.

For more than two days they navigated the straits between Sweden and Denmark, stopping only to pay tolls at Elsinore, where Bayard, though feverish with a cold, roused himself at four on a cold morning for a walk through Hamlet's castle and garden. By Friday, June 25, they were strolling the streets of Copenhagen.

The Danish capital, unlike rural Gothenburg, was a large and varied city, and Gallatin and Bayard and their entourage spent nearly a week enjoying its cosmopolitan offerings. They toured parks and palaces and the estates of wealthy Danes, ate handsomely, visited museums and libraries, and met the King and members of his cabinet. Copenhagen too was a vortex of news and hearsay. Napoleon was supposed to have agreed to an armistice with the opposing alliance of Russia, Prussia, Austria, and England. Neither American minister was an advocate of Bonaparte's, but if the French Emperor assented to a peace or were defeated England's hands would be free to throttle America. Even more disquieting, although Bayard and Gallatin did not believe it, was the rumor that Great Britain would not consider Russian mediation of her dispute with the United States.

From Copenhagen the route led across the Baltic to the Gulf of Finland, and for two weeks the *Neptune* made slow progress against persistent headwinds. July 4, a holiday that the commissioners had hoped to celebrate in St. Petersburg, was commemorated aboard ship instead. The July weather was wintry, and Bayard's fever and cough, which he attributed to the removal of his long underwear when he was in port, returned to rack his body. When the *Neptune* reached Revel on the 15th Bayard was still too feeble to leave his bed for more than a few hours.

Revel, the ancient walled city that guarded the entrance to the Gulf of Finland, had not been intended as a port of call, but the wind, blowing steadily from the East, locked the *Neptune* in the harbor. For three days, Gallatin, and Bayard when he was able, tasted of Revel's society. By Saturday, with the *Neptune* still at anchor, they found the delay intolerable. Wearied by a trip of almost five thousand miles and anxious to reach their destination and get on with their vital business, they bought carriages and hired horses, and at seven in the evening of Sunday, July 18, set out over the post road for St. Petersburg, carrying as much of their baggage as they could.

Day and night, with only infrequent and brief stops for food and a few hours of rest, they traveled through an indolent summer countryside, lush with ripening fields of rye and oats and barley, broken occasionally by small clumps of birch. To the left of the smooth, hard-packed road they glimpsed blue patches of the Gulf of Finland, sparkling in sunlight that lasted from before four in the morning until after nine in the evening. Every fourteen miles or so they were forced to stop at stinking posthouses—community centers and shelters for filthy and vermin-infested men and animals—to change their horses and take their meals, but on Wednesday morning their carriages rolled away from the last of the rude places, only twelve miles from St. Petersburg. They had not gone two miles before they encountered the carriage of Levett Harris, American consul, and Bayard and Gallatin, transferring from their carriage to his, jolted off at a faster trot for the city. By midafternoon, bearers of the tender American hope for peace with honor, they were finally at the court of the Czar.

CHAPTER

⤞ 2 ⟞

The Emperor's Court

St. Petersburg was the glory of Peter the Great. Its granite foundations, its wide boulevards with their tree-shaded walks, its spacious squares lay majestically on a bed of mud and the rotting bones of thousands of reluctant workmen whose sweat and blood had polished its marble into splendor. The River Neva and the three great canals flowing through it had contributed to its reputation as the "Venice of the North." It was a dream city of monuments and breathtaking palaces and hundreds of ornate bridges. It was also a graveyard for those susceptible to tuberculosis. From November to April the waterways that surrounded and divided it were pavements dense with ice and black in an everlasting winter, but in summer the sun returned, driving the night almost out of existence. It was an unpredictable city— capital at once of enchantment and anguish, of the noble and the base, of the exceedingly rich and the unbelievably poor, of hope and disillusionment.

On evenings when day and night were indistinguishable and pillows of steam covered the canals and on those when few men moved far from the barely sufficient warmth of red-hot stoves, a lonely, preoccupied figure pursued a resolute course along the quay that bordered the Neva. Sometimes the metronomic beat of his regular footsteps reverberated from the walls that lined quiet side streets, and sometimes he walked swiftly down the Czarskozelo Road, but almost always he avoided the places where people congregated.

Occasionally this American met another, younger man—a Russian, also alone, also lost in contemplation—and for a few mo-

ments the two would stop and chat. They would discuss the
weather and the war in Europe or the war in America or items of
court gossip. The Russian would inquire after the health of the
American's wife and that of his father, the ex-President. If it
were spring the Russian would ask the American what his plans
were for the summer. In winter the Russian observed that the
stocky American was the only man braving the cold of St. Petersburg without gloves. The two men, so different in nature and
background, liked and respected one another. One was Alexander
Pavlovich of St. Petersburg, Russia, and the other John Quincy
Adams of Quincy, Massachusetts. One was the Emperor; the
other was American minister to the Emperor's court.

Even the Czar, whose knowledge and opinions of the American minister came primarily from such chance meetings on the
banks of the Neva and the infrequent official consultations, would
probably have described Adams as a man of purpose and pre-
cision. Adams's days knew not a moment of waste or indolence.
Nearly every morning he rose between the hours of four and five
—to study the Bible, to read Horace, to argue with the philosophy of Voltaire, to write with aching fingers in a cold that solidi-
fied the water in the basin on his dressing table.

By his own measure, he knew that his height was "five feet
seven inches, English." His pace was exactly "two feet six inches
and eighty-eight one-hundredths of an inch." Ordinarily he
walked "one hundred and twenty steps to a minute," and on one
cold morning he did "thirteen hundred and sixty-six paces" in
eleven minutes. He knew just how far it was between the bridges
that spanned the river and the canals, how far between islands,
how far from one end of the Hermitage Palace to the other. If
anyone wished to know, he could also name and locate every star
in the heavens.

In the privacy of his home he was a sensitive, reflective, sometimes passionate man. In society he was awkward and cold and
domineering. His erudition was overpowering. He had written
learned books and pamphlets. He had been a Harvard professor,
a member of Congress, a United States Senator, minister to the
Netherlands, and minister to Prussia. Since 1809 he had served
at his post in Russia. Though he was lawyer, statesman, and
diplomat, he nevertheless castigated himself for having wasted
the forty-six years of his life.

Long before the United States declared war on Great Britain Adams anticipated and feared its coming. Unlike Madison, who expected unity from a common cause, Adams, with a bitter memory, was apprehensive that the political and economic differences that divided the men of New England from other Americans would grow deeper and wider. News of the war and its military disappointments came for Adams at a time of personal sadness over the loss of his infant daughter. For Russia it came at a time of tragedy. The great French plague had swept through the country, leaving scorched fields and rutted villages and the mangled bodies of thousands of Russians; it had paused, seemingly invincible, before the gates of Moscow. Fearing the worst, the diplomatic corps fled from St. Petersburg, and Adams debated whether to follow them with his wife Louisa and his son Charles; as it turned out it was Adams who stayed and Napoleon who left.

Even before the little Corsican had reached the funeral pyre that was Moscow, the Russian government had expressed official interest in the Anglo-American hostilities. On the evening of September 21, 1812, Adams hurried to keep his appointment at the home of Count Romanzoff, Russian Minister for Foreign Affairs. Not long after Adams arrived there, the courtly, solicitous Chancellor, Adams's friend and confidant, disclosed the purpose of their meeting. He reminded Adams that although Russia was allied with England in the struggle against the hated Bonaparte she cherished her friendship with the United States. Not only that, but at the moment when Russia was threatened with destruction the American war had cut off a precious supply of goods and foodstuffs. Neither the United States nor Britain appeared eager to continue the war, said Romanzoff, and the Emperor hoped that both sides would favorably consider an offer of mediation. A note on the subject had already been dispatched to London. Did Adams anticipate any opposition on the part of his country? Adams, although he lacked instructions on the matter, assured Romanzoff that he did not, and a month later, after news of the failure of attempted armistice had come from London and while Napoleon vacillated midst the eerie and ominous winds that scoured Moscow's vacant skeleton, the proposal of mediation was sent to Washington.

In the months that followed, Bonaparte's retreating troops

were transformed into statues of ice—a grisly tableau that de-
filed more than five hundred miles of Russian plains. Within a
few weeks, forty thousand Frenchmen surrendered to the terrible cold, the wolves, or the Russians. With his Russian friends
and neighbors Adams rejoiced in the deliverance of the country,
but at the same time he learned of Hull's surrender at Detroit
and was stunned. "The honor of my country," began the lament
in his diary, "O God! suffer it not to go unredeemed!"

Napoleon's retreat was almost as much of a relief to the British
as to the Russians, and when Lord Liverpool and his government
became aware of the fiasco of the American invasion of Canada
they reacted like men who had been promised a tale of calamity
and told a joke. Napoleon was still the principal target. The up-
start Americans could wait for their peace or punishment, whichever was probable or advisable. Nor was it necessary to be
prompt or definite concerning Alexander's suggested mediation.
The Emperor, too, the English were sure, had more important
things to think about than the silly antics or the modest trade of
the Americans.

On December 3, 1812, Romanzoff notified Adams of the first
indication of the British attitude. It seemed that the British had
not rejected the offer but had intimated that the Americans
might do so—that America might be more receptive after the
national election—when, it was presumed, Madison would lose
ground if not his actual office to the Federalists.

As things turned out, Madison did not go down in the election,
but neither did the British lose their faith in the prospect of
American dissolution, nor were they persuaded to seek peace. In
June, 1813, as Gallatin and Bayard were suffering the boisterous
temper of the Atlantic, Adams read in the London *Courier* that
the British government intended to refuse the Czar's overture.
To complicate matters, a little more than a week later came the
news that the United States had accepted, and Romanzoff, while
not certain of British aims, was unable to see how the English
could decline. Only seven days later he was a wiser man; for, as
Gallatin and Bayard were departing from Gothenburg, Romanzoff was sorrowfully explaining to Adams that the British had
said no, that, according to the word from London, the difficulties
with the United States were internal and not subject to outside
interference, however well-intended. Perhaps, though, sug-

gested Romanzoff, genuinely eager to help the Americans and hopeful of fortifying his own weakening position, the Emperor could try again.

John Quincy Adams, a pessimist without peer, was hardly shocked by the miscarriage of mediation; already in deep despair, he could sink no lower. At the first hint of British intransigence Adams was convinced that the omen was an unhappy one. What he could not credit was a simultaneous report that Gallatin and Bayard had been appointed to the American peace commission. He argued with Romanzoff that Gallatin could not be spared from the Treasury and that Bayard, member of the irreconcilable party of opposition, would naturally sabotage any peace effort entrusted to him. Romanzoff, for his part an optimist without equal, rationalized the nominations of both men, and in this case it was he who proved to be right. The *Neptune* was passing the Hebrides on the day that Adams read of its anticipated departure from the United States in the *National Intelligencer,* the leading mouthpiece of Madison's administration. On July 3, while the *Neptune* wallowed in the Baltic, Adams received a note, written by Gallatin and Bayard when in Gothenburg, informing him of their appointments and his as Envoys Extraordinary and Ministers Plenipotentiary. From that day on, Adams waited for the arrival of his colleagues with ever-increasing anxiety. Perhaps, he let himself believe, the peace attempt could be salvaged or a new one, as Romanzoff intimated, be started. In any case, it would be cheering to enjoy once again the company of fellow Americans. For days he expected them hourly, and, fearful of their meeting with some dreadful accident, he persistently pestered Levett Harris, the consul and now secretary to the commission, for any available information. Late in the afternoon of Wednesday, July 21, Harris rode by to tell Adams that Gallatin and Bayard had arrived. Relieved and pleased, the minister to Russia hurried off to see them.

Bayard and Gallatin, who had not slept for three nights, regretfully turned down Adams's invitation to dinner, but for an hour the three envoys pooled their meager collections of news and information, and Adams, when he returned home, cast aside the bonds of habit and stayed up until the sinful hour of ten, reading letters and dispatches. The war disasters were worse than even the conjectures of his gloomy imagination, and his substantiation of the story of British rejection, heard by Gallatin and Bayard in Copenhagen, was no more cheerful a revelation to them. Having just arrived, they at once concerned themselves with the problems of getting home. It was midsummer, but the Emperor was in Germany, matching wits with Napoleon, and London was a distant sail. Correspondence to and from both places exhausted weeks. In September the roads would be transformed into channels of sodden, impassable brown muck and then, overnight, the northern world would become a vast panorama of ice and snow; ships would freeze in their harbors and travelers be threatened with death.

Throughout Thursday and Friday the three ministers exchanged views, and Adams advised Gallatin and Bayard on dress and deportment for their interview with Romanzoff on Saturday. In more leisurely moments, Harris, who was not fond of Adams and hoped to impress his new masters, conducted a tour of St. Petersburg's pleasures and palaces, topping things off with dinner at his lavish apartment on Friday evening. Promptly at eleven on Saturday morning Adams called for the other two commissioners, and, uncomfortably resplendent in their newly designed and never-used uniforms of blue with gold embroidery and buttons, the three men trooped off to see the Chancellor of the Empire.

The tall, mellow Romanzoff, at ease in his more elaborate uniform, was the epitome of grace and consideration. He had the day before promised Adams to query the Czar about renewing his offer, and this understanding was the unstated theme of the brief meeting of introduction. Gallatin, head of the mission, submitted copies of its credentials and replied to Romanzoff's questions on the progress of the war. Romanzoff ended the interview by inviting them to dinner on Wednesday, and, fifteen minutes after they had arrived, the Americans, having agreed to present their government's intentions in writing, retreated through an endless suite of rooms and down long flights of stairs to the street and their waiting carriages.

Throughout the following weeks Romanzoff made every effort to pay suitable respect to the envoys' rank and to make them feel at home. At the court dinner on Wednesday he placed the Americans before all other members of the diplomatic corps, although strictly speaking Gallatin and Bayard could not be accredited until they had been received by the Emperor. The Americans' note, explanatory of their position, was delivered to the Chancellor on Friday, and two days later, on August 1, having acceded to their request for a special audience, Romanzoff entertained Gallatin and Bayard at his country château.

The Americans were obviously seeking some definite word on the possibility of British participation in a mediation, and Romanzoff began by repeating the British argument that American "pretentions" were not the business of a third party, that England before now had made every effort to reach a settlement. Also, for the first time, Romanzoff disclosed that the Russian minister in London had been told of the British refusal in November, 1812, long before the American government had even been apprised of the offer. The revelation added weight to what Adams, who was not at the meeting, was beginning to suspect: correspondence was sent to and decisions were made at Alexander's headquarters in Germany, and Romanzoff, who no longer held the Czar's confidence, was the last to be informed.

In answer to the British statements, Gallatin and Bayard gave a long history of impressment and its abuses, and agreed, at Romanzoff's urging, to state their arguments in an unofficial note to go directly to the Emperor. The Chancellor said that he had already recommended renewal of the mediation offer to the Czar and that he would now draw up such a proposal to be reviewed by both the Emperor and the American commission. Romanzoff did not think that the British answer was meant to be final. He did not see how that country could reject a second offer without incurring the displeasure both of Alexander and the opposition party in England. On the other hand, he added as an afterthought, if mediation were not accepted there might be other possibilities.

Both Gallatin and Bayard, perplexed by the uncertainties and contradictions of Romanzoff's assurances, hastened to tell him that their powers were limited to mediation. Romanzoff assured them blandly that they might remain in Russia until they received greater powers. On that note the meeting at the château on the Peterhof road came to an end.

The session was to become but one of many occasions on which Romanzoff's kindly interest in the Americans and their cause overwhelmed the accuracy of his judgment and went beyond the bounds of his control of foreign affairs. On August 10 he summoned Adams to tell him that the Czar had approved the renewal of the mediation offer, and, while Gallatin and Bayard enjoyed a gala dinner at Princess Beloselsky's, a social affair glutted with the cream of society and intriguing to Bayard for what he thought was the brazen presence of the husband of the Emperor's mistress, Adams listened patiently to Romanzoff's monologue on the importance to him of an American history of the causes of the war, to be used in drawing up a new mediation proposal. Four days later the lengthy document was in Romanzoff's hands, and on the 19th he once more, by special request, had Adams before him.

Romanzoff began by describing the American note on the history of the Anglo-American dispute as a model of moderation and logic which the British could not ignore. He was especially impressed by the American Act of March 3, 1813, which laid the basis for a reciprocal agreement on the nonemployment by one country of the other's mariners. If the English, however, wished to transfer the negotiations to London would the American envoys consent?

The startled Adams reminded the Chancellor of the limitations of the mission's powers. If they could go at all, the commissioners could only go to London for mediation under the Czar, not for direct negotiation. In any case, noted Adams, the British had rejected mediation once because, as Romanzoff himself had told Adams in June, the war was "an internal affair." Why should they accept a second offer? But Romanzoff could not recall his statement, made only two months earlier. The British had given no such reason, as far as Romanzoff now knew, nor was he certain that they had flatly rejected the first offer. It was a bewildered Adams indeed who took his leave a few minutes later.

Whatever were the torturous meanderings of Romanzoff's thoughts and memory in that summer of 1813, he persisted in his plans to draft a dispatch to the Russian minister, Count Lieven, in London. On the 24th he read his proposition to the three Americans, reluctantly incorporating into it changes which Gallatin suggested. Presumably, if the Count kept his word, copies of the document would be on their separate ways to the Czar and to Lieven before August gave way to September.

The opinions of the Americans and their acute desire to get on with their mission or go home mattered little. They were at the mercy of the Russian court that had yet to officially acknowledge their presence. Until the Emperor recognized them only Adams was accredited as a diplomat—as minister to Russia, and not as a peace commissioner. Until the Czar declared that mediation efforts were at an end and until he dismissed them the American representatives could not, without creating a diplomatic incident, go home. As far as they could make out, their fate was in the hands of a sickly, well-intentioned Foreign Minister who was hated by the English and had been forgotten by his distant master.

Purveyors of peace in a country which apparently had no outlet for their product, the American ministers, especially Gallatin and Bayard, turned down the paths of tourists and partook of the social life to which their rank entitled them. It was not the gayest of St. Petersburg's social seasons. The loss of a son or a brother or a husband or a lover provided an almost daily justification for a *Te Deum* in one of the cathedrals, and absence dulled dinner-party luster when death or mutilation did not actually stain it; for the principal members of the resplendent court of the Emperor were encamped with him in Germany. But it was a life, a culture, no matter who was missing or dying, that knew no equal in the frontier atmosphere of Washington and was reflected only astigmatically in the puritanical mirror of Boston. To Adams it was the devil's beckoning-away from the wholesome pursuits of knowledge, industry, and exercise. To the aristocratic Gallatin it was a reminder of the transplanted French culture of his Genevan youth. To the provincial, homesick Bayard it was a novel, if not altogether pleasing, experience that in all its facets, of similarities or differences, reminded him of Wilmington, Delaware.

Romanzoff and Adams opened the doors, and Harris, the consul with feverish aspirations, provided the experience of a seasoned and sophisticated guide. He led Bayard and Gallatin first through the Hermitage and the Winter Palace, adjoining monuments of luxury and culture that cast their shadows on the Neva, and the ministers looked up in awe at the gold-plated ceilings and were transfixed by the magnificence of the paintings that

covered the walls. At St. Michael's, where Alexander's father, the
Emperor Paul, had been ruthlessly strangled to Alexander's benefit and with his knowledge, Bayard imagined he could see the
spot where blood had oozed from Paul's lifeless body, even
though he knew that the original floor had been replaced, "in
order that that should not remain which had been stained with
the blood of an Emperor." And early one morning in late August
the commissioners took their carriages eighteen miles out of St.
Petersburg to the Peterhof Palace, overlooking the port of Cronstadt, where the *Neptune* was anchored in the Gulf of Finland.
Fascinated as are most tourists with a glimpse into the accom-
modations of notables, they viewed the beds of the Emperor and
Empress and peeked in at Alexander's shower bath. They marveled at the gardens, a fairyland of fountains supplied by aque-
ducts that spanned twenty miles. Spouts of water shot forty feet
into the air, formed geometric shapes, turned bushes and trees
into watery sprays, exploded silvery particles into a fishpond six
hundred feet long. From a doorway, they uneasily observed the
damp humiliation of servants caught, for the ministers' supposed
pleasure, in a room whose floor masked hidden jets.

Even Adams, who although he had been in Russia for four
years had seldom left St. Petersburg, occasionally joined the
others and enjoyed the picnic atmosphere of their excursions.
He went with Bayard and Gallatin on their trip to Czarskozelo,
the rural retreat of the Empress, and was as excited as they when
his carriage entered the grounds through elaborate carved granite arches, proceeded down a broad avenue curling through
dense woods and exquisite gardens, and passed a row of Chinese
temples, to come suddenly upon the massive façade of the palace.

The rooms of the palace, some with walls of amber, others
with doors of mother-of-pearl, left them speechless, and equally
overwhelming were the grounds and the vast artificial lake upon
which the ministers were rowed by four Russian sailors. They
were shown a concert hall on an island in the middle of the lake,
and the statues and gravestones of nobles and dogs, all favorites
of the Empress. With malicious humor Adams observed that the
dogs had received larger stones and longer inscriptions than the
nobles.

There are gravestones for three greyhounds, with inscriptions as long, probably much more ingenious, and certainly more intelligible, for they are in French, than those in honor of Romanzoff [the Chancellor's father] and Orloff. The dogs were Sir Tom Anderson, Duchesse, and Zemire. The epitaph of the last is in very elegant French verse, by the Count de Segur; they say that Zemire loved very much her whom everybody else loved . . . and, finally, that the gods, witnessing her tenderness, had given her immortality. . . . I believe there is nothing like this for Orloff and Romanzoff.

Gallatin and Bayard learned soon enough that St. Petersburg society began its day at two in the afternoon and ended it shortly before four in the morning. Nearly every night there was a dinner party—the diplomatic dinners of Romanzoff, open house on Tuesday evenings at Princess Beloselsky's, Thursday and Friday night suppers at the Myers' or the Pflugs', members of St. Petersburg's extensive German community of merchants and engineers. The ritual seldom varied. A lengthy dinner was followed by cordials and coffee and a turn around the garden. Next came boston, a game resembling whist, which, interspersed with conversation and more walking, gave way to supper at the hour when every self-respecting Cinderella had already turned in her slippers. It was not until two or three in the morning that drivers switched their impatient horses and carriages creaked homeward.

After years of Jeffersonian simplicity in a city that considered Dolly Madison's home-style dinner parties the epitome of elegance, Gallatin willingly adjusted his sleeping and eating habits to conform to the night life of St. Petersburg. He was witty and charming and spoke French, the language of the court, fluently. For Bayard, whose halting French was sometimes unintentionally funny and whose mode of living approached the regularity of Adams's ways, immersion in the social pond was less complete and not nearly as comfortable. The continental dinners, served dish by dish, were exasperating and interminable. Bayard, ignorant of the complete menu, seldom knew how much to take of the dish being offered. Even getting to and from the dining room posed a problem, for he invariably tendered the wrong arm to the lady of the moment and was several times corrected for doing so. With little aptitude for garden chitchat in an alien tongue and with almost no desire for an evening of boston, he often took what he called "french leave" and, with Colonel Milligan, his secretary, or some other young member of the commission, went to a public house for dinner or to the theater.

The days, when time was not occupied by the scant business of the mission or tours of palaces, were given over to walks through the parks and along the boulevards or to visits to orphanages or schools or model factories established by some member of the royal family, or to one or more of the many Greek Orthodox churches and cathedrals. Loss of a noble life or the winning of a battle occasioned many days on which all three envoys stood for hours in the hot and steamy interiors of the cathedrals, awaiting the arrival of the Empress or the Empress-Mother and the beginning of the service. The splendor and solemnity of the churches impressed the Americans, whose own edifices and religious ceremonies were much quieter and simpler, but Bayard noted that the nobles in attendance at the *Te Deums* "were as merry and as noisy as if they had been in a coffee house," and he remarked also that "the greek christians are said to be very superstitious without being very honest." As *Te Deum* followed *Te Deum*, Bayard's awe at the impressiveness of decoration and the ritual of the mass and his annoyance at the levity of the worshipers gave way before the elementary but uncomfortable observation that "there is no place to set down in a greek church." This, in time, was the thing that impressed Bayard most about the religion of the Russians.

More than business or boredom it was the drinking water of the Neva that broke the routine of tours, walks, rides, and dinners. One after another, each of the men who had traveled aboard the *Neptune* took to his bed, weakened by diarrhea. Bayard, especially, was unable to leave his room for days at a time and had more cause than the others to consult Dr. Galloway, a transplanted Scot who believed tincture of rhubarb to be a panacea. Debilitated by an infection he could never quite shake, Bayard became more intemperate than usual. He took delight in criticizing Adams's contributions to their joint notes; he taunted Milligan, his secretary; he sneered at Gallatin for sleeping until noon.

A hot August gave way to a milder but rainy September which, in turn, surrendered its tenure to an October that was alternately awash or thick with snow. Practical men, the Americans knew that no official word, good or bad, could be expected from the

British before November and that when it came, no matter what its import, it meant a chilly and isolated winter in St. Petersburg. But their unrealistic desire to see either peace or their families and that of Adams not to spend another winter in Russia died slowly before the inevitable impact of a truth they had long known, and as false hope breathed its last they became more intolerant of one another.

Adams's initial delight at being with other Americans had been relatively brief. He noticed, or thought he noticed, a tendency on the part of Bayard and Gallatin to bypass him and take matters into their own hands. He had not known of the August 1 session with Romanzoff until two days after it had occurred, and in time there were more incidents that ruffled his seldom-placid composure. He was no better able than the other two to understand the perplexing assurances of Romanzoff or the silence of the Czar, but, however great his own annoyance and anxiety, Russia was his province, and, like a man who resents uncomplimentary references to the wife he himself freely criticizes, he grew impatient with the harsh comments of his fellow envoys.

Most infuriating of all was the time and effort wasted in preparing notes for Romanzoff or reports to Secretary of State Monroe. It took a week or more to complete what could be done by one of them, so Adams believed, in two hours. "It is a sufficient specimen," he told his uncomplaining diary, "of the method of negotiating by commissions. In the multitude of counselors there is safety, but there is not despatch." Particularly galling was Bayard's and sometimes Gallatin's criticism of his contributions to their joint letters. Adams thought that Bayard was simply being spiteful, and, certain in any case that both men wished to ignore him, he coldly informed them that he would be willing to translate or do "anything of mere labor" but that they must do the drafting. Neither Gallatin nor Bayard was so naive as to believe him.

For that matter, nothing that Adams might have said or done would have been surprising to Bayard, who had formed an unflattering opinion of the New Englander almost from the beginning. Adams, he had decided, "has little talent for society and does not appear to enjoy it. His address is singularly cold and repulsive. His manners are harsh and you seldom perceive the least effort to please any one." Bayard's judgment of Gallatin

was not so damning, but neither did he and the Secretary of the
Treasury have much in common or much to discuss. They had
separate apartments in the same house, separate carriages, different hours for rising and eating and retiring. One was sophisticated, complex, taciturn; the other was a simple Delaware lawyer,
a man who gaped in wonder at the table settings of a court dinner and was ill at ease when presented with a finger bowl. Bayard was as comfortable with Gallatin as is a country lawyer with
the member of a big city firm, and all Bayard wished to know of
Russian society could have been condensed into a weekend. The
Russian women talked of politics and philosophy as if they were
men; dinners were "laborious"; and by mid-October there no
longer was novelty to St. Petersburg, and nothing remained "to
compensate for the separation from my family & friends."

Even Gallatin, composed and temperate by comparison to
Adams and Bayard, felt keenly the growing pressures of uncertainty and helplessness and isolation. In moments when he had
been too long dependent on his own resources and was too much
under the influence of wine he gave vent to sarcasm—although
softly spoken—and became indiscreet about some of the inner
doings of the administration, and at such times Bayard felt more
at home with him and more his equal. All three ministers were
impatient and fretful under their sentence of inertia and ignorance, and on Gallatin, head of the mission and key member of
Madison's government, the burden was heaviest. But until such
time as Romanzoff should receive a precise answer from London
and from the Czar there was nothing Gallatin could do but wait
and try to jolly Adams and comfort Bayard and lose himself in
the glitter and play of the Russian court.

It was not that Gallatin and Adams and Bayard were altogether without word from England or America or the Continent,
but the messages that did penetrate the Baltic were uncertain
or unpromising. In the English newspapers there was news that
the Senate had yet to confirm the ministers' appointments. There
was a story of the ill-fated *Chesapeake*, that she had again and
for the last time surrendered to a British warship. And in letter
and newsprint there was confirmation of a new American campaign on the Canadian border but no hint as to its outcome. It
was now known that Napoleon was no longer the man of almost

all victories and no defeats, but chances for a European peace that would stand America alone against Great Britain were anyone's guess. Perhaps the most definite, least encouraging information concerning mediation came in a private letter to Gallatin from London.

It was the day after the gay excursion to Czarskozelo that Gallatin received Alexander Baring's answer to the letter written from Gothenburg. At thirty-eight, Alexander Baring, Member of Parliament, husband of the daughter of an ex-Senator of the United States, was head of one of the leading banking houses of Europe. To him the United States meant income, friends, and family. He profited little by a war between his own country and one of his best customers. It was he who had authored the "Inquiry into the Causes and Consequences of the Orders in Council," and it was he, also, who, in the spring of 1812, had worked successfully but belatedly for the repeal of the Orders. He wrote to Gallatin as one sound banker and honest man to another, and Gallatin knew that whatever Baring had to say was a paraphrase of the words of Lord Castlereagh, British Foreign Secretary.

"The mediation of Russia was offered, not sought," wrote Baring, gratuitously acquitting the United States of any clandestine agreement:

it was fairly and frankly accepted. I do not see how America could with any consistency refuse it; but to the eyes of a European politician it was clear that such an interference could produce no practical benefit. The only question now seriously at issue between us is one purely of a domestic nature . . . no foreign government can fairly judge of it. . . . On the other hand what a handle does such a subject offer for fomenting discord on points totally foreign from it. . . . It is a sort of family quarrel where foreign interference can only do harm. . . .

Baring went on to say, in no uncertain terms, that mediation was definitely out of the question, that England would, however, negotiate directly in Gothenburg or London, preferably the latter, for it was obvious that both sides wanted peace. It was also clear, continued Baring, with a jab at American pretensions, that both sides could tease but not really harm each other and that a useless, apathetic, expensive war was being continued solely because of impressment, so unlikely a cause for hostilities that "the prevalent opinion here was that the war was a war of passion . . . and that concession would only show weakness." If America insisted on discussing impressment Great Britain would agree to do so, but she never could fully give in to the United States without losing her navy. "It is useless," concluded Baring, "to discuss the abstract question of right when it is one of necessity." Gallatin was given to understand that the practice could be examined but that the right of impressment would never be surrendered.

Although nothing that Baring wrote was new or unexpected, his letter was the first clear and direct proof of the attitude of the British government. Baring's arguments were carefully transcribed long before London could have known of Russia's intention to renew the offer of mediation, but it took a clouded view of reality to support the opinion that Britain would look more favorably upon a second attempt than she had upon the first. And on September 1 came unnecessary corroboration to the statements of Alexander Baring. General Moreau, once aide to Napoleon, then exile in America, and now lieutenant to the Czar, wrote from the Emperor's camp to Gallatin that Cathcart, the British minister, had made it very clear that Britain would not accept mediation.

Both letters were further rungs on a lengthening ladder of frustration and futility, but, in the absence of an official notification from the Russian government ending their mission, the American commissioners could do nothing but argue the cause of mediation and outwardly maintain an appearance of hope. In the belief that Moreau's proximity to the Czar might be important Gallatin wrote first to him, requesting his good offices. But Moreau was never to read the letter. He was on his way to St. Petersburg, in his casket, for his own *Te Deum.*

The chances of directly swaying the British government appeared to be appreciably less than those of using the Czar; in consequence, Gallatin delayed his answer to Baring, while he and Bayard and Adams debated but did not resolve a course of action. It was not until late October that Gallatin took matters into his own hands and dispatched George M. Dallas, one of his young secretaries and a future Vice-President of the United States, to London—with detailed instructions to disclose nothing about the mission except that it could treat only under mediation and to listen carefully without appearing to snoop. He was to relay all information, not "vague rumors," to St. Petersburg and Washington, especially any word on the final rejection of mediation and any offer of direct negotiation. Dallas was also to carry a letter to Baring, a letter in which Gallatin bemoaned the fact that the mission would probably be trapped in Russia for the winter and in which he damned the British government for not officially notifying the United States of her refusal of mediation. This procrastination, Gallatin reasoned, was the cause of the continuance of useless bloodshed, and her guilt should compel England, if she retained any honor, to give serious consideration to the Czar's second offer.

It is doubtful that Gallatin anticipated any happy results from his efforts, and it is certain that Adams and Bayard, reluctant brothers in misery, feared for the worst. Only Romanzoff apparently was serene in his conviction that all would end well that had already ended or would never begin. On October 1, as water from a fresh snowfall squished in Bayard's boots and brought on the sneezes of a new cold, Romanzoff assured Gallatin and Bayard that he expected a favorable answer in two to three weeks. The Americans would be rewarded, said Romanzoff, for remaining in St. Petersburg for the winter.

Bayard's most immediate reward was an aching head and a tormenting cough, and, taking to his bed, he had ample time to study the raindrops that pocked his windowpane and made a slippery gruel of the layer of snow. The distress in his nose and chest subsided with the demise of inclement weather, but the depression of his spirit lingered, untouched and unhealed by the happy predictions of Romanzoff. After a week of snow and rain and slush, on the first fine day of October, Bayard, lost in reflection, walked the boulevards. "I was occupied with my own thoughts which respected our errand in Russia," he wrote when he got home, having decided to set his thoughts down for later verification. He predicted that England would not accept mediation, nor would that country "give either an immediate or a decisive answer," but he believed it probable that in the spring there would be direct negotiation in London—that peace might result from this negotiation but that it would be a peace fashioned entirely on British terms.

In the midst of gloomy meditations on the part of the three American ministers came word from Romanzoff. The Emperor had finally written to his Foreign Minister, directing him officially to receive the American envoys and to see that they were presented to the Empresses. Bayard sullenly commented that they could simultaneously take their leave, but his suggestion received nothing more than a cold glance from Adams, and on October 12, nearly three months after their arrival in Russia, Gallatin and Bayard, in the company of Adams, marched stiffly past a saluting guard of honor and came to a staggered halt before a beaming and bemedaled Romanzoff. Adams, in his embroidered uniform an improbable picture of a ship's captain, stepped forward, presented the mission's genuine credentials, and "seemed disposed to make a short address." Romanzoff, however, gently cut him short, and, after a few words of official welcome, told the Americans that they were now fully accredited.

Five days later the commissioners once more donned their uniforms, and, with secretaries and messengers in tow, went off to the Winter Palace. Met at the front entrance by a gaudily dressed and plumed page, they were escorted through one suite after another and transferred from page to chamberlain, until, dizzied from the blurred magnificence of endless rooms and exhausted from climbing long flights of marble steps, they found themselves bowing three times in unsteady unison before the Empress. She greeted them, asked them about their transatlantic trip, discussed American and Russian weather, and wished them a pleasant stay in her capital. She then offered her hand for each minister to kiss, and Adams, Bayard, and Gallatin bowed low and, as well as each could, backed out of the room. For whatever it was worth, they were now fully recognized as emissaries to treat for peace with Great Britain under the mediation of Alexander I. They had every reason to believe that the privilege was not worth much, and they returned to their quarters, unmoved by their few moments of splendor, to brief Dallas for his journey to the land of the enemy.

A Tangled Web

As the American ministers exchanged conversational trifles with the Russian Empress at the Winter Palace in St. Petersburg, nearly three hundred rain-swept bateaux, gorged with the men and supplies and armaments of an invading army, departed the shelter of Sackett's Harbor, New York, and headed precariously into the choppy waters of Lake Ontario. Under the faltering command of Major General James Wilkinson, described by one of his brigadiers as "much indisposed in mind and body," this American force of about four thousand men was supposed to descend the St. Lawrence, join with an army of nearly equal numbers under Major General Wade Hampton (a man who loathed Wilkinson and was in turn hated by him), and take Montreal. That neither general was capable of such an undertaking and that neither they nor the Secretary of War anticipated success did not prevent the launching of the futile effort.

Wilkinson exhausted two weeks merely getting his men and boats into the river, and then, leaving his troops to straggle along the New York State border as well as they could, he took to his floating bed, sick with a fever that diminished such limited faculties as he possessed. He was still bedridden and out of touch with his staff when, on the afternoon of November 11 at Chrystler's Farm near Massena, New York, a considerable portion of his army was badly whipped and driven from the field by a small band of British and Canadians. Two days later the remainder of Wilkinson's sorry expedition was immobile in its winter quarters not far from Malone, while at the same time, slightly to the east, Hampton's army, which had penetrated Canada and suf-

fered defeat in a slight skirmish, was on its way back to its winter
lodgings at Plattsburgh on Lake Champlain. In such an inspired
manner did the northern campaign of 1813 come to its end.

In contrast to the American despair at these momentous defeats
was the English rapture over the successes of their savior, the
Duke of Wellington. Throughout the summer he had swept
French armies from the plains and mountains of Spain, and in
October and November, having crossed the Spanish frontier, he
was fighting his way through southern France. And his were not
the only victories that cheered the British and presaged the
eventual end of the detested Bonaparte—for as the three Americans in St. Petersburg pressed their lips to the plump hand of
the Empress, as they later attended a celebration dinner at Count
Romanzoff's, as they said farewell to George Dallas, three hundred thousand Russians, Prussians, Austrians, and Swedes hurled
themselves vindictively at the confused and almost surrounded
army of Napoleon in eastern Germany. On October 19 the terrible battle of Leipzig came to an end, and throughout that night
and on the following day Napoleon and his badly mauled troops
limped away from the Elbe in the direction of the Rhine.

It was the same day of the French retreat—a dark, cold, rainy
Wednesday in St. Petersburg—that Albert Gallatin was told by
John Payne Todd, the only one courageous or callous enough to
do so, that the Senate of the United States had rejected his appointment to the peace commission.

The news of the Senate's action had come the day before, enclosed in separate letters to Bayard, Adams, and Harris, providing the three of them with a dilemma as to how and when to inform Gallatin. Bayard, already somewhat frantic because of
illness, worry, and suspense, and aware that he, as Gallatin's
housemate, was expected to convey the news, proposed that
Adams put the information in a letter. Adams, almost unable to
believe what he had heard, gruffly said he would do so if Bayard
would deliver the letter, but Bayard quickly declined and, after
taking his leave of Adams, decided that it might be better to
wait for the official dispatch. He fretted over the matter throughout the afternoon, carefully avoiding Gallatin, and in the evening
was back at Adams's house, convinced that the news could not be
withheld indefinitely. By this time Adams was more sensible of
the strain on Bayard, and he gently advised him to wait for an

appropriate moment. Their concern was academic, for by Wednesday morning the unpleasant tidings were secret only to Gallatin, and Todd shortly corrected that.

When all had heard of the rejection, the least excited and surprised member of the group was Gallatin himself. He calmly acknowledged the news repeated by Todd, and the only sign of any disquiet on his part was his greater indulgence in conversation and gossip. On Thursday night, with sheets of rain still slashing against the side of the house, Gallatin quietly sat with Bayard and told him he had sought the nomination against Madison's wishes—that Madison had argued that Gallatin was more important in the Treasury, and Gallatin had replied that he could no longer raise money and might more successfully try to make peace. He was not startled by the Senate's repudiation, although he had expected to lose his position as Secretary of the Treasury, not that as minister. As the man with the longest service in Republican cabinets, he had, he reminded Bayard, earned the enmity of Bayard's Federalist party and the jealousy of the dissident elements of his own. In some ways the rejection was a relief. He was once more a private citizen; when snow and ice came to stay and sleds could travel he could go home.

The collective depression over Gallatin's dismissal by the Senate was, in view of his own equanimity, relatively brief. In a matter of days, sympathy gave way to envy or annoyance, depending on the occasion. When Gallatin took the initiative on a matter or gave freely of his opinion Adams and Bayard muttered to themselves or to one another that Gallatin no longer possessed the right to take part in matters of the mission. When Gallatin acceded to this judgment his two companions complained that he was shirking responsibility. On the whole, the three of them alternated between moments of compassion and respect for one another and moods of anger and despair. As the month of October—snow one day, rain the next—wasted away, the American ministers, who would have been astonished had Britain accepted the second offer of mediation, continued to cling to the tatters of hope for this unlikely occurrence and, at the same time, wished for some improvement in the anemic possibility that any one of them would depart from Russia before winter, England, Romanzoff, or the Czar had run their exasperating courses.

"The present," confided Bayard to his diary, "is considered as the most disagreeable season of the year. The sun is not to be seen, the atmosphere is damp and chilly, the ground wet, and the appearance of everything calculated to inspire sombre reflections." Into their "sombre reflections" came the realization that if the *Neptune* were not quickly moved from her anchorage at Cronstadt her passengers might be stranded in St. Petersburg until June. Consequently, Captain Lloyd Jones was ordered to get under sail as quickly as possible for Gothenburg, and Bayard added to his many worries the fear that headwinds would prevent Jones from accomplishing his assignment.

To the doubts and melancholy and preparation for unknown eventualities the Russian court offered a cheerful appearance of optimism. On the last day of October the ministers were presented to the Empress-Mother in a ceremony that outlasted and surpassed in grandeur the audience with her daughter-in-law, and whenever he was seen or heard from Romanzoff repeated his assertions of a happy ending for American trials and tribulations. It was November 1 that brought ice to the Neva and clear, cold truth to St. Petersburg. On that day Levett Harris escorted Daniel Bailey, the British consul, to the apartments of Bayard and Gallatin, and once introduced, Bailey spoke the words that Lord Walpole, English ambassador to Russia, recently arrived from the Czar's headquarters, had authorized: mediation was "explicitly refused by the British Government."

Adams, Bayard, and Gallatin were never to receive a very coherent story of Britain's reaction to Russia's offer of mediation, but they were to see Walpole time and again for the next few months—until they cringed at the very sight of him. He was a coarse, garrulous man who boasted to the Americans that "he never heard from his government, he never wrote to them, he never read newspapers excepting articles about murders, could not bear to look at births or marriages, he never wore boots, never walked, hated music and dancing," and he took delight in telling the proper Adams that on Goose Day, the day when Members of Parliament dined with their constituents, "we do not get drunk—but something devilish near it." While in his crude, outspoken way he openly commiserated with the Americans, he also obviously relished his role as bearer of sad tidings. With or without urging, he reiterated in detail Britain's steps in the refusal of Russian mediation, and, although his memory for dates

and events was haphazard, his listeners never ceased to be irked
or intrigued by his retelling of the story.

While Walpole's recitals of the measures his government took
to shun mediation were garnished by an inconsistency that transfixed his American audience, two of the dates and events held
special fascination. Walpole several times insisted that the British government had not known of the first Russian offer until
August 5, 1813, when they received a dispatch from Admiral Bor-
lase Warren, commander of the fleet blockading the United
States, informing the cabinet that he had issued passports for the
voyage of Gallatin and Bayard to Russia. Walpole also was
adamant in his assertion that the Czar knew of England's inflexible rejection by August 22 and that shortly thereafter Alexander told Romanzoff to give his regrets to the American
commission. Other aspects of Walpole's variations on a theme
required inattention or gullibility for acceptance, but one thing
was certain: there would be no mediation of Anglo-American
differences.

If Walpole's veracity were open to question, Alexander Baring's
was not, and his second letter to Gallatin arrived in St. Petersburg in mid-November. Baring restated British desires for peace
and the government's determination to negotiate directly or not
at all, adding that Gallatin's arguments in favor of mediation
were "very ingenious, and no inference of insincerity is drawn
from America's adopting this mode." Great Britain, Baring again
told Gallatin, would have to insist on its rights of search and
impressment, but Baring was sure that his government would be
"reasonable," for "I feel the more convinced that the existing
difficulties are more difficulties of form than of substance." In
other words, Britain, if she negotiated at all, would not discuss
the principle of impressment, the eradication of which was a
sine qua non of American agreement to a peace treaty, the cause
for which Americans continued to spill their blood.

Most interesting and pathetic of all the reactions to the messages which came out of England was that of Romanzoff. Harris
and Gallatin hastened to see him on November 2, and Romanzoff
readily admitted that Count Lieven had written from London,
saying he had not submitted the second offer of mediation because of the finality with which the British government had refused the first. Romanzoff, however, "did not feel himself at

liberty" to say that mediation was over, nor would he agree that Gallatin was no longer a minister. Neither fact could be recognized until Romanzoff received official notification from the Emperor.

In the matter of details, Romanzoff's words, like those of Walpole, suffered not the chains of consistency. The Count was vehement in stating that the Czar had, with his own hand, written a letter on August 22 approving the renewal of the offer of mediation. According to Walpole, Alexander had been informed of Britain's refusal by this date, although Walpole, if his alternate versions were to be credited, also had the Czar being informed in July, weeks before England had heard (said Walpole at other times) of mediation.

Only Adams struggled endlessly and fruitlessly to put together the pieces of what were really separate puzzles, for neither Romanzoff nor Walpole had the full confidence of his superiors or was well informed on the actions of his government. Gallatin and Bayard, after some modest attempts to discern the truth, put the riddle aside and turned to the problems of leaving St. Petersburg, a step that could be taken as soon as the commission received official notice from the Emperor of Britain's rejection and as soon as snow formed a lasting pavement over the mud of the roads.

In the meantime, suppers, games of boston, courts of reception, and official dinners filled the social routine with dreary regularity, and day after day passed without news from the Czar, a situation that caused "much impatience and embarrassment." An unpredictable November surrendered its unruly lease to December, and Bayard and Gallatin finally fitted out their sleds, but the Czar remained silent. On December 15, at a diplomatic dinner, Romanzoff, for probably the twentieth time, said he should have an answer from the Emperor in a few days. Bayard, eyeing the antics of Walpole, who was animatedly relating one of his many anecdotes, scarcely troubled to acknowledge his remark with a nod.

The day before Romanzoff's dinner, Lord Castlereagh, the tall, handsome Foreign Secretary of Great Britain, had crossed the floor of the House of Commons to confront Alexander Baring. What was this, the indignant Castlereagh wanted to know, about some American named George Dallas's being in London? Having already asked the same question of Count Lieven, as Baring knew, the Foreign Secretary was only venting his anger over the American problem, a petty annoyance not worth the efforts of a Foreign Office clerk but a distasteful ingredient, nevertheless, in a European stew that was already unpalatable enough. Baring assured Castlereagh that Dallas was there and offered to take personal responsibility for him while he remained in England. Castlereagh muttered that it was "extreme condescension" on his part to allow Dallas to stay, but he said little more and soon went back to his own bench. For what good it might do, Dallas was free to remain in the enemy's capital.

As Reuben Beasley, agent for American prisoners of war and his country's only official representative in Britain, later wrote to Bayard, the arrival of Dallas "made a considerable noise." Dallas, in late November, set foot in a land that thought of its American involvement only periodically—when American privateers cut out an excessive amount of British shipping, when a United States frigate sailed home with a British warship as its prize, when an American army blundered back and forth across the Canadian border and made heroes of His Majesty's officers. The real threat lay beyond the Channel, in the person of the unprincipled little Corsican who wanted nothing less than the world. But Napoleon was in the twilight of his career, and Britons were becoming more conscious of the paltry but sensitive wounds inflicted by the Americans. It was embarrassing to have a nondescript group of ex-colonies prey on English shipping as if England's navy were no more menacing than Portugal's. It was infuriating to have Americans running in and out of Canada, boasting that that colony would soon be divided into states. It was an example of American effrontery that one of them should come uninvited during a time of war to London. Did it mean that the Americans and the Czar were cooking up some new and evil brew, or was it a sign, as a British newspaper thought, "that the Yankeys had come down on their marrow bones?"

The government of Lords Liverpool and Castlereagh leaned toward the latter possibility, with no little justification, but it was a belief derived less from knowledge of the facts of the American war than of refusal to recognize that their colonial offspring had come of age and asserted its independence from the crown.

The American Revolution had concluded with the Peace of 1783, a bad treaty in British eyes and one not necessarily definitive or permanent. As the conviction "once an Englishman, always an Englishman" excused the practice of impressment, the inability to accept the successful revolt of the thirteen American colonies prompted successive British governments to think of American relations as more of a Colonial than a Foreign Office matter. The American declaration of war in 1812, although English diplomats had predicted it for six months, came as a rude and incredible shock. The British government had made reparation for the *Chesapeake* affair; it had repealed the Orders in Council; it could not, as all the world must know, give up impressment without losing its navy, which depended for its manpower on such patriotically inspired slavery, or its honor, which by this time was as closely involved with a continuance of impressment as was the navy. Only one conclusion was possible: the Americans, "less popular and less esteemed . . . than the base and bigotted Portugueze, or the ferocious and ignorant Russians," were in the embrace of an unholy alliance with Napoleon.

Such a restricted and forbidding outlook boded ill for the American armistice attempts of 1812, efforts which fell entirely on the shoulders of Jonathan Russell, chargé d'affaires and the highest-ranking American in England. Russell, not a mild-mannered or soft-spoken man, had a capacity for reaping weeds of ill will from soils that normally grew daisies of harmony, and London's loam did not favor happy results. But even if Russell had been a Benjamin Franklin or a Talleyrand his task would have been impossible from the beginning. His first instructions, received in August, 1812, directed him to propose an armistice on the basis that Great Britain affirm her repeal of the Orders in Council and that she discontinue impressment and release those sailors already impressed, in return for a reciprocal law prohibiting employment by each nation of the other's seamen. Russell submitted a note embodying these propositions to Castlereagh on August 24. Just five days later he had the Foreign Minister's answer. The terms for an armistice were "absolutely inadmissible."

Madison and Monroe apparently had second thoughts about their first instructions to Russell; for Monroe wrote again a few weeks later, still insisting on the same acts of compliance on the part of the British but asking now for a "clear and distinct understanding," not a formal declaration, on the points before an armistice could take place. The dispatch reached Russell on the morning of September 12, and by that afternoon his restatement of the propositions was on its way to the Foreign Office. Silence pervaded the London autumn until 3 P.M. on the 16th, when Russell received a brief note from William Hamilton, one of Castlereagh's subordinates, informing him that his Lordship could not reply to Russell for a few days. Minutes later, Russell, fuming with ire and impatience, was sealing his reply, a message that bluntly stated that he would stay no later than Sunday, the 20th, "unless some special and satisfactory reason be assigned for a longer delay." Less than two hours passed before a Foreign Office messenger was back with a request that Russell be at Castlereagh's home in St. James's Square at nine that evening. Promptly at the appointed hour Russell was ushered into a richly paneled room in which Castlereagh and Hamilton sat behind a long table brimming with documents on relations with the United States.

The room may have been mellow in the soft light of candles and crackling fire, but the subject was war, and after a brief exchange of polite conversation the talk was pointed and not always temperate. Castlereagh first demanded the American's powers, and Russell handed over Monroe's most recent letter. As the Foreign Secretary carefully examined the words of the Secretary of State, Hamilton and Russell kept an uneasy silence. It was some time before Castlereagh spoke. He could not see, he said, that Russell's powers or instructions were any greater than or different from what they had been a few weeks ago. Russell could not commit the United States to an agreement; yet Castlereagh, placed on "unequal ground," was expected to pledge his own government. It could not be done. Furthermore, Russell's instructions were probably drafted before the United States had learned of the repeal of the Orders in Council. Even if this were not so, Russell and his government seemed to underestimate the difficulties of solving the problems of impressment. "Even our friends in Congress," Russell later recorded Castlereagh as saying,

I mean (observing, perhaps, some alteration in my countenance)

those who were opposed to going to war with us, have been so confident in this mistake, that they have ascribed the failure of such an arrangement solely to the misconduct of the American Government. . . . You are not aware of the great sensibility and jealousy of the people of England on this subject; and no administration could expect to remain in power that should consent to renounce the right of impressment, or to suspend the practice, without the certainty of an arrangement which should obviously be calculated most unequivocally to secure its object. Whether such an arrangement can be devised is extremely doubtful, but it is very certain that you have no sufficient powers for its accomplishment.

Castlereagh's statement was not only an honest appraisal of the English political situation, but if stated by an American of Americans in a New England or Southern village it would have won the respect of native politicians who, even in 1812, knew that principle was not to be confused with power or the source of power. Russell was not the least of politicians, but on that September evening he was a diplomat in St. James's Square, and Americans have frequently denied the political facts of life upon leaving their own shores. Russell asserted that his powers were sufficient for the business at hand—to reach an informal agreement—and insisted also that impressment difficulties were less alarming than Castlereagh implied. Perhaps, Russell admitted, his government had not known of the repeal of the Orders in Council when Monroe wrote his dispatch, but repeal was expected, and, in any case, this was "generally considered to be of minor importance" when compared to impressment.

Castlereagh and Hamilton remained impassive. You say, Russel abruptly told Castlereagh, that the British people are sensitive about impressment. What of the citizens of the United States who are the victims, the hostages who may have to fight their own people? I am astonished, he said, that you can get so upset about the slave trade and not about impressment. For a moment he paused, and then, in milder tones, he described the proposed American law that would prohibit employment of each other's seamen. Castlereagh said nothing, showed nothing, and Hamilton interrupted only to ask if the suggested law meant that the United States would give up British citizens who had become naturalized Americans. Russell stared at him in disbelief. To do so, he said tersely, would be a national disgrace.

When Russell had exhausted his emotions and arguments Castlereagh eyed him coldly and told him that neither Hamilton nor he had anything to add. He concluded by saying that if the United States was "so anxious *to get rid of the war*" they could do so when they heard of and accepted the repeal of the Orders in Council—Britain's fullest extent of compromise. Minutes later Russell was dismissed, and two days later Castlereagh sent his final note, declaring that Monroe's more recent instructions sought the same end as his earlier set "in a more covert, and, therefore, in a more objectionable manner." Russell answered as well as he could, but on the following afternoon he left London; he was not to return until many years had passed and much blood had been shed.

The principal British attempt to achieve an armistice was transmitted through Admiral Warren at Halifax, Nova Scotia. Warren's dispatch to James Monroe assumed that Britain's suspension of the Orders in Council was sufficient action on her part and demanded that the United States "instantly recall letters of marque and reprisal" and revoke her military orders as her share of the preface to a cessation of hostilities. In late October Monroe replied, repeating the gist of his instructions to Russell— the failure of whose mission was as yet unknown to Monroe, and who was at the moment nearing New York—and emphasizing the necessity for some curtailment of impressment. Whatever trials she might suffer, America meant to continue the war until seamen such as Jesse Bates—"about five feet nine inches high, dark hair and complexion, dark snapping eyes, has an impediment in his speech, and at times affects lunacy; has a wife and family in Boston, Massachusetts"—were released from British prisons and ships and need never again fear seizure by the British navy. It was, as Russell clearly knew, the one demand that England intended not to accept under any circumstances. Except for the interference of the Czar, whose proposition was not yet known, war was to continue unabated.

For England the American war came at the worst possible time. Liverpool's newly formed cabinet of undistinguished politicians was on trial before the British people; it was also confronted with Napoleon, seemingly at the height of his power, master of the Continent and its goods and foodstuffs, and con-

queror of Russia and its supplies. When the United States broke
its ties with and closed its doors to its mother country, Great
Britain rocked on the edge of disaster. Mills closed by the hundreds; wages dwindled into insignificance as food prices became
nearly twice what they had been in the spring; men were reduced to beggary or starved in the streets. In Portugal, Wellington waited impatiently and in vain for reinforcements. The troops
that he should have received were sent instead to Scotland and
northern England to quell rioting mobs of unemployed workmen.
America's feeble incursions into Canada amused British officers
and Members of Parliament, but want of food and raw materials
came close to turning a nuisance into a calamity, and to make
matters worse British papers were filled with accounts of the
infuriatingly successful accomplishments of American ships.

The autumn of 1812 was marked in England by flooding
rivers and visions of doom, and the winter that followed came
early and stayed late, but, even before life returned to English
gardens, hope and arrogance had come once more to the fore.
The French Emperor who had done so much to get America into
a war removed the sting of her blows by wasting his own army
and fortunes in Russia. As spring turned to summer Continental
ports began to open and pour forth their goods, and Wellington
started his triumphant drive through Spain. With the news becoming more promising day by day, the United States was all
but forgotten. To be sure, peace would be better than war, but
America, it became increasingly clear, posed as much of a threat
to Canada as she did to Scotland. As a result, peace, whenever
it came, would be dictated, not negotiated.

Castlereagh, engrossed with the troubles of a wavering European alliance, gave little thought to the difficulties with the
United States, but he dwelt on them enough to determine that the
spice of the New World should not be added to the boiling stew
of the Old. As the strength of Napoleon receded that of Great
Britain and the Continental nations grew, but in the death struggle of Bonaparte's Empire old problems came to life and new
ones were born. Sweden and Russia, now that their ships could
again sail the seas, recalled their sufferings from British maritime restrictions and were reminded of their sympathy with
American principles. Thus Britain, unravaged by land warfare
and more powerful than ever, became the object of the fears and

jealousies of her allies. Just as Napoleon was to be feared for his propensity and ability to wage war, England was to be heeded for her powerful tendency to regulate and profit from the fruits of peace. Castlereagh—an Englishman pure and, in this case, simple—recognized the symptoms of developing Allied suspicion and hostility even if he could not fathom the causes, and he and the rest of the British cabinet knew from the first suggestion of the possibility that mediation should not be.

Contrary to the later inventions, hallucinations, or guesses of Walpole and Romanzoff, Great Britain was notified of the Russian offer in October, 1812. The first reaction of Prime Minister Liverpool and Foreign Minister Castlereagh was to treat the overture as they did domestic and colonial and American problems—to ignore it in hopes that it might conveniently be forgotten, but they were plagued by the persistence of Count Lieven, the Russian ambassador, and by the necessity of keeping up their diplomatic friendship with Alexander. In consequence, Castlereagh, in November, resorted to the unlikely excuse of probable American rejection as reason for British delay. In a winter of uncertainty, filled with the rigors of war and climate, no one but John Quincy Adams, who scarcely mattered, bothered to debate the point.

In the spring of 1813, however, it was obvious to the English and, more significantly, to the Russians that the United States did not mean to cast mediation aside, and, in May, Castlereagh undertook the painful task of explaining to Count Lieven what Romanzoff later repeated to Adams—that Britain considered the American unpleasantness a private matter which did not lend itself to even the kindest of outside interference. What the British Foreign Minister had thus verbally communicated Lieven conscientiously relayed to Romanzoff and the Czar.

The answer may have satisfied the very busy Alexander, at least temporarily, but it could not have been and was not known by the American government, and Castlereagh was no little exasperated to learn, during the first days of July, that Gallatin and Bayard had touched the shores of Europe, determined on their innocent mission of peace. At first word of this unfortunate proximity of American envoys Castlereagh moved quickly to put the British stand in writing. On July 5, as the *Neptune* fought headwinds in the Baltic, the British Secretary for Foreign Affairs

drafted instructions to Lord Cathcart, British minister attendant
on the Emperor's roving court, telling Cathcart that he "should
lose no time" in getting an "explicit understanding" with the
Czar that Great Britain would not participate in mediation.
Neither would she be willing to have maritime matters discussed
in a general European congress. "It is to be lamented," continued
Castlereagh, in an effort to rewrite history, "that the formal offer
was made to America before the disposition of the British Government was previously sounded as to its acceptance of a mediation," for the mediation proposal had given Madison a chance to
offer the United States "a vague expectation of peace. . . . This
evil, however, cannot now be avoided, and it only remains to
prevent this question from producing any embarrassment between Great Britain and Russia."

Castlereagh was only technically right in saying that the British government had not been "previously sounded as to its acceptance of a mediation," for he chose to ignore the fact that
Britain had received and orally replied to the formal proposition
long before that proposition had traversed the Atlantic. Adams in
St. Petersburg knew of Castlereagh's parrying statement on possible American rejection months before Monroe or Madison in
Washington had been offered the opportunity to accept or reject.
But although Castlereagh's facts were somewhat distorted his
lament was genuine.

The British cabinet, which anticipated the eventual collapse
or submission of Madison's administration in the face of antago-
nistic American public opinion, would much rather have preferred to allow the American issue to lie neglected until it
expired of its own accord or until Napoleon was deposed and
European politics were less unsettled. To be forced by Alexander
to treat with the United States was a galling matter, but even
worse was the apprehension that Russia, the Scandinavian countries, and France—whose own complaints against Great Britain
read like a slightly more moderate version of the American declaration of war—might call a truce, combine forces, and fasten
their attention on maritime affairs. Only Napoleon's violence kept
much of Europe from deciding that England was, in the long
run, more to be feared than France, and the British cabinet
could not be sure that the weakened French leader might not
make the most of Allied dissensions and adopt a policy of sweet-

ness and light with the Continental powers as a means of saving
what was left of his Empire and of gaining time to restore his
forces.

Castlereagh realized that Bonaparte and Alexander were the
key figures in deciding the probable direction of international
affairs, and dissatisfied with the steps he had so far taken or failed
to take, he spent the second week of July, 1813, mulling over the
possibilities that lay before him. In view of the chaotic condition
of the Russian government and the jealousies among ministers in
that government, the English could obscure their refusal of mediation and trust that it would be some time, if ever, before Lieven,
Nesselrode, who was with the Emperor and had the prerogatives,
if not the title, of Minister of State, and Romanzoff, who was far
from the Czar and had the title but no longer the powers of
Minister of State, would be able to clarify matters. This Castlereagh had already attempted in his note of July 5 and in his
verbal replies to Lieven. But if pressure were to be put on Alexander to keep maritime matters out of a European congress he
must be assured that Britain meant to negotiate with the Americans.

Consideration of the American question could be delayed but
could no longer be avoided, and Castlereagh, uncertain of the
success of his first letter, sat down on July 14 to pen further instructions to Lord Cathcart—instructions that mixed firmness on
maritime matters with a willingness to talk with representatives
of the United States.

The first and most important thing for Cathcart to do was to
again impress upon the Emperor that Great Britain did not want
maritime questions brought into European negotiations. "Great
Britain may be driven out of a Congress," wrote Castlereagh,
knowing that Cathcart would repeat his message word for word
to Nesselrode or the Czar, "but not out of her maritime rights,
and, if the Continental Powers know their own interests, they
will not hazard this." So much for threat and bluster. Castlereagh
next turned to the American problem, and here his words were
intended to serve Cathcart merely as a guide, not as a set speech.
"It is of great importance," advised Castlereagh, "to strip any
negotiation between America and us even of the *appearance* of
foreign intervention . . . the mere fact of an arrangement being
made through the intervention of a third Power would probably

decide the nation against it." Cathcart was to tell the Czar of England's readiness to negotiate directly with the Americans, either at London or Gothenburg, preferably the former. It had to be one place or the other and Castlereagh's further directions to his minister concerning the site underlined his sensitivity to European reaction to Britain's reasons for declining mediation. "Any place near the Russian court, or the seat of other negotiations," warned the Foreign Minister, "would give to our refusal of the mediation the air of a shabby pretence."

Castlereagh, having been apprised of the letter Gallatin had written to Baring from Gothenburg, communicated essentially the same story to the head of the British banking house, and Baring included some of the details in the letter which Gallatin received in St. Petersburg in mid-August. It took longer to get an official statement into the hands of the Czar, although Alexander had heard of the British attitude from Lieven in July. Cathcart did deliver a verbal message about August 20, but not until the dust had settled from the battle of Dresden, a defeat for the Allies, was the British Minister able to hand Nesselrode a formal note of rejection on September 1. To all such messages, oral or written, the Emperor replied that the matter was at an end and he would pursue it no further, but to Romanzoff's suggestion of a second offer of mediation he responded affirmatively in late July and again on September 20.

These contradictions threw Cathcart into a state of utter bewilderment, which he conveyed in thoroughly unintelligible messages to his masters in London. Nesselrode was no longer certain of what the Czar had in mind, nor was Lieven, but Lieven knew full well the attitude of the British, and he flatly refused to announce the second proposal. Consequently, no second offer of mediation was ever made, and the Americans in St. Petersburg waited in vain.

What the Emperor intended remained a mystery, perhaps even to him, for it is less likely that he was dabbling in some sinister diplomatic move than that he had his hands full with the business of war and had neither the time nor inclination to attend to other matters. It is possible that he meant for Romanzoff to take charge of the situation, but forgot, amid the constant demands made on him, to give his Minister for Foreign Affairs the necessary powers. It is possible, too, that Romanzoff and Nesselrode, in their struggle against one another, used the mediation affair in an attempt to gain supremacy. It is certain that the British blamed Romanzoff and that the Americans in St. Petersburg, who knew almost nothing of what was occurring, doubted Romanzoff, were perplexed by the silence of the Czar, and knew not whom to blame.

Castlereagh was no better able to penetrate Russian inscrutability than was Cathcart, but he was adamant in his stand against mediation and was prepared to keep his part of the bargain—direct negotiation—especially when this meant even greater delays and less chance than ever of American success. Castlereagh took his time, and it was not until November 4—a day when Walpole at a diplomatic dinner at Romanzoff's was feeding Bayard helpings of misinformation—that he signed a dispatch to be sent to Secretary of State Monroe. In it he enclosed Cathcart's note to Nesselrode of September 1, saying that Cathcart had been told to present the message as soon as Great Britain had learned of the appointment of an American commission. This statement, while true, once more ignored the fact that Britain had known of the offer of mediation long before the American government.

Castlereagh came shortly to the point and proposed direct negotiation, and, calling on his knack for fiction where fact was insufficient or contrary to his wishes, added that the American ministers had already been apprised of the British offer and "have intimated, in reply to this overture" that they had no objection to London and were as desirous as was the British government "that this business should not be mixed with the affairs of the continent of Europe." It can be assumed that Castlereagh paused at this point to admire his creation. He then went on to conclude that Great Britain was willing to negotiate with the United States "for the conciliatory adjustment of the differences subsisting between the two States, with an earnest desire on their part to bring them to a favorable issue, upon principles of perfect reciprocity, not inconsistent with the established maxims of Public Law, and with the maritime rights of the British Empire." In short, Great Britain would treat, but she would not discuss the principles that underlay her Orders in Council, and she most certainly would not surrender the right of impressment. It remained to be seen if such was the understanding of James Monroe or James Madison.

Castlereagh's dispatch to Monroe preceded George Dallas's arrival in London, and as soon as the young American became aware of English intentions he dutifully wrote of them to the ministers in St. Petersburg. It was wasted effort, for his letters remained icebound throughout the winter, and it was not until spring, long after Gallatin and Bayard had fled the chilly Russian wastes, that the mail was delivered. In December, when news from the outside world was feverishly prayed for, Adams, Gallatin, and Bayard heard nothing. They no longer hoped for a revival of mediation but knew not what next, and they waited impatiently on Romanzoff for word that would release them from the confinement of St. Petersburg.

It was not until the middle of December that heavy snow and ice and bone-chilling cold came to stay. Before then, weeks of snow had alternated with periods of drizzle and slush, and the river and the canals were one day solid and covered with a layer of ice and the next day choked with ugly, grinding chunks. Almost always it was damp and dark and dismal, with midday affording only a brownish twilight and with the curtain of night falling shortly after three in the afternoon. The season of joy approached unheralded. On Christmas Day Bayard sat in his lonely room, forlornly thinking of his family in far-off Delaware. "In all other Christian Countries," he dejectedly wrote in his diary, "this is Christmas, but in Russia it is the 13th day of the month."

The evening before—Christmas Eve to the Americans, the night of the Emperor's birthday to the Russians—the three envoys had attended a diplomatic dinner at Romanzoff's. For nearly an hour, while dinner cooled and patience expired, the assembled company had awaited the tardy arrival of Lord Walpole, who took this opportunity to express his contempt for the Count. The episode was, to Adams, Bayard, and Gallatin, one more example of British opposition to Romanzoff and his policies and another bit of evidence that Romanzoff had lost his influence with the Czar. It was becoming more and more unlikely that Romanzoff would ever be able to give the American commissioners official word on the outcome of the mediation proposals. What little the Americans knew or suspected came from unofficial letters or clippings from English newspapers or from the involved, contrary, unofficial ramblings of Walpole and Romanzoff. Not only had there been no authoritative word from the Russian government on mediation but Gallatin had yet to hear from his own government on the Senate's rejection of his nomination. It was not that doubt or hope lingered concerning either of these matters, but, unless they wished to risk a diplomatic affront, Bayard could not leave Russia until the Emperor had dismissed him, and Gallatin required either the Czar's farewell or formal notification from Monroe or Madison on the disapproval of his appointment.

Only Adams, who was not going anywhere unless he received a new and unexpected commission from his government, burrowed in for the winter and settled down with his books. He reflected to himself that the desire to do noble things is not enough, that " the spark from heaven is given to few. It is not to be obtained by entreaty or by toil. To be profitable to my children seems to be within the compass of my powers." Spurred by this humble perception, he gave over five hours a day to the reading of tomes on science—up at six and in bed by ten, social and diplomatic functions allowing. He was as anxious as the others for an official statement from the Russian government, but he divorced himself as much as possible from the anguished projects and comings and goings of Gallatin and Bayard.

Adams's attitude toward the plight of Bayard and Gallatin seemed strangely inconsistent. He agreed with them that mediation was at an end; he sympathized with their desire to depart and to do so before spring rains turned the countryside and the roads into a mucilaginous morass; and his faith in Romanzoff, like theirs, had been stretched beyond endurance. Yet he became tiresomely insistent on the necessity for observing diplomatic niceties, on the necessity for official confirmation of what everyone knew. He turned a deaf ear and a cold shoulder to every plan that Gallatin and Bayard proposed.

As early as November, Gallatin and Bayard conceived the idea of heading ostensibly for home via London, where, they supposed, they could obtain more precise news of the possibilities of direct negotiation and perhaps accelerate moves toward such peace talks. Apart from the ravings of Walpole, their only evidence that England was entertaining thoughts of direct negotiation appeared in the letters of Alexander Baring. When the matter was broached to Adams he insisted that his colleagues' intentions and the statements of Baring be included in the next dispatch to Monroe. Bayard and Gallatin demurred. They had, after all, only limited knowledge of British plans and were not yet certain of their own. Furthermore, American publication of Baring's remarks, always a possibility, might be injurious to him. They could, they told Adams, suggest their intentions to Monroe now and write more fully and positively later.

Adams thought not, and his anger and hurt over the project that had gone so far without the benefit of his advice was evident in the lecture which he proceeded to give and later entered in his diary. To ascertain how far the British "persevered in their principles," said Adams sternly,

> and also what they proposed as expedients to guard against the abuse, as they called it, of impressment, was sufficient in my mind, to justify their touching in England, and they were to judge for themselves as to the responsibility which they assumed by it in regard to our Government. I thought that responsibility not inconsiderable, as, without any powers to treat at all, they were going to treat with a full knowledge that it must be upon a basis directly in the face of our instructions.

Clearly, Adams had little tolerance for an unauthorized trip to the capital of the enemy, a visit that might effectively negate his position on the commission.

Gallatin listened soberly and controlled his annoyance but not his tendency to twit Adams or Bayard whenever the opportunity offered. He pointed out that only Bayard bore official responsibility for such a journey, that he, Gallatin, was no longer a member of the commission and could go wherever he pleased without giving a damn whether the United States government liked it or not. In any event, he said more reasonably, the purpose of the visit was to determine if the British government would consider the question of impressment if it were otherwise or properly presented and to convince them that they must treat on this problem or not at all.

Bayard, not always quick to catch the reason behind the line of Gallatin's argument, disagreed, saying he thought they could negotiate and even settle all "principles and articles of a treaty."

He added that both would share responsibility since both would again be private citizens when they left Russia.

This was too much for Adams. At some length, he advised Bayard of his responsibilities, which, he claimed, did not end until Bayard arrived back in the United States. More pointedly, he reminded both gentlemen that they already had a good idea of British intentions. To say that they were going to England to ascertain these intentions was but a feeble suppression of what should be and were their real aims. If they went to England at all, they should go to convince that government that she must change her ways. Bayard and Gallatin withered before the on-slaught and assented, and Adams, still furious, stalked from the house.

Adams knew full well that, aside from improbable missionary accomplishments, the envisioned trip was vague in its purpose. Gallatin, especially, nourished the fancy that somehow his mere presence in the enemy's capital would be salutary. To Adams this belief was extreme presumption, and, knowing that Bayard was willing to forgo an agreement on the renunciation or curtail-ment of impressment and suspecting that Gallatin might share a similar disposition, Adams feared the results that a visit to Lon-don might produce. But beyond that, what irritated him more was Bayard's and Gallatin's neglect of him. Adams learned of their schemes and doings only belatedly and often inadvertently —and then usually because Bayard, who was seldom able to con-fide in Gallatin, could no longer contain himself or desperately needed the reassurance of someone, even Adams. To worsen the situation, Gallatin and Bayard used Harris, Adams's refractory subordinate, as their emissary to Romanzoff and as their aide-de-camp.

It was Levett Harris who came to Adams's home on the last day of the year to inform the minister that Gallatin, who no longer made any pretense of waiting for official dismissal, had recently outlined a route to London that allowed for a wide sweep to include the Czar's headquarters in Frankfort and Gal-latin's ancestral home in Geneva. It was as the two men were discussing this latest variation in Gallatin's plans for his journey that Harris innocently dropped his opinion that he thought it strange that Bayard, instead of joining Gallatin as he had in-tended, would, because of his responsibility to the mission, re-

main in St. Petersburg, waiting for a document from the Emperor
that would probably never come. Adams wondered at the import
of Harris's aside but made no comment. On the following evening Bayard visited until well after Adams's bedtime, and before
he left he had proposed a meeting of the commission for January
3, to fix a time beyond which the ministers would not wait for a
formal notice of British rejection of the mediation.

Monday afternoon, January 3, the three of them gathered in
John Quincy's home. They had only a minor squabble in deciding to send a note to Romanzoff, requesting a definite answer
on the British stand, but in the course of discussing the matter,
Gallatin, to Adams's uneasy interest, disclosed that he had already seen Romanzoff to arrange for his own departure. Before
Adams could thoroughly digest this bit of news, Bayard and
Gallatin informed him of what Harris had already partly revealed—that both ministers planned to leave together and were
considering stopping at the Czar's headquarters to confer with
Nesselrode. Adams nodded but said nothing. The silence was
thunderous. It was Bayard who broke and asked Adams for his
opinion. Adams promptly and bluntly gave it. It was not, he said
emphatically, a proper thing to do.

> Both . . . gentlemen appeared to be very strongly affected by . . .
> my opinion. They both started instantly from their seats, and
> walked to and fro in the chamber, in directions crossing each other,
> and in great apparent agitation. I observed that there was no
> proper channel of communication for them with the Emperor at
> headquarters. Mr. Bayard said there was Nesselrode. I said he was
> not Minister of Foreign Affairs, and would certainly receive no
> communication from them without an express order from the
> Emperor.

When Adams quieted, Gallatin suggested that Bayard and he
could go close enough to headquarters to send Harris, assuming
Harris would go, and not actually go themselves. Bayard quickly
asserted that Harris was quite willing to go, a fact that Gallatin
confirmed. Adams did not doubt it. He knew now that Harris had
come on the 31st to sound him out; he suspected that the scheme
was entirely of Gallatin's making and that Bayard was irreso-
lutely playing a role that had been created for him. Adams was
incensed at all of them, but as they left to go into the dark-blue
cold of the late afternoon he also felt alone and deserted.

It was Bayard who by Adams's insistence had been assigned to draft the note to Romanzoff, and during the next week he wrote and rewrote, struggling mightily to incorporate the editing suggestions of Adams and Gallatin. It was more than a week later before the three ministers met again in an effort to reach some final agreement on the statement which Bayard scarcely recognized as stemming from his original. The remaining point in dispute was a paragraph Adams had added, ending with a comment that if they received no clear answer from Romanzoff, Bayard would ask for his passport, "leaving to the other [Adams] the care of receiving and transmitting the Answer. . . . " Bayard protested that Adams's paragraph made it seem as if he, Bayard, were shirking his duty, whereas the real purpose of his leaving was to bring the mission to an end.

Adams reminded him that this could be done only by the United States or Russian government, not by any one or all of the commissioners, and on the subject of duty he was vitriolic. He said that Bayard had thought himself "competent to go alone to the Emperor's head-quarters . . . without needing my cooperation," that he had believed himself "competent to go to England alone, and there make a treaty, without needing any concurrence of mine." If, therefore, Bayard "could perform separately duties . . . of that magnitude," Adams could not "conceive that the mere act of receiving and transmitting an official paper was such" that Bayard, "without any desertion of his duty," could not allow Adams to do it alone.

Bayard, confused and dispirited by Adams's attack, argued feebly that his visit to the Czar's headquarters was uncertain and that he would appear in England in an unofficial role. Adams refused to answer him. Convinced that he had been disregarded, "as if I had never been joined in the commission," he sat sullenly through the rest of the meeting, but under Gallatin's patient and deft persuasion he finally allowed the offending paragraph to be struck, and, as the afternoon waned, the three of them achieved uneasy accord on the note to Romanzoff.

From that moment it was but a matter of concluding preparations and participating in the ceremonies of leave-taking before Gallatin and Bayard could be on their way. The note to Romanzoff served mainly as justification to their own government of the step which the American ministers were taking. No satisfactory answer—one that clearly and officially stated the British response to the offer of mediation—was anticipated and none ever was received. Harris, at Bayard's request, called on Romanzoff the day after the American note had been delivered. The consul found the Count pale and weak from an illness of body and spirit. The old man said that he had yet to read the note, and he asked Harris to summarize the contents. Harris did so and Romanzoff said that he would dispatch the message to the Czar. He said, also, that he was sad and mortified over the way the American ministers and he had been treated by the Czar.

A few days later Romanzoff sent for Harris to come again, and, when Harris appeared before him, the Count said he appreciated Bayard's predicament and would not oppose his leaving. He refused, however, to put his opinion in writing, as Harris requested, and he volunteered his belief that the United States "had shewn rather too much ardour in pursuing peace," but he was sure, nevertheless, that a just peace eventually would be obtained. Harris advised him, as Romanzoff by now understood, that Bayard would probably consider Romanzoff's words justification for his departure, and Romanzoff nodded his assent. Harris rushed to repeat the conversation to Bayard, and, after the homesick Senator from Delaware had heard, he confessed that "no words can express my joy at the prospect" of leaving.

Two weeks elapsed between the completion of the note to Romanzoff and the day of departure—time enough to bring the personal relations between the American commissioners to an almost irreparable state. Adams and Bayard renewed their harsh or anguished comments to one another over a second note to Romanzoff, one that announced Bayard's intention to depart, and over a final dispatch to Monroe, which Bayard insisted Adams write and which Adams, in a fit of pique, succeeded in writing in three terse lines. Adams was only slightly less pleased with Gallatin, but, however annoyed he became with him, he could not help but respect the man for his obvious intelligence and remarkable self-control. When Adams sulked or became abusive Gallatin simply smiled and joked about it, and Adams, bewildered by such a reception, soon forgot the cause of his tirade.

It was less easy to forget and forgive the blunders of James Bayard, for Bayard, in the grip of melancholy and indecision, lost whatever composure or reason he had possessed. Night after night, despite the mistreatment he received, he made himself a guest in Adams's home, and there, when Adams was not lecturing him on duty or the error of his ways, Bayard admitted his doubts and misgivings about the mission and the administration and complained about the faults of Gallatin, whom, he indicated, he did not trust and whose air of superiority he found intolerable. Adams seldom committed himself, but he was revolted by these indiscretions of Bayard, and he shook with fury when he later learned from Harris, who shifted his allegiance as his ambition dictated, that Bayard had also uttered many unkind words about him. After Bayard had departed St. Petersburg Adams expressed the hope he should never have to associate with the man again.

It was fortunate that Bayard and Gallatin left soon. Gallatin, who was more certain than Bayard of his intentions, completed his ceremonial rounds early, and on Sunday, January 23, Bayard passed his final hurdle when he took farewell leave of the Empress-Mother. She apologized to him for the Czar's absence and the consequent lack of social life and announced her hope for peace between England and the United States. Bayard muttered his thanks, kissed her hand, and, for the last time, backed slowly out of the throne room of the Winter Palace. Harris shared in the leave-taking audience, but the visit to the Emperor's headquarters had been abandoned, and Harris would not be going for a few weeks.

On Tuesday afternoon, after attending court in honor of the Empress Elizabeth's birthday, Adams stopped at his colleagues' house to say good-by. He did not stay long, and when he had left, Gallatin and Bayard returned to their packing. It was not until ten thirty that night that the horses snorted in the icy air and heaved against their burdens, and the runners of the three sleds—one carrying Gallatin, another Bayard, and a third servants and baggage—crunched into the hard-packed snow and began to glide through the streets of St. Petersburg. Soon after midnight, Bayard's and the servants' sleds were far in front of Gallatin's, slipping through the silent and awesome countryside, along the narrow strip of road that was barely outlined in the mountainous drifts of snow. St. Petersburg was a scene of the past.

PART TWO

Confusion and Delay

Winter: 1813–1814

To President Madison and his Secretary of State James Monroe the Russian offer of mediation had come as unexpected and unsolicited assistance. Hull's failure at Detroit, in the opening maneuver of the war, was a setback so terrible that it was incomprehensible, and, more than a year after its occurrence, Madison still grieved and talked about it, as if his deepest desire were to go back and start over again. Whatever illusions he had nourished concerning American ambitions and their fulfillment, he had been practical enough to realize that, with a small army and uncertain funds, success depended on a quick, bold stroke. That lightning thrust had barely sparked, however, before it was doused by the threat of Indian butchery, and, soon after he had learned of Hull's incompetence and possible cowardice, Madison had aged perceptibly.

It was, perhaps, fortunate for the United States that warfare in the early nineteenth century was largely confined to that part of the year between the spring rains and the autumn frosts. Throughout the winter of 1812–1813 the defeats of summer and fall receded in men's memories, and months of inactivity bred cautious hope and kept the American army from blundering into further calamity. Assurance of easy victory had vanished, but the ambitions held by a majority of Americans remained. What was to have taken weeks would now take months, even, some conceded, a year or two, and though the spirits of Madison and Monroe did not revive as fully as those of the leaders of the West and South, the two men were convinced that their cause was just, and the President and his principal cabinet member surrendered not one of their intentions. It was into this reviving atmosphere that the Czar's proposition entered—not as a means of rescue but as a complementary force for bringing the British to terms. From this overture and other signs, it was quite evident to Madison and Monroe that other nations, Russia and Sweden especially, shared both America's complaints and goals.

As a consequence of their belief that England would at some time be compelled to recognize the inevitable, Madison and Monroe agreed upon and Monroe copiously composed instructions to the peace commission that were the dictates of an assuredly victorious nation. It was impressment, of course, that received the greatest attention. Monroe wrote again and again, page after page, on the subject. Unless the British should "stipulate, in some adequate manner, to terminate or forbear the practice of impressment from American vessels" there could be no peace, for not to accomplish this, "after all that has passed on the subject, would be to give up the cause." Furthermore, "as a necessary incident to an adjustment on the principle . . . it is expected that all American Seamen who have been impressed, will be discharged, and that those who have been naturalized, under the British laws, by compulsive service, will be permitted to withdraw."

After the commissioners had settled this preliminary condition to peace they were to introduce a series of other demands. They were to push for definitions of blockade and neutral rights, although, since Great Britain had removed her Orders in Council and consequently her "illegal blockades" which excused high-seas marauding, this was no more a *sine qua non*. England was no longer to be allowed to trade with Indian tribes within the jurisdiction of the United States, and she must recognize the right of the United States to keep a superior naval force on the Great Lakes. For all this Britain was to be granted reciprocal restoration of territory, a distinct advantage for her, thought Monroe, considering "the probable state of the War at the date of the Treaty." Monroe advised also that the American ministers keep the Russian and Swedish governments abreast of the negotiation, for he was sure these governments would have more than an impartial interest in neutral rights.

These instructions seemed more rational to their creators than to Gallatin and Bayard, their initial recipients. Bayard, surprised by his appointment and unwilling to disappoint the administration that had selected him, did not make his reservations officially known, although he partially confided them to Gallatin. Precisely what Gallatin thought Gallatin kept to himself, but he did transmit Bayard's doubts about getting an agreement on impressment, in such a manner that Monroe was undecided whether Gallatin was acting as translator or co-author.

To insure that Gallatin and Bayard would not depart from American shores in a state of confusion Monroe added more words to the thousands he had already penned on impressment. "It would be deplorable," he wrote to Gallatin,

> . . . if we did all that we could and received nothing but the informal promise of the British commissioners . . . to do what is otherwise their duty to do. I believe that such an arrangement would not only ruin the present Administration, but the Republican party, and even the cause. . . . It would be considered by Europe that we had no government whatever, and they would all begin immediately to trample us underfoot. The expulsion of the present people from office . . . would be among its least important effects. The opposition coming in on its principles—I speak of many of its leaders—could not resist the British pretensions, though I should not be surprised in the temper of the nation, under such circumstances, if we should be visited by other and greater calamities.

That Monroe overstated the case is, with the benefit of hindsight, not to be doubted, but he was entirely sincere in his beliefs. He feared too much the ravings of the "war hawks," and both he and Madison depended too heavily on these men for the military power that would transform the demands on England into realities. That England might not be pressured into compliance under any circumstances was a possibility scarcely considered by Madison and Monroe, despite their knowledge of four hundred years of British insistence on the policy of impressment, and in defiance of the more recent correspondence between Jonathan Russell and Lord Castlereagh. Nearly every American outside New England was certain that rectitude in Anglo-American affairs was an exclusive virtue of the United States, and not for the first time, nor the last, did the American government believe right to be a potent weapon in the conduct of foreign affairs. Don't the good men always win out over the bad?

Had he been asked, Gallatin would have smiled and not answered the question, and Bayard, simple though he sometimes could be, would have scowled. Neither man further disclosed his feelings to the President or the Secretary of State, but Bayard confided to his cousin that "if we are to continue to fight till the point [impressment] is conceded to us, you and I at least will grow grey in the war."

Monroe was undaunted by signs of doubt among the peace commissioners, and, both before and after the envoys sailed, he continued to add to their instructions. The ministers were to make clear to Great Britain the validity of American claims to East and West Florida, claims which Gallatin and Bayard and possibly Monroe seriously questioned. A treaty of commerce and amity was to be negotiated with Russia, and, peace having been obtained, a like agreement was to be pursued with Great Britain. In addition, the ministers should press claims for indemnity for all instances in which Britain had violated American territorial jurisdiction, a category of transgressions almost impossible to catalogue, let alone avenge.

It was in June, when the administration mistakenly thought conquest was in the offing, that Monroe wrote of the "fair prospect" of taking "all Upper Canada," and, this being the case, he advised the commissioners that "it may be worth while to bring to view the advantages to both Countries which is promised by a transfer of the upper parts and even the whole of Canada to the U.S." This bit of fantasy and faulty grammar was consigned to paper on the day the *Neptune* was beating between Gothenburg and Elsinore, and the message arrived in St. Petersburg on August 30, when the American commissioners already knew that mediation was as likely as a cotton field in Scotland. Gallatin, when he read Adams's decoding of the State Department's cipher, commented that Monroe "might have saved himself the trouble of writing the whole letter."

If Monroe was a fool he was not more so than many of his countrymen, whose notions of victory and conquest were equally unrealistic. Furthermore, his motives and beliefs were extensively fashioned by his ambition and by his singular position in Madison's administration. After some earlier disagreements and bitterness, particularly over the conduct of foreign affairs during Jefferson's Presidency and over Monroe's role as an envoy to England in 1806, Monroe had opposed Madison in the Presidential election of 1808, only to lose emphatically. In the next few years Madison attempted several times to bridge the gulf that separated the two men, and in 1811 he finally brought Monroe into the cabinet, partly because he needed and wanted him and partly because he preferred to have Monroe with rather than against him.

Monroe accepted the appointment as Secretary of State with the hope that he could further his Presidential aspirations and in the belief that he could negotiate an agreement with Great Britain. It was not long after he assumed office that he gave up the latter goal, convinced that war with England was a certainty, and by 1813 he also viewed his connections with the administration as a liability for his prospective candidacy. Government inefficiency and hesitancy filled him with impatience; cabinet intrigues and jealousies repelled and enticed him. He was torn between having as little to do with the administration as possible and assuming the role of the indispensable man. Events, his ambition, and his capabilities pushed him in the direction of greater responsibility. Twice he took over the War Department between outgoing and incoming Secretaries, and he could not resist giving gratuitous advice even when military matters were not under his direct control. He came to respect Madison, if not his leadership, but his faith in his own talents and aptitude for command was overwhelming, and he was agonized by the way the government of which he was a part botched nearly everything it attempted. What kept him going was a belief in his country's cause and his own—this and a somewhat limited imagination and the unwavering support of his Virginia friends.

Monroe's assumption that 1813 would be a better year than 1812 and his confidence that Britain would bow before superior and more righteous forces remained relatively firm through the time he wrote to the peace commissioners that it would be to England's gain to cede Canada. In June the campaign on the Canadian border had met with some success and appeared to hold promise. If military advances were not sufficient to dismay the British, Madison and Monroe were unshaken in their persuasion that Napoleon's setbacks were temporary, and they were innocently immersed in their trust in the Czar. Neither American was fully confident that the British would accept mediation, but, one way or the other, they expected the Russian offer to bear fruit. "Whether England will accede to the mediation, or do so with evasive purposes, remains to be seen," wrote Madison to Jefferson.

> That she has brought it about I cannot readily suppose, because I think she would not promote our political intercourse with the Baltic, where she apprehends a sympathy with our maritime doctrines, and not with hers. The present occasion proves the good policy of having cultivated the favorable dispositions of the Emperor Alexander. We have good reason to believe that Sweden is as well inclined towards us as Russia.

Exactly how Russia might benefit the United States if mediation were rejected by England was a question that Madison and Monroe never attempted to resolve. It apparently did not occur to them that the Czar, overburdened with his own enormous problems, might not be disposed to fight America's war as well.

Whatever the political agreement between Washington and St. Petersburg in the summer of 1813, the two capitals were unfortunately similar in climate. Washington's physical atmosphere was not salubrious in any season. In summer it was especially damp and oppressive and unhealthy. In mid-June Madison contracted what Monroe called a "bilious attack," and Dolly and the President's doctors feared he might be near death. Not until the end of September was he sufficiently recovered to assume the full burden of his duties; Monroe was forced in the interim to take over many Presidential obligations. And as Madison's health had waned so had the encouraging omens of spring.

The first sign of trouble came not from abroad but from the assembled members of the Senate. Gallatin's appointment to the commission, while he continued to hold the office of Secretary of the Treasury, provided the Federalists and the anti-administration Republicans with an excellent opportunity to oppose and embarrass the executive branch of the government. No sooner had the commissioners' appointments been sent to the Senate for ratification than Federalist Senator Rufus King, ex-minister to England and Presidential hopeful, demanded an inquiry into the manner in which the Treasury was to be administered in Gallatin's absence. Madison answered that the Secretary of the

Navy was supervising the Treasury Department as well as his own. This, of course, the Senate knew, just as Madison was aware that his reply would not suffice. The issue was not Gallatin's appointment, nor even the propriety of sending a cabinet member on a diplomatic mission, and the Senate, pursuing its real object, created a special committee to meet with the President and hand the administration a defeat.

Insofar as his health allowed, Madison met several times with the committee, but he flatly refused to negotiate with them on equal terms, suspecting that their primary intention was to weaken the executive power. As early as June 7 Monroe predicted the outcome, and on July 19, when Gallatin and Bayard were on the road between Revel and St. Petersburg, the Senate, by a vote of 18 to 17, made Gallatin's trip unnecessary. Two weeks later, Madison wrote to him of "the painful manner in which the Senate have mutilated the mission to St. Petersburg," and this was not the only discouraging news he had to relate. English newspapers and travelers returning from that country told of the likelihood that Britain would reject the mediation. Madison, in that first week of August, 1813, could see only one favorable aspect in all that had lately occurred: Gallatin should soon be returning home where he was sorely needed.

For some time, though, Madison and Monroe refused to accept as conclusive the signs indicating that England would not send a commission to St. Petersburg. Adams and Bayard were sent new credentials and advised to continue with their negotiation, if their mission were not already accomplished or terminated. Gallatin, who was expected in Washington before Christmas, was told to sail immediately aboard the *Neptune,* leaving Bayard to get home as well as he could. None of these instructions, however, arrived in St. Petersburg until long after Bayard and Gallatin had set off through the snow for Amsterdam and London. In Washington, leaves fell and men woke to frost but there was no sign of the missing Secretary of the Treasury, and on November 27 Monroe wrote to Hannah, Albert Gallatin's wife, to say that the only news of the peace commission since its departure from America had come by a letter from George Dallas, then in London, to his father—and this was so brief and out-of-date as to tell them almost nothing.

As December came to the Potomac, Madison and Monroe

waited in vain for the arrival of Gallatin and for final news of mediation. About military matters they no longer had expectations, good or bad, for the campaign of 1813 had come to its undistinguished close. York (Toronto), the capital of Upper Canada, had been raided and burned, but no occupation had taken place and some deserved guilt and retaliation were the only consequences of the action. A violent invasion of the Niagara frontier followed, but all that had been gained was eventually lost, and at the end of December American rapacity was to be repaid in kind with the burning of the villages of Black Rock and Buffalo.

To the west, results were more impressive and lasting. Commander Oliver Hazard Perry crowned more than six months of carefully planned and devoted labor by winning, on September 10, a wild, seesawing, bloody naval battle near Put in Bay on Lake Erie, giving his country at least one bona fide hero and her history books a deathless sentence—"We have met the enemy, and they are ours"—with which to lend luster to a war that was otherwise somewhat inglorious. More important, Perry opened the way for General William Henry Harrison, the hero (of sorts) of Tippecanoe, to sweep the British from the Canadian shore of the lake. Detroit was once more American, and much of West Canada was under her influence.

These victories, while not trifling, were insignificant compared to the failures, and, when Generals James Wilkinson and Wade Hampton crawled into their winter encampments in New York, Canada, though no longer untouched, was hardly abused. The President and his Secretary of State were not insensitive to the dismal harvest of their military sowing, and they sought refuge in what they did not know for sure: no official word had yet been received on mediation; Napoleon, the last the United States had heard, could still win battles. Things could change for the better, and 1814 might find a nation that was wiser and stronger as a result of its trying experiences. This, at least, was what Madison stated in his December 7 Message to Congress.

> The war has proved . . . that our free government, like other free governments, though slow in its early movements, acquires in its progress a force proportional to its freedom; and that the Union of these States, the guardian of the freedom and safety of all and of each, is strengthened by every occasion that puts it to the test. In

fine, the war with its vicissitudes is illustrating the capacity and the destiny of the United States to be a great, a flourishing, and a powerful nation.

Having said this, Madison hoped for the best, but he was reminded that the only part of the nation that was "flourishing" and "powerful" was New England, which contributed neither men nor money to the nation's cause and which gladly sold her goods to the British and Canadians, thus drawing the rest of the country's limited specie into her banks. To be sure, this illustrated "capacity" and probably "destiny," but such activities had little to do with "Union," and they were not what Madison had in mind when he delivered his message to Congress. Consequently, he sent another, secret message to that body two days after the first, asking for an embargo—a trade restriction which, in view of the British blockade that sealed off the coast from New London southward, could only be aimed at the states of the Northeast. Congress immediately complied, and, as a new year approached, the first warlike action of the United States was a punitive measure against one of its own parts. The reaction in New England was ugly and soon to be more frightening.

What, among other things, encouraged the Federalists to oppose and defy the embargo was the news that came aboard the British ship *Bramble* of the Allied victory at Leipzig. Napoleon's fortunes plainly were ebbing; European ports were or soon would be open, begging for trade; Britain's troops might shortly be free to concentrate on America. All the information that came on that December 30 conspired to strengthen the unco-operative role of New England and to diminish the freedom of action of the administration. Not least of the messages brought by the *Bramble* was Castlereagh's dispatch of November 4, announcing the refusal of mediation and proposing direct negotiation. Madison and Monroe could accept or they could pin all their hopes on a new campaign that would almost certainly face odds much greater than those of 1812 and 1813.

The President and his Secretary of State did not take long to reach a decision, but it was not a verdict of despair. Every defeat the United States had experienced Madison and Monroe shunted aside. They convinced themselves that the failure of mediation was a good omen that spoke of English fear of

Russian and French power—that England had rejected mediation "because she dreaded it" and had offered direct negotiation
because she wished to keep the United States away from Russia
and Sweden. Monroe was so obsessed with this idea that he
began to pity Great Britain and promised himself that the
United States government would not join in a coalition against
her enemy if that country co-operated. Proud of his magnanimity
and confident in the unknown force that would save his country,
Monroe replied to Castlereagh less than a week after the British
Minister's proposal had been received.

In his official letter of January 5, Monroe told Castlereagh that
the United States regretted "the new obstacle to the commencement of a negotiation." The Czar, after all, was an impartial man
and the ally of Great Britain. Knowing this, the President of the
United States had never doubted that Britain would accept the
mediation. England, under the circumstances, had nothing to
fear. It was the United States that had reason to know caution;
yet she had placed her confidence in the Czar so that peace
would not be delayed. Nevertheless, continued Monroe, his government was willing to treat "on conditions of reciprocity consistent with the rights of both parties as sovereign and independent nations, and calculated not only to establish present
harmony, but to provide as far as possible, against future collisions which might interrupt it." Monroe could not realize how
much Great Britain would agree with this last suggestion. Even
less could he suspect the means by which England would attempt
to guard against such "future collisions." In this case, his desire
was Castlereagh's command.

Only one note of uncertainty crept into Monroe's acceptance
of direct negotiation at Gothenburg. He admitted to Castlereagh
that he and Madison wished they had heard from the American
ministers before making their decision. The administration was
still without word from Adams, Bayard, and Gallatin when it
appointed and the Senate confirmed a new commission headed
by Adams and further composed of Bayard, Henry Clay, the
leader of the West and Speaker of the House of Representatives,
and Jonathan Russell, former chargé d'affaires in London and
the new minister to Sweden. Gallatin, whose appearance at home
was yet thought to be imminent, was omitted. It was not until
a week later, in a letter to Hannah Gallatin, that Dolly Madison

excitedly wrote that she had received a note from her son, dated September 15, saying that all were well but still in official ignorance of the British stand on mediation. A few days later, more mail from the Baltic broke the long silence, and Madison and Monroe, sure now that Gallatin was not returning, added him to the new peace commission. The year 1814 was barely entering its third month when the leaders of the American government stirred themselves to fresh efforts that, they trusted, would lead to victory and peace.

It was but a few days after Dolly Madison wrote to Hannah Gallatin, sending the first real news of the ministers, that Bayard and Gallatin began their journey from St. Petersburg. During the night of January 25 Bayard's carriage, outdistancing the others, made steady progress through the snow, stopping only at Strelna and Kiepena to change horses. By midmorning of the 26th Bayard was warming himself in the posthouse at Kaskovo, the first of the group to arrive there. The carriage carrying the servants and the baggage came soon after, but there was no sign of Gallatin, and Bayard, again suffering from fever, a cough, and a stabbing pain in his chest, entertained dire suppositions of Gallatin's fate. Perhaps, he thought, the German servants hired in St. Petersburg and assigned to Gallatin's carriage had robbed him and left him dying in the snow. For three hours Bayard tortured himself with worry, but shortly after noon a team of horses came pounding up the whitened road, pulling the carriage of Gallatin and the Germans. The travelers had, it developed, been stuck in the snow shortly after leaving St. Petersburg, but all were well, and in fact much healthier than Bayard.

From Kaskovo the route followed the southern shore of the Gulf of Finland to Narva and then turned south past Lake Peipus and once more west to Riga. Snowfall was almost constant, making an accumulation that sometimes reached to the horses' bellies and slowed them unmercifully. One day it took eight horses per carriage to cover fourteen miles in thirteen hours, and the road could be distinguished from the rest of the countryside only because previous travelers and local residents had placed green branches along the shoulders. When there was no such greenery or it had been misplaced or when it was necessary to pull aside for sleds coming in the opposite direction there

were sometimes dangerous and chilling spills into towering
drifts.

Some nights were spent on the road, but in the worst weather
or when they could no longer go on Gallatin and Bayard and
their party sought refuge in the filthy, reeking, overheated inns
and posthouses. They spent one night sitting up in a kitchen, the
only unoccupied room in the house, the stink and slop of which
almost nauseated them. Bayard's illness grew worse, bringing
visions of death, and he was reminded of Joel Barlow, American
author and diplomat, who, following Napoleon in his retreat
from Moscow, had perished not far from Warsaw on Christmas
Eve of 1812. Fortunately, the group came to an inn where Bayard
was able to spend the night bundled in blankets on a sofa. He
could not sleep, but by morning he was soaked with perspiration,
and, although the cough and chest pains persisted, his fever
had subsided. On Thursday, February 3, at eleven in the morning, their carriages slid through the streets of Riga and up to
the doors of the "Hotel da St. Petersburg," haven for a few days
of rest and recuperation.

From Riga the ministers pursued a course through Russia's
Lithuanian province and then through the Kingdom of Prussia
to Berlin, a trip that took more than two weeks. The intense
snowfall continued, making bushes and trees and scattered
houses little more than white humps and grotesque shapes in a
dreary, colorless landscape. It was a frigid February 21 when
the party reached Berlin and its shelter and comfort and theaters
and—most important of all—news from and of other Americans.
On their third day there, Gallatin and Bayard received a letter
from Sylvanus Bourne, American consul in Amsterdam, saying
he had recently heard from Reuben Beasley, agent for prisoners
of war in London. Beasley had written of Castlereagh's proposal
of direct negotiation at Gothenburg and of America's acceptance
and the appointment of Gallatin and Bayard to the new commission. In the pages of Bourne's letter months of rumor and
supposition found acknowledgment, and, eager to begin their
new mission, Gallatin and Bayard, at six that evening, started to
Potsdam, where they spent a night and a day before setting out
over the shortest route for Amsterdam.

In a spell of milder weather, the trip from Potsdam to Amsterdam took but a week, and Bayard and Gallatin arrived on March

4 to find an accumulation of mail that had been frozen in port or gone back and forth across the Baltic or been held by British censors. For the first time in nearly ten months the Americans learned authoritatively of events in their own country and in Britain, and on Saturday evening, March 5, Nathaniel Strong, the new consul to Gothenburg, arrived with a packet from Washington. Strong, stumbling lethargically and unconcernedly toward his destination, had left some of the dispatches consigned to his care in his cabin on the *Fair American,* but Gallatin and Bayard were for a few days none the wiser until the consul departed for St. Petersburg, leaving behind papers intended for Adams. Fortunately, others following after Strong brought copies of the messages he had carelessly misplaced.

In addition to largely discouraging accounts of the campaign of 1813, Bayard and Gallatin received copies of the correspondence that had passed between Castlereagh and Monroe and some of that which had been exchanged by the British Foreign Minister and Cathcart. These dispatches did not entirely clarify the mysterious events which had kept the American ministers anxious and unenlightened for six months in Russia, and Castlereagh's little inventions were infuriating, but the official letters that Gallatin and Bayard read in Amsterdam did justify their having left Russia without formal notification from the Czar.

Gallatin learned more of the details of the rejection of his appointment by the Senate, and, since the news which had reached Amsterdam was complete only to the end of January, he discovered that his name was not included, as Beasley had thought, among those named to the new commission. This was the most disheartening word he had received since leaving the United States. He still planned to visit London, but he determined that his stay there would be regulated by the length of time it took the *Neptune* to free herself from the ice of Gothenburg. When that ship made England he would board her for the sad return home.

Bayard, with mixed feelings, gave his attention to his new assignment. He thought it probable that he would reach Gothenburg before Clay and Russell could sail there from the United States and before John Quincy Adams could chip his way out of the Gulf of Finland. He did not, therefore, feel compelled to rush to Sweden, but Monroe's insistence that his instructions of

1813 were still valid and the composition of the new commission gave Bayard cause for concern and heightened for him the importance of a visit to London to determine British intentions. Nothing that Bayard read encouraged a belief that England would look more favorably than before upon a renunciation of impressment, and all indications made preposterous the notion, yet harbored by Monroe, that the enemy could be induced to cede all or at least Upper Canada to the United States. That Clay and Russell had been chosen because they shared these expectations seemed likely, and Bayard was no more cheered to hear from Senator William Hunter of Rhode Island that Russell was "cold, reserved, *artful*" and that his rank and performance "have certainly not entitled him to the high situation to which he is raised."

Even less encouraging was news from Beasley that Great Britain had taken no steps to appoint a commission and that she would probably not do so until she heard formally from the American commission. Furthermore, wrote Beasley, England now seemed to prefer The Hague rather than Gothenburg as a site for negotiation. Bayard, who looked upon Gothenburg as "a vile place," shared the British preference, but neither he nor Gallatin could guess at the British reasons for wishing a change. Even without evidence it was well, they thought, to be suspicious of British motives.

Despite their eagerness to seek firsthand information in London, Gallatin and Bayard remained for three weeks in Amsterdam, recuperating from the rigors of their long journey and making preparation for what lay ahead. Colonel Milligan, Bayard's secretary, and John Payne Todd, both of whom had preceded the ministers from St. Petersburg, arrived from Sweden. Levett Harris, who had followed from the Russian capital, came soon after and paused briefly before continuing to England as advance agent, and, finally, George Dallas crossed the Channel, after nearly five months on the banks of the Thames. Each brought news and rumor and uncertain tidings of English intentions, but Amsterdam, though under the English shadow, was an inviting place that encouraged procrastination, and Bayard and Gallatin lingered there.

The Americans were quickly taken in tow by the partners of Willink & Company, the Dutch banking house that co-operated with Baring Brothers in serving American interests, and Bayard and Gallatin were entertained at the theater and wined and dined. On March 25, William, Prince of Orange, quietly returned from his forced exile in England. The Americans were received by him the next day, and on the following evening they were flattered by the Prince's attentions at a court dinner. William's warm consideration was gratifying to Gallatin and Bayard but without political significance, for he, even more than they, was at the mercy of British power. Only ten miles from Amsterdam the French continued a stubborn resistance against Dutch troops who were dependent on English arms and supplies, and on idle mornings Bayard would walk far enough out the Naarden road to view the siege from a safe distance, passing the litterborne dead and wounded on his way.

Finally, a letter came from Alexander Baring, saying the Americans were welcome in England and that he would expedite their passage through customs. On the heels of this message came another report from Reuben Beasley, warning of difficulties ahead. No British peace commission had yet been appointed, and, as far as Beasley could determine, the British still were in no hurry. The matter could wait until Castlereagh returned from his mission to the Continent. Also, wrote Beasley, the enemy was planning harsh demands to be presented when negotiation did take place: the United States must renounce all trade beyond the Cape of Good Hope and with the West Indies; they must give up their right to dry fish on the shores of Newfoundland. Britain, in other words, was offering peace, but for a stiff price.

Bayard, after the receipt of Beasley's letter, wasted no time. He left Amsterdam on March 29 and on the evening of the 30th was in Rotterdam. Gallatin tarried for a few days, hoping the *Neptune* might make her appearance, but on Friday, April 1, he left a note directing Captain Jones to Falmouth and wrote to Baring that he would be on his way to London in the morning. Three days later he, his son, Milligan, and Todd were with Bayard in Rotterdam, and on the evening of April 6 all of them were in their bunks on a ship off the Dutch port of Hellevoetsluis, waiting for the tide to come in. Two days later they landed at Harwich, a long way from home, an unknown distance from peace, and in the land of the enemy.

England Triumphant

On February 13, 1814, when Gallatin and Bayard were fighting their way through blizzards between Riga and Berlin, Henry Clay sat in his room in New York City, awaiting the tardy arrival of Jonathan Russell. It was Sunday and Clay wrote to Monroe to tell him, among other things, what rumors of European events were current in that part of the country. It was not that Clay himself much cared, for his faith in American—especially Western—capacity was almost without limit, and he viewed the pressures of Europe as crumbling dikes against an irreversible tide. This is not to say, however, that Clay, who played the political game as well as he played cards, was insensible to the political realities of 1814. He was only biding his time until the call came to play the last hand. "The *state* of things is undergoing continual changes," he had written to a friend, "and we must judge of the conditions of peace, when peace comes, not by the present state, but by that state of things which shall exist when it is negotiated." How favorable conditions might be at that time Henry Clay would decide for himself.

With no minimum of thought as to the political consequences, this tall, loose-jointed Kentuckian had resigned his position as Speaker of the House of Representatives to accept an appointment to the peace commission. He was a man of the common people—one who knew his cards and his horses and could hold his liquor, one who could move into a street-corner gathering and win its attention and adherence with wit and affability and unpretentious speech—and he had no intention of endangering this popular support. Instrumental in bringing about the declaration of war against Great Britain, he expected to be no less influential in arranging an honorable and profitable peace. There was no telling what the future would bring, but in the final act the powerful British nation would be reduced to a handful of men sitting across the bargaining table, and under these circumstances Henry Clay gave ground to no man or nation.

For more than a week, Clay's light-colored mane could be seen about the streets of New York. Christopher Hughes, secretary to the mission, and the messengers and private secretaries had arrived, but still there was no sign of Russell. Monroe, in Washington, receiving Clay's reports and words of advice, grew fretful over the delay. Even Clay began to fear that Gallatin and Bayard, unaware of their new assignment, would pass their credentials and associates in midocean. It was not until the last week of February, soon after Clay had received Monroe's most recent and frantic letter, telling him to sail immediately with or without Russell, that that gentleman made his appearance. A few days later the *John Adams*, Captain Samuel Angus in command, put to sea.

It was April 13 when the *John Adams* anchored off Gothenburg's ice-clogged harbor, and on the next day Clay and Russell rushed into town, afraid that the negotiation might have already commenced. When they reached the inn, they were astonished to find no other American ministers and no British commission there. No one had even heard of the negotiation or the negotiators, and Clay and Russell could only speculate on where their colleagues might be and what they might know. Assuming that Gallatin and Bayard were in Amsterdam, their last known destination, and Adams still in St. Petersburg, Russell and Clay directed letters to these places and settled down to wait.

Their ignorance was not dispelled for a week—not until Captain Jones, whose *Neptune* was still locked in Gothenburg's harbor, received a letter from Gallatin in London, ordering Jones to make sail for Harwich. For a moment Clay lost his composure. It was inconceivable to him that Gallatin and Bayard could for any justifiable reason be in the enemy's capital. Russell was equally perplexed as to Gallatin's and Bayard's motives, but, realizing that the negotiation could not now possibly begin for several weeks, he set out for Stockholm to fulfill the second of his assignments and present his credentials as United States minister to Sweden.

Before Russell had started on his journey, however, other news reached Gothenburg that reduced the surprising word of Gallatin's and Bayard's whereabouts very nearly to unimportance. From France came stories of what Clay called "wonderful events." On March 31 the Allies had entered Paris, and at Fontainebleau, on April 11, Napoleon, the forlorn ex-Emperor of France, had said farewell to his troops and begun his humiliating journey to Elba. Twenty years of nearly incessant warfare had ended. Towns from the Mediterranean to the Arctic Circle went wild with celebration. Rockets filled the night sky with vari-colored flame. Grown men wept with joy. "A new epoch has thus arisen," wrote Clay to Monroe, "the first effect of which will be an European peace. It will doubtless lead to totally new relations, political as well as commercial." Beyond this Clay did not venture to predict. No American close to the administration, not even Henry Clay, had anticipated such a rapid and vast change in European affairs.

The next message Clay received from Gallatin and Bayard was as disconcerting as the unexpected news from the Continent. Colonel Milligan arrived from London on the 30th with a message that seemed to bear out Clay's misgivings about the wisdom of Gallatin's and Bayard's presence in England. They wrote proposing a change in site from Gothenburg to the Netherlands city of Ghent, and the urgency with which they requested Clay's opinion convinced him that he would not have time to consult with Russell or the missing Adams. For more than a day Clay wrestled with his decision, and when he consented to the change, Milligan could not help noting the minister's reluctance. "The fact is," Milligan later wrote to Bayard, "his Excellency is very commodiously and handsomely established, and either dislikes the idea of moving, or thinks it will occasion delay in commencing the negotiation. He is far from believing we stand in as much need of peace, as I think, your much better judgement is impressed with."

Milligan's loyalty to Bayard and his distaste for Clay misled him in assessing Clay's aversion to a new site for the negotiation. However "commodious" Clay's new quarters were compared to his rooms at the inn, he had no love for the limited attractions of Gothenburg. He was certain, though, that change meant delay and feared also that it signified the commission's first surrender to the British. It was, he thought, what one might expect from Gallatin's and Bayard's foolhardy visit to London, and, to whatever else Clay might agree, he would not under any circumstances join them there.

"With regard to changing the place of negotiation," Clay wrote to Gallatin and Bayard, "it appears to me to be a measure attended with some difficulty, and requiring, on our part, great delicacy." He pointed out that Great Britain had on April 9 asked Sweden's permission to hold the negotiation in Gothenburg, and Russell, when he arrived in Stockholm, had followed suit on behalf of the United States. If a change in site were now to be made it must appear to be at the insistence of the British. The shift must not, in any event, jeopardize Sweden's friendship for the United States. "Such explanations may be made to Sweden as will not only retain to us her friendship, but cast upon the other party all the unfriendly consequences, should there be any, growing out of the measure."

It was Clay's hesitant opinion that neither Madison nor Monroe would oppose a move to Ghent if they were aware of the startling events that had taken place in Europe. For his part, Clay was not for a moment in doubt that the commissioners could do as they pleased. "I am prepared in this instance, and in all others, to give to our instructions a liberal interpretation." He warned, however, that the commission must be firm. Britain might not be so able, as it then seemed, to do as she pleased. Clay expected the proposed Allied conference in Vienna to be to the United States' eventual benefit; for, with France out of the picture, the rest of Europe would not be indifferent to British power and pretensions and would impose some limits. He added somewhat sarcastically, "but I forbear; indeed, I ought to apologize for touching at all on a subject on which you are so much more competent to judge."

The next day, May 4, Milligan and Hughes, the commission's secretary, "*whose health* [Clay] *feared would be impaired*" by Clay's continued opposition to his going to the inviting city of London, boarded a packet to Harwich. Other couriers had left previously to carry dispatches to Adams in St. Petersburg and to William Harris Crawford, minister to France, in Paris, and Clay was left alone and impatient in Gothenburg. A few days later, without further information from abroad, he complained in a letter to Russell that "I am still in the most painful uncertainty as to the duration of my probation."

For almost three weeks Clay was to remain in this unaccustomed state of solitude and virtual ignorance, holding the fort until his colleagues should appear or be heard from. His only companion was Captain Angus of the *John Adams,* and Angus, who had been severely wounded in the war, suffered many days when he had a "violent fever with mental derangement." Near the end of the month, Clay's anxiety and feeling of claustrophobia became "inexpressibly distressing." He wrote to and heard from Russell frequently, but Russell, with little in the way of positive information, could only disconcert Clay more with his accounts of the dismal forebodings that came in letters from Reuben Beasley. "Perhaps never," added Russell in one of his notes, "was a joint mission so disjointed and scattered." Clay firmly and sadly agreed, but he was powerless to effect a solution. The responsibility rested with Bayard and Gallatin in London.

And that responsibility was onerous. London, in the spring of 1814, was not a salutary place for ministers representing the rebellious ex-colonies of America. Gallatin and Bayard set foot in Harwich three days after news had crossed the Channel of the Allied entrance into Paris, and no sooner were the two men established in London than excited messengers brought the details of Napoleon's abdication. England became a delirious nation. For months, happy throngs filled London's streets, splitting the air with cheers at the slightest provocation, releasing exuberance that had been contained for twenty fearful years. For some men it was the first time in their conscious lives that they were without dread of the physical and economic threats of Bonaparte. For a time nothing else mattered. The King was as mad as a summer blizzard. His son, the Prince Regent, was a fat, disgusting fop. But what difference did it make? Long live the King! Long live England! And God help any man or nation that should stand in her way.

The excitement, the relief, the unbounded joy were all the greater for the months and events that had immediately preceded the French Empire's downfall. In December, 1813, Castlereagh had been forced to hurry to the Continent to correct the blunders of his ministers and to hold the Allies together before the skillful evasions and the vicious, diabolical counterattacks of Napoleon. There were those among the Allies who would have left Bonaparte in power, who would have been content to bargain with him concerning French boundaries.

By the end of January Castlereagh had convinced the others that they must push on to victory and reduce French territory, and he also had obtained their agreement to leave the question of maritime rights out of their discussions. This latter accord relieved Britain's fears that the United States would become the object of Russian and Swedish and French sympathy and support, and it confirmed a decision the British cabinet had made a few weeks earlier: Great Britain would be willing to sign a peace with the United States "without involving in such treaty any decision upon the points in dispute at the commencement of hostilities."

But in the first part of February, Castlereagh saw all his work, other than the commitments relating to America, come to naught, as Napoleon rallied his armies and drove wedges through the Allied lines. For a time the Allies were divided and desperate, and the whole movement faltered badly when Napoleon threatened again at the end of the month. To the Allied nations the world seemed black and hopeless. Even nature was unco-operative. In England snowdrifts built to an unbelievable height of twenty feet, and the waters of the Thames, which should have been lapping at the first flowers of spring, remained solidly frozen. Only Wellington continued to pound his way through southern France.

For Castlereagh it was a nauseating period of near-tragedy, but he remained outwardly calm, holding out to the Allies bright hopes of the future on one hand and threatening them with a loss of subsidies on the other. He stilled the beginning clamor over the division of the French Empire's spoils, and finally, after the Treaty of Chaumont, which called for no separate peace with Napoleon and contained secret clauses realigning Europe, the Allies drew together and thrust relentlessly forward. Their momentum did not seriously diminish until Napoleon, in disguise for his own protection, was on his way to Elba. Then Europe went wild.

Though the members of the American commission knew that

their country now had even less than usual cause to celebrate, they could not help but be moved by one of the most exultant moments of history. From his hotel window looking out on Albemarle Street, Bayard watched the surging crowds by day and the fireworks by night. He walked through Hyde Park and stood at the edge of the raving multitudes to see the gross Louis XVIII pass through London on his way to Paris where British, Prussian, and Russian arms would restore his and the Bourbon throne. The Americans came and went and ogled without hindrance. No one, save a pickpocket who encountered George Dallas, paid the slightest heed to them.

And their reception in private circles was courteous and friendly. In view of the fact that Castlereagh was still on the Continent and out of respect for diplomatic propriety, no member of the British cabinet made a move for direct consultation, but channels of communication were usually open through Alexander Baring or Reuben Beasley or sometimes Count Lieven, the Russian minister. Lieven and Baring met with Gallatin and Bayard shortly after the arrival of the latter two in London, and in the following weeks the Americans were entertained frequently and well. Special tours were arranged through Westminster Abbey and the British Museum; there were pleasant, leisurely excursions into the burgeoning countryside, dinners at Madame de Staël's, visits to the Court of Chancery, to Windsor Castle, to sessions of the House of Commons. On Saturday, April 16, the two American ministers were presented to the Grand Duchess Catherine of Russia, and a few days later they enjoyed dinner with a half dozen Members of Parliament who were openly sympathetic to the American cause. On the whole, London was a gracious host to the country's enemies, but the shrill cry of the newspapers and the well-founded rumors sounded the real essence of England's attitude: the major score with France had been settled; the lesser one with the United States remained to be dealt with—with the same finality. "In the intoxication of an unexpected success, which they ascribe to themselves," wrote Gallatin, "the English people eagerly wish that their pride may be fully gratified by what they call the 'punishment of America.'"

Precise knowledge of the specific details of that "punishment" would have to await the summer's campaign and the commencement of the negotiation, but broad hints of what lay in store were abundant and unavoidable. Reuben Beasley, who circulated most freely in English society and was the one American to have official contact with the English government, dutifully noted what he saw and heard—and reported pessimistically to all the American commissioners in London, Gothenburg, Stockholm, and St. Petersburg. Near the end of April he relayed to Russell news that was already well known to Gallatin and Bayard. It was stated by authoritative persons in London that the United States must restore British hostages to regular prisoner-of-war status before the negotiation could begin. The absurd practice of naming certain prisoners as hostages had begun early in the war, when Britain held for trial some American prisoners as deserters from His Majesty's Army or Navy. The American response was to confine and threaten death to an equal number of English prisoners. Britain answered by naming twice as many American hostages, and for a time, until the limited number of prisoners was exhausted, each side proceeded to retaliate in geometric proportions. By 1814 both belligerents were weary of the game and eager to end it, but, as far as Beasley could determine, Great Britain intended to salvage her pride and insist that the United States make the first move as a prelude to peace talks.

According to other information that Beasley had heard, it appeared doubtful that the negotiation would be profitable in any case. Twenty-five thousand veteran troops were massing in Atlantic ports, from whence they would sail to America to enforce British demands that would throttle American trade beyond the Cape of Good Hope, that would drive American fishermen from Newfoundland's Grand Banks, that would sever the United States permanently from the Great Lakes. "There are so many people who live by war fever," said Beasley. "It will be no easy matter to bring about an honorable Peace." It was confidently expected by the British that their arms and diplomacy and American disunion, spearheaded by the New England Federalists, would send America groveling and begging for peace.

Throughout April and May, Beasley's reports grew ever more dismal, usually concluding on the note that peace was impossible. At times, Bayard shared these dark forebodings, but he and Gallatin clung to the hope that favorable results would come from compromise on both sides. While they shared Beasley's concern over troop movements and possible British demands, they were worried even more that Madison and Monroe would insist on unattainable American goals. In the first week of May they wrote to Monroe, describing the profound change in the European situation and repeating the rumors of large armies of destruction destined for America and unpleasant surprises planned for the peace talks. With all this, they assured Monroe, there was no chance of obtaining an end to impressment. "We think that we may at all events distinctly state that for our government the alternative only remains either to resolve on a vigorous prosecution of the war under an expectation of probable success, or to forego for the present the assertion of our rights on what was the principal remaining object of the war."

The American commission was scattered; the British commission had not been appointed; future negotiation was still uncertain; and yet two of the American ministers advised their government that the only stated principle for which the war was being fought should be surrendered. Gallatin and Bayard did not even consider the elusive plum of Canada. For them the fiery year of 1812 belonged to a past era.

At least Gallatin knew officially, by the time he and Bayard wrote to the Secretary of State, that he was a member of the commission. Upon arriving in England, Gallatin had been shown newspaper accounts that mentioned his replacement as Secretary of the Treasury, but the first letter from Clay and Russell in Gothenburg arrived on April 20, and, although it was addressed to both Americans in London, it failed to speak of Gallatin's appointment. It was not until Milligan had completed his round trip from London to Gothenburg that Gallatin knew authoritatively that he had been added to the original roster of four.

When Milligan returned to England he brought with him the mission's official credentials, not only to comfort Gallatin but to assure the British cabinet that an American commission had been named and was waiting to negotiate. In his repeated visits to the Foreign Office, Beasley was told that it was probable that no British commission would be selected until Castlereagh returned from the Continent, and it was definite that no such appointments would occur until the British government had been apprised of the creation of an American commission. Clay was annoyed at the request and felt that the Americans should not comply, but, when Milligan and Harris departed Sweden's shores, the Kentuckian handed over the necessary documents.

The British government had been first to decide that some spot in the Netherlands would be preferable to Gothenburg as a site for the negotiation, but Gallatin and Bayard arrived in London similarly convinced and without any official word from the English on the subject. A letter from Beasley, written in early February, had arrived in Amsterdam in March, saying that a member of the Foreign Office had evidenced a preference for the Low Countries. Once they overcame their initial suspicion, the two Americans had to agree that the suggestion perfectly suited their own inclinations. They were singularly unimpressed with Gothenburg, and they believed that a place more accessible to London would speed the negotiation. The necessity for such dispatch was heightened by what they saw and heard when they reached the British capital, for it became obvious that whoever was appointed to the British commission would be a mere messenger for decisions made by the cabinet. London itself, Gallatin and Bayard were convinced, would be an even better place, but they were not sure of the reactions of Clay and Russell. Consequently, on their own initiative Gallatin and Bayard mentioned London but specifically proposed Ghent to their colleagues, believing, and virtually assured, that the British would agree.

Clay's conditional comments on a possible change in site, however, discouraged Gallatin and Bayard from saying anything about the matter when they sent copies of their commissions to the British Foreign Office on May 13. Lord Bathurst, in Castlereagh's stead, replied on the 16th and, having heard through Beasley that both sides were mutually agreed, recommended Ghent for their common deliberations. Bayard and Gallatin, their desire accomplished, and happy that any onus for the change would fall on Great Britain, thus satisfying the demands of Clay, immediately accepted. Britain, for her part, looked forward to negotiating in a city that was under her military and political control and on the route to Paris. Gallatin, Bayard, and the British Foreign Office were pleased with the change. Clay, Russell, and Adams might react differently, but, whatever their attitude, they would be presented with a *fait accompli*.

In his letter of May 16 Bathurst made no mention of a British commission except to say that one would be appointed "forth-with." In keeping with the mystery and delay with which the British surrounded the negotiation, nothing else was said on the subject at that time, but the indefatigable Beasley had already pried from William Hamilton of the Foreign Office the informa-tion that "Admiral Lord Gambier, Mr. Adams a gentleman of the Law, and Mr. Gouldsbourn one of the Secretaries of the Colonial Department" would be the British ministers, and he reported this knowledge to the American commissioners on the 13th. These appointments bore out the expectation of Gallatin and Bayard that all important decisions would be made by Prime Minister Liverpool, Foreign Minister Castlereagh, and Colonial Secretary Bathurst. Gambier was an Admiralty joke who had seldom been to sea and was best known for his leader-ship of an expedition that had bombarded and gutted defenseless Copenhagen. Adams was an obscure admiralty lawyer who was destined to justify his obscurity, and Goulburn, a youthful under-ling in the Colonial Department, was so little known that Beasley was uncertain how to spell his name. To confer with five prom-inent Americans, Britain apparently intended to send three non-entities.

This evidence of Britain's disdainful attitude toward the United States disturbed Gallatin and Bayard but failed to surprise them. The leaders of Great Britain were not as violent in their attitude toward the United States as the populace they supposedly led, but all literate elements in British society accepted Federalist accusations and threats as gospel and looked confidently toward American collapse. To whip up popular hatred toward the United States, wrote Gallatin to Crawford, "the Ministerial papers have had nothing more to do than to transcribe American Federal speeches and newspapers." The effect of the speeches was such that even Gallatin and Bayard began to fear New England's proclivity to pursue its own stubborn course. Clay scoffed at Gallatin's warning that "above all, our own divisions and the hos-tile attitude of the Eastern States give room to apprehend that a continuance of the war might prove vitally fatal to the United States," but Gallatin, more than Clay, had reason to know that faction could transcend reasonable bounds.

More appalling were signs that England was planning a crush-ing military campaign for some time in the summer. She had thousands of idle troops who could be either released to probable pauperism or utilized in America. It did not take a prophet to predict England's choice. Beasley's numerous sources constantly reported this or that troop transport sailing for Canada or Bermuda. Regiments of Wellington's hardened veterans were known to be gathering in Continental ports. Furthermore, little if any help for the United States could be expected from Sweden or France. Neither country was enamored of Great Britain, but both depended on the island country for their existence. The only conceivable hope of foreign assistance was the Emperor Alexander, despite his apparent indifference during the preceding year, and Gallatin wrote to William Crawford and America's venerable friend, the Marquis de Lafayette, in Paris, asking both to intercede with the Czar or his ministers. Gallatin was not optimistic, but he dreaded to think what would happen if the Emperor did not use his influence and strength to check Britain's burgeoning power. One way or another, America's future was closely intertwined with the actions of the Russian despot.

Once a site had been finally determined and a British commission selected, Bayard became restless to start for Ghent and spend some time in Paris before the meeting, and on May 23 he set out from London to Dover. The Channel crossing from Dover to Calais was tempestuous; passengers were "sick and puking in all parts of the vessel," but France, when its shores were gained, was a pleasant change from the land of the enemy, and the ride to Paris was through a glorious, ripening countryside, with fields that were "a perpetual wave, and the lofty hills cultivated to their summits." On Saturday, May 28, Bayard was in Paris.

Gallatin remained behind in the English capital, waiting for letters from Crawford and Lafayette and hoping himself to see the Czar when that mystical ruler should pay his visit to London in June. Gallatin intended also to report the movements of the American ministers to the Foreign Office and to prod the English government into dispatching her own commissioners to Ghent. While he waited he hoped to pick up more valuable hints concerning English treaty demands and military strategy. His vigil promised little in the way of happy results, but opportunity, if it came at all, would probably come in London.

An Uncertain Spring

Of the five members of the American commission the head of
the group knew least and last the events which were so dramati-
cally shaping the commission's future. In distant St. Petersburg,
John Quincy Adams dourly and drearily spent the months following the departure of Gallatin and Bayard waiting for spring and
information. He continued to rise at three on snowy mornings to
study the stars; he tended to the occasional duties of his Russian
ministry; he made the rounds of courts and *Te Deums* and receptions. Separated by hundreds of miles of ice and snow from
the center of European activity, Adams was engulfed by splendid
trivia and furiously engaged in personal and patriotic vendettas
which, for the most part, had ceased to have any real importance.

Wherever Adams went, there, too, like a bad conscience, went
Lord Walpole, and Adams, annoyed and amazed, ever noted and
reacted to the Englishman's aberrations. At one meeting, Walpole
complained to Adams of the frequent delays at court receptions;
at another, he said that his only regret over Romanzoff's decline
was that the man would no longer be giving his excellent diplomatic dinners. And he continued to fill Adams with improbable
stories concerning mediation and direct negotiation. One day,
with an astonished Adams standing nearby, Walpole grew
tired of waiting for a tardy Duchess Anne to appear at the Winter
Palace and "lay down on the steps of the throne" to rest. Everything that Adams hated about Great Britain was, to him, epito-
mized in her minister to the Czar's court.

Adams could well have done without Lord Walpole. He had

not been sorry either to see Gallatin and Bayard go. Without them his life was lonely and with limited purpose, but his capacity for remembering and reliving slights and innuendo was almost without limit, and, under pressure, Levett Harris, the consul, unfolded tales that confirmed Adams's belief that he would do well to avoid both Gallatin and Bayard, especially the latter, in the future.

Less than a week after Gallatin and Bayard had commenced their icy sleigh ride, Romanzoff summoned Adams to show him a dispatch from Count Lieven, containing information on Castlereagh's offer of direct negotiation. Romanzoff told Adams that Gallatin, through Harris, had requested that any important news be transmitted via Harris who, at that time, was to leave for Amsterdam about a week later. Romanzoff refused to comply, telling the consul that Adams was the only one authorized to receive such information. Adams, naturally enough, emphatically agreed.

Later that day Harris confirmed Romanzoff's account of Gallatin's instructions, and, before the consul left for Amsterdam, he and Adams washed all that remained of the mediation commission's dirty linen. Adams learned that Bayard had said as many unkind words about him as about Gallatin. He learned also that Bayard had hinted to Harris that Adams thought little of the consul and had wanted his own nephew to be legation secretary. Adams, in a lengthy denunciation of Bayard, denied that this was so, and, digging deeper, extracted from Harris an unflattering comment about Harris's masculinity, uttered by Gallatin when under the influence of too much wine. Under considerable prodding, Harris—whom Hughes, secretary to the new commission, was to describe as "a very neat little man"—retold the whole, not very sordid story, a story which Adams, in any case, already knew. Swaying with the immediate political breeze, Harris agreed with Adams that Gallatin was very capable but sometimes indiscreet and that Bayard was both useless and unpleasant.

As Adams learned more of what Gallatin and Bayard had said and done his emotions grew almost uncontrollable. He was still brooding about these matters when he wrote to Gallatin later in February. "After you left this City," he told Gallatin, "I was made acquainted with certain Circumstances, which I am

to regret not having known before, as they would have inclined
me to ask a conversation with you upon subjects, about which it
may be inadvisable at such a distance to write. Should it be my
good Fortune to meet you again, I shall explicitly state to you
the Circumstances to which I allude." Gallatin, of course, could
easily guess that Harris, who had by this time begun his journey
to Holland, was the source of Adams's knowledge of the "Circumstances." It was to be fortunate for Harris that Gallatin
placed less store in such things than did Adams.

With Harris gone, Adams had no immediate adversaries, save
Walpole, and he grew more despondent over almost everything.
Romanzoff, his good friend, was definitely on the way out, and,
on February 23, Adams, along with other members of the diplomatic corps, received a circular letter from the Count, announcing that ill health had forced him to resign. Adams was
sincerely grieved over Romanzoff's plight and spent long hours
with the ex-Minister of State, trying to console him and listening
to his expressions of desire to start a new life in America if only
he were younger. The last official business between the two was
to explode, to Adams's satisfaction, Castlereagh's allegation that
the American mediation commission had agreed with the British
government that Anglo-American affairs should not be mixed
with European problems or nations—that they had therefore accepted direct negotiation as a better course.

Shortly after Romanzoff passed from the scene, Adams fell ill
with jaundice and for weeks was confined to his house and his
bed. Dr. Galloway came, predicted confidently that John Quincy
would get yellower, and prescribed a "vial of Sacred Elixir."
Father Bryozowsky, head of the Jesuit movement in Russia, came
also and tried to convert Adams to his church, but Adams,
though feeble in body, was strong in mind and prejudice. His
debility lasted through most of March, but he struggled to keep
to his strenuous schedule of reading and studying and—when he
was barely able—walking. He read in Sully's memoirs of the life
of the French King Henry IV, even though it pained him to
learn of the lurid details of Henry's only vice, "his passion for
women; which was so excessive that, in my mind, it casts a foul
and indelible stain upon his character." And sick as Adams was,
he lamented that "time is too short for me, rather than too long.
If the day were of forty-eight hours instead of twenty-four, I

could employ them all, so I had but eyes and hands to read and write."

It was not until April 1 that Adams learned definitively of the new peace commission and his role in it. On the morning of that day Nathaniel Strong drifted into St. Petersburg, like the last leaf of autumn, out of season but bearing at least some of the tidings that were his to transport. What mail he remembered to bring corroborated the news Adams had heard nearly two weeks before—that he, Bayard, Clay, and Russell were appointed to the commission for direct negotiation. He learned, too, that Gallatin and Bayard had safely reached Amsterdam, and, forgetting his resentments, he regretted that Gallatin was not among the four commissioners named to the new commission. He would be missed, Adams wrote his mother, for "his quickness of understanding, his sagacity and penetration, and the soundness of his judgement."

It took Adams nearly a month to wind up his affairs in St. Petersburg and be on his way. He was both eager and reluctant to take up his new duties. If fortune smiled upon him he hoped never again to experience Russia's hostile climate, and perhaps before the dawn of a new year he and his wife and son would once again be in Quincy. On the other hand, "the prospect of a wandering life" violated his devotion to systematic endeavor, and he already felt burdened by the "cares and duties which will probably for many months absorb all my time and faculties." Humbly he prayed to God for guidance.

Beasley had written that Clay and Russell would most likely not leave the United States before April 1, and Adams, therefore, felt no urge other than his own impatience to begin his journey. He submitted his orders to Senator Wedemeyer, Romanzoff's temporary replacement, and provided that gentleman with a detailed account of Castlereagh's inventions relating to mediation. Without expecting one, he asked for an acknowledgment of the veracity of the American version, and, more within the bounds of Wedemeyer's jurisdiction, requested leave-taking audiences with the Empresses. He summoned Harris to return and dispatched his last messages from St. Petersburg to Monroe, merely alluding to the fears he felt for the outcome of the negotiation, which, so far as he then knew, would take place in Gothenburg.

In the week before Adams's departure, word came to St.

Petersburg of the fall of Paris and Napoleon's abdication. As had Bayard and Gallatin in London and Clay and Russell in Sweden, Adams witnessed the celebration of a people who had for years known death and destruction and misery as their neighbors. Rockets flung their burdens of crazy brilliance into the night sky; the thudding of cannon endured for hours in the caverns of the narrow streets, and each church and cathedral swung its bells unremittingly. To Adams the news was not altogether pleasing. He shuddered at the thought of the fury Britain could now release on the United States. More than ever it seemed improbable that Britain could be induced to suffer curtailment of impressment, even in principle, and Adams did not believe that America could recognize England's seizure of mariners. It seemed to Adams, as he packed his bags for his trip, that the only possibility, if Madison and Monroe allowed, was to negotiate a treaty that neglected to mention the subject. Even with this compromise, Adams thought that America's success depended on the help of the Czar and on some split occurring among the Allies.

At one thirty in the afternoon of April 28, Adams, his wife, Louisa, and his son Charles rode out from St. Petersburg to the first stage stop at Strelna, where they had dinner. The day was cold and clear, and the roads, though mostly free of snow, were deeply rutted. After dinner, Adams got into his carriage and Louisa and Charles took their places in theirs. At four thirty, the father started off down the road to Revel, and mother and son turned their backs and undertook their painful return to the loneliness and isolation of the Russian capital.

The trip from the posthouse at Strelna to the medieval city of Revel took three nights and two days. Not far from Strelna the roads were white-coated, and by evening of the next day the sky was freckled with a fresh snowfall. The flurries continued throughout the morning of the 30th, and it was not until Adams neared the outskirts of Revel that early spring vegetation spread a tentative carpet to the Gulf of Finland. As had Gallatin and Bayard before him, Adams made do with dirty beds and revolting food. Only the coffee, which Adams pronounced excellent, cheered the stops at the wayside shelters. At eleven on the morning of May 1, after a night's fruitless efforts to recover the baggage stolen from his servant, Adams was being greeted by friends in Revel.

He lost little time in arranging passage aboard Captain Brinkman's *Ulysses,* but that ship like the others was imprisoned in the harbor by adverse winds and grinding mounds of ice, and Adams was forced to bide his time in a city which, although not unpleasantly, reminded him of the twelfth century. To a man less driven by duty the delay would have been enjoyable, and, at that, it was returning to his silent apartment after an evening at dinner or the theater or the opera that intensified his longing to be on his way; for his days and evenings were filled with visits and strolls about the city. He was entertained by the principal members of the local government. He was often at the home of Christian Rodde, the American consul, where he took delight in Rodde's "very pretty" younger daughter. Through Rodde, he rediscovered his old friend, General Norberg, a Swedish man-of-the-world and sometime inventor. The General proudly displayed his latest creation, a "lazy susan," but Adams thought it a "gimcrack" that would never make money.

More than a week passed, but the *Ulysses* sat stolidly in the harbor, even though Adams frequently climbed the hill outside the town and stared furiously at the ice. On clear afternoons he circled the city's walls completely, covering the two and two-thirds miles in exactly forty-seven minutes, except when he wove in and out of the seven gates that punctuated the ancient walls. When this form of amusement palled, he returned to Sully and the indiscretions of Henry IV. It was not until May 15 that the wind shifted and the ice began to drift into the Baltic, and that evening Adams moved his belongings aboard ship. By next day, however, the breeze had died, leaving a frozen barrier across the harbor's mouth. For four days the wind was fickle, bringing rain and snow and cold, shuttling the ice in and out of the harbor, but on the 20th the *Ulysses* fought her way into the Baltic and began her slow progress toward Stockholm. At sunrise on the 25th the Swedish coast came into view, and by evening, with customs inspection behind him, Adams was being shown to his room at the English Tavern in Stockholm.

While Adams was still battling Baltic ice floes, Clay and Russell in Sweden daily anticipated his arrival and waited impatiently for some final word from the commissioners in London. May, 1814, was one of the most trying periods of Clay's life. Normally a self-assured man of action, he found himself alone in Gothenburg, the only American commissioner at the place originally designated for negotiation, without friends, adequate information, or power. He did not surrender to the near-panic that plagued some of his colleagues; he continued to believe that the United States would prosper and emerge triumphant, but the rapidity of change in European fortunes was shocking even to him. When he left home, as he wrote to Crawford, European peace was anticipated, "but no human sagacity could then have foreseen the astonishing events which have since occurred in France—events which have put the mind more in that state of amazement which attends a deep dramatic performance, or an agitating dream, than belongs to the sober condition of real transactions."

It was the disappointing wait for news that would "throw a cheerful light around me" that accentuated his despair and feeling of helplessness. He awoke every day expecting the appearance of Adams or the arrival of a packet from England bringing word from Gallatin and Bayard. The cartel *Chauncey* made port from New York, but she carried news that was unexciting or difficult to assess. Monroe transmitted new instructions which merely rephrased earlier ones and urged the commissioners to make haste. Letters and newspapers told of the probable repeal of the embargo, a step which Monroe thought would swing neutral commerce toward the United States. Clay was doubtful, but, far from his accustomed haunts in Congress, he was unable to pass judgment. More distracting than the contents of dispatches from home were the rumors that filtered in from England and France. One of these named Lord Gambier and unknown others as members of the British peace commission, and Clay wrote to Bayard and Gallatin for confirmation. From France came suggestions that the Allies had secretly agreed not to interfere in Anglo-American affairs. "I cannot credit it," Clay told Russell. "Such a stipulation would have been dishonorable on the part of any of them, disgraceful to the Emperor Alexander."

For both Clay and Russell, May exhausted its tenure with the speed of glacial erosion, and, as the last days of the month approached, with no sign of Adams and no note from Gallatin and

Bayard, both men in Sweden began to weaken before what seemed a conspiracy of silence and inactivity—although Russell, distracted somewhat by his mission to the Swedish government, felt less acutely the "ignorance and solitude" which were crushing the spirit of Clay. Russell, in any case, was more concerned about himself than about more impersonal matters. It was not that he was unpatriotic or lacking in devotion to the cause of peace, but so engrossed was he in the cause of Jonathan Russell that his attachment to other causes and forces suffered accordingly.

His self-involvement, however, did not prevent some penetrating glances elsewhere, and, measuring other men by his own standards, he was often possessed of an uncanny ability to peel layers of human camouflage from naked reality. He was, for instance, quick to perceive that Gallatin and Bayard were the innovators of a change in the site of the negotiation, regardless of a like preference on the part of the British, and he lost little time in informing Monroe of his opinion. With similar shrewdness and some knowledge of Beasley's youthful excitability, Russell partially discounted that gentleman's "dismal forebodings." He was accurate, also, in appraising the diplomatic climate in Stockholm, and here his judgment was perversely sharpened by his proclivity to suffer a personal affront where probably none was intended. After an initially warm reception, Russell ran into cooler treatment from the Swedish government. His credentials were criticized, and he was told by the Swedish Foreign Minister that in the future his letters must be in French, not English. Smarting because of the Swedish government's tendency to be "fastidious in matters of mere etiquette," Russell correctly assumed that the United States could expect little assistance in this quarter. In time, he more rationally perceived the degree of Sweden's dependence on England—a reliance which caused her to repress expression of agreement with American principles.

Although kept busy by his personal and ministerial affairs, he was delighted when Adams appeared on the evening of May 25. Russell invited Adams to room in the house where he lodged, and the next day, while the two dined together, Russell communicated all—or almost all—he knew. By the evening of the 27th Adams had spent hours closely questioning Russell and more hours reading a mountainous collection of letters and dispatches. Spending that evening alone in his new lodgings, Adams thought seriously on the subjects of the documents he had received, "not without much perplexity of mind and doubt whether I ought not, instead of proceeding any further, immediately to return to St. Petersburg."

For three days, when not attending dinners and receptions or delivering his opinions to Russell, Adams walked the streets, seeking solace and decision and courage. He had expected to arrive in Sweden on the eve of the negotiation. He found, instead, that the British were dragging their feet and planning a massive military and diplomatic offensive. And the actions of Gallatin and Bayard sickened him. By going to London and supporting a move for a change in site they had, believed Adams, helped the cause of the enemy as effectively as a regiment of Wellington's troops. "For a multitude of reasons" Adams deplored going to Ghent, and he poured out his bitterness and reluctance in letters to his wife and his mother and the Secretary of State. He nearly drove Russell to his wits' end, and, on top of this, Russell received the most depressing of Clay's many letters. Russell responded to Clay immediately. "My distress at the delay which our joint errand has encountered has almost become intolerable & the kind of comfort I have received from Mr. Adams has afforded very little relief. His apprehensions are rather of a gloomy cast with regard to the result of our labours, in which I hope however he will be disappointed."

As Russell thus wrote to Clay, Adams was loading his baggage into his carriage for the trip to Gothenburg. Threatening one moment to return to St. Petersburg, he could not the next moment be restrained from going forward. He could not even wait for Russell to take leave of the Swedish court and join him, and at six thirty on the evening of June 2 he, his servant, and his driver left Stockholm at a fast trot.

The first stop, at two in the morning, was at the small village of Gran, where Adams alighted from his carriage to be greeted by John Connell, a courier who had come on the *John Adams* with Clay and Russell. Connell happily relieved himself of a bundle of thirty letters and dispatches, pointing out a recent one from Clay. Adams opened and read it. Clay had left for Paris and Ghent on the 1st, but the *John Adams* remained in port for the use of Adams and Russell, who would be so kind as to take charge of Clay's baggage. Enclosed was the dispatch from Bayard and Gallatin which had prompted Clay's sudden departure. The negotiation would definitely take place in Ghent, and, according to Clay, the British commissioners were "Admiral Gambier, Mr. Golsby and Mr. Adams."

Adams's hopes of meeting with Clay and perhaps having the opportunity to fulfill some part of his role as head of the mission were extinguished in the time it took him to read Clay's letter. Contrary to Adams's understanding of Monroe's orders, Gallatin and Bayard had connived with the British to change the site and had, most likely, agreed to more serious proposals. For a few moments Adams sat in the posthouse, sipping his coffee in silence, and Connell, across from him, uneasily studied the older man's reddening features. When Adams spoke he was harsh and decisive. He ordered Connell to hasten to Stockholm and tell Russell to leave without further delay. Connell departed like a man who had been sitting on embers. Adams himself wasted no time. He noted that he was already three hours behind schedule, and at three in the morning his weary servant and driver swore at the horses and whipped them into a dash down the road to Örebro. Determined to reach Ghent and restore order and firmness to the American commission, Adams felt that he had not a moment to lose.

For two nights and days the carriage kept a feverish pace, flashing through fields and woods and towns like a maddened specter, stopping only to pick up fresh horses and snacks. Adams finally called a halt of two hours for breakfast on the morning of the 5th, only because his driver kept falling asleep at the reins. At that, they were eight hours behind Adams's impossible schedule, and after his driver had briefly rested, Adams ordered him back to his job, and the three men rode on through the day and into the night until they reached Trollhättan at 10 P.M. and could stand no more. They stayed until morning, but by ten thirty the following night they had traversed the remaining distance to Gothenburg.

After such furious haste, Adams was forced to wait four days for Russell and his son to arrive and nearly a week for the *John Adams* to sail. Futhermore, by arriving in Gothenburg at night, he aroused the suspicion of the local constabulary, who apparently thought such travel habits characterized less sensible or less honest men. No sooner had Adams settled into his room at Seger-lind's Inn than a soldier appeared at the door and, despite Adams's outspoken reluctance, insisted on escorting him to the lieutenant at the guardhouse. The lieutenant and Adams failed, and perhaps did not really try, to understand one another, and Adams was led from the guardhouse to the home of the com-mandant. From his bed, the commandant interviewed the irate New Englander and sleepily demanded the surrender of his pass-port. At midnight, Adams was allowed to return to his room and be alone with his fury.

After the Russells had arrived and before the members of the mission boarded the *John Adams,* the ministers considered but finally refused the applications to sail with them of a number of American seamen who had escaped from impressment aboard British ships. Despite their desire to help the men, both Adams and Russell feared that such an act might have repercussions in the negotiation. Adams also dismissed his servant, Axel, who was unwilling to travel with Adams so far from his Russian home. While Axel was not immediately replaced, one applicant pre-sented himself and nearly secured the job. "I believe I should have taken him," wrote Adams to his wife, "but for his extraor-dinary talents. For he assured me that he was one of the great-est coiffeurs that ever was bred at Paris; that he had dressed the head of the Crown Prince and of all the royal family at Stock-holm; that he could make one a wig that it would be a pleasure to wear; and besides that he had a most uncommon talent *pour la danse.* He had been four years in this country, but the climate did not agree with his health, and he must say, there was no encouragement or reward for talents in Sweden."

Without the gifted applicant, Adams, in company with Russell and his son, was received aboard the *John Adams* with a thirteen-gun salute. Also welcoming them was Captain Angus, somewhat improved in spirits and sanity. At four the next morning, June 12, the sails of the *John Adams* rippled in a light breeze, and the ship began her cautious passage through the narrow channel. The next day, in brilliant weather, the vessel moved into the North Sea, and Adams, vicariously living the role of an able-bodied officer aboard a ship named for his illustrious father, sniffed the salt air and for the first time in weeks felt wonderful.

A few hours before John Quincy Adams was led away by a suspicious soldier to see the lieutenant of the guard in Gothenburg, the Emperor of Russia, the King of Prussia, Prince Metternich of Austria, and a host of generals and ministers and hangers-on stepped ashore at Dover, England, and were given a royal welcome by the Scots Greys and the 43rd, 52nd, and 95th regiments of His Majesty's Army. The next morning the group proceeded to London, the Czar in his "bottle-green uniform" leading the way, and by midafternoon, having parted from the others and circled the city and its waiting mobs and dignitaries, Alexander was in reunion at the Pulteney Hotel with his sister, the Grand Duchess Catherine, while throngs gathered in the streets outside and shouted his name.

For more than two weeks, the Czar disrupted the normal flow of life in the English capital. Everywhere he went multitudes followed and cheered him, and his effect on the upper classes and members of the government was as pronounced if not always as pleasant. He started off on a sour note by making his sister, not the British government and its citizens, the object of his visit, and he joined her in snubbing the Prince Regent and bestowing his favor upon politicians who were not in power. He was rude to the Prince Regent's current mistress and overly attentive to his former one, and it took supreme effort on the part of Count Lieven to keep Alexander from visiting George's estranged wife, the Princess of Wales. Furthermore, he refused to discuss European political questions with Castlereagh, whose spirits and patience were depleted more by each ball and dinner. The Emperor had no comment to make about the explosive problem of Poland, and insisted on returning home after his visit to London ended, thus indefinitely postponing the opening of the Congress of Vienna and allowing European tensions to grow and gather momentum.

"For three nights the Metropolis was illuminated, Lord Eldon's house in Bedford Square displaying in large letters formed of lamps the words: THANKS TO GOD. Transparencies, fireworks, and bonfires surrounded by ill-regulated and often drunken mobs met the visitors at every turn." Near the end of his stay, the Czar wore out his welcome among all classes of English people, but for the better part of a fortnight London was a gigantic carnival, and wherever Albert Gallatin went he saw signs of the festivities.

Gallatin steered clear of the mobs and was not, of course, invited to any of the official functions. He talked to Members of Parliament, however, and quietly gathered information and espoused the American cause, but the more he learned the more discouraged he became.

During the first two weeks of June he received several letters from Crawford and some from Lafayette. So far as Crawford could determine in Paris, the Americans were not to be encouraged by the expectation of any assistance from members of the Allied governments. Crawford even thought he saw signs of England's having motivated a systematic effort against the United States. He had failed in his efforts to see the Czar. He was purposely not presented to Louis XVIII. He was certain that the Allies would not discuss maritime questions. Even worse, Crawford had heard that French troops would be among the English regiments sailing for America.

Through Lafayette and his friends, Crawford eventually got a statement of American arguments to the Czar, and both Crawford and Lafayette later reported their achievement to Gallatin. Lafayette had gone even further and conversed with the Emperor, with whom he was much impressed. The Czar told him he had read Crawford's statement, but he was afraid the United States was being defeated by her own internal situation. Lafayette attempted to explain this away by saying it was simply part of the American party system, that what Europe thought were bitter internal divisions were merely mild factional expressions of the "happiest and freest people upon earth." Lafayette continued by stating the American case against Great Britain, and the Emperor agreed that, if the extent of current military preparations was indicative, England certainly was hostile to the United States. At this, Lafayette reminded the Czar that it was Britain that had rejected and the United States that had accepted mediation, and he called for the Czar to make a third attempt. " 'Well,' says he, 'I promise you I will. My journey to London affords opportunities, and I will do the best I can.' "

It was primarily to determine and, if possible, reinforce the effect of this conversation that Gallatin remained in London. While waiting for a chance to see or communicate with the Czar, he kept his finger on the quickening pulse of British hostility toward America, and on June 13 he penned a warning to the Secretary of State. Admiral Warren, former commander in American waters, had told Levett Harris that the new orders for the British forces in North America were very different and more serious than previous ones. Rumors of fifteen to twenty thousand troops on their way or about to sail across the Atlantic confirmed Warren's statement. Great Britain, thought Gallatin, meant "to inflict on America a chastisement that will teach her that war is not to be declared against Great Britain with impunity." He believed the enemy would probably aim at splitting the Union, attempting in the process to occupy the state of New York, and would most likely loose predatory invasions along the American coast, that would include efforts to capture New York City, Washington, Norfolk, and Baltimore. At the peace table England would demand the cession of American territory, the end of the fisheries right off the Grand Banks, and the curtailment of American commerce. Against this military and diplomatic on- slaught, the United States, in Gallatin's opinion, could expect no help from friendly powers in Europe, including Russia. The Czar, Gallatin predicted, would do what he could, but it would not be enough. Gallatin was convinced "that under the existing unpropitious circumstances of the world, America [could not] by a continuance of the war compel Great Britain to yield any of the maritime points in dispute, and particularly to agree to any satis- factory arrangement on the subject of impressment; and that the most favorable terms of peace that [could] be expected [were those of] the status quo ante bellum."

Knowing that his letter, more than those of any other American commissioner, would receive close attention in Washington, Gal- latin had waited until mid-June to write what was, perhaps, the most discouraging letter of his life. He had not cast aside all hope of American success, but he knew that the mission would need more latitude than the instructions of Monroe allowed, and he feared that the administration was woefully unprepared for what was coming. Believing herself to be in the right, America supposed that no real harm could come to her. In Gallatin's opinion it was time for an awakening.

Soon after writing to Monroe, Gallatin composed a statement to be presented to the Emperor of Russia. He not only reviewed the causes and history of the war and argued against the English practice of impressment, but, foreseeing British demands at the negotiation, he stated a case for confining the talks to the principles for which the war had been declared. And without precisely saying so, Gallatin suggested that his country would settle for a treaty that recognized conditions as they existed before the war. In doing so, he assumed that Monroe and Madison would act affirmatively on his letter of the 13th. It was a bold, perhaps foolhardy, decision, but Gallatin could honestly see no other possibility.

While Gallatin labored over his message to the Czar, Levett Harris, who had remained in London specifically for that reason, renewed his friendship with the Emperor's ministers. As a result, Gallatin and Harris had an audience with Alexander on the 17th. For the first time, after so many months in the Czar's shadow, Gallatin looked at the tall, round-faced man before him and, speaking in French, with all the persuasiveness he possessed, pleaded the American position in the war against Great Britain. The Emperor listened attentively, and, when Gallatin had concluded, Alexander reaffirmed his friendship for the United States, but, he added, he did not know whether he could be of help. Gallatin thanked him, smiled, and politely withdrew.

On the 19th the Czar received Gallatin's written statement, and, on the following day, Gallatin, having done all that he could, prepared to leave for Paris and Ghent. Before setting out for Dover, he wrote one more letter to Monroe. He informed the Secretary that all the American commissioners would shortly be in Ghent, and that Mr. Peter Irving, substituting for Beasley, who was enjoying his honeymoon on the Continent, had heard from Hamilton of the Foreign Office that the British mission would sail about July 1. Gallatin briefly described his interview with the Czar but said little more. He had issued his warning and his advice, and he hoped that Madison and Monroe would profit thereby. There was nothing else to add. The test would come simultaneously in America and Ghent, and Gallatin was off to join his colleagues in facing that part of the struggle that would occur hard by the canals of the Flemish city.

Americans in Ghent

About the same time that Albert Gallatin was introduced to the Emperor Alexander in London, the *John Adams,* five days out of Gothenburg, approached her anchorage near Texel, a barrier island for the Zuider Zee. The cruise had been without incident and in perfect weather. Adams and Russell, at ease with one another and the limited world that confronted them, were only mildly disturbed when, after they had anchored, an officious Dutch port officer boarded and told them that it would take four days to obtain a landing permit. The young man, however, shortly was reprimanded and overruled by his commander, and later that day, when Russell went ashore to arrange for the hire of carriages, the Dutch fleet and the *John Adams* exchanged a deafening barrage of salutes.

The next evening, after a day-long trip through lush fields and past busy canals and pretty, antiseptic little towns, the plenipotentiaries were comfortably settled in their rooms at the Arms of Amsterdam, a hostelry in the city of that name—a city that had been host to generations of Adamses. For three days the travelers remained there, while Russell entered his son in a local school and Adams, enjoying what amounted to a homecoming, wandered the streets and noted the changes wrought by time. Henry Clay arrived on the evening of the 21st and talked to Russell, but Adams, who had gone to the opera, missed him, and, since the rigorous schedule called for early departure the following morning, Adams and Russell were on their way to The Hague before Clay opened his eyes to daylight.

The first part of the trip from Amsterdam was accomplished in close quarters and chilling silence. To save money, Russell, now without the company of his son, had released his carriage and invited himself to join Adams. As a consequence, the latter had been forced to send his baggage and his servant, hired in Amsterdam, back to the *John Adams* to proceed to Ghent by sea. Furthermore, he had learned something the previous day that suggested that Russell was withholding information. Two Americans Adams had met in Amsterdam had been surprised that he had not known of the appointment of a minister to Spain. Russell, when asked by Adams why he had not told him this, had answered that he was "not at liberty." Therefore, on the morning of June 22, with Russell sitting unconcernedly at his side, Adams was doubly annoyed.

His mood changed drastically, however, when the carriage entered The Hague. He had first visited the city thirty-three years before, when he had been only thirteen and traveling with his father, then minister to the Netherlands. He had come again in 1783 and 1784. In 1794 he returned to take up the post his father had held. Now twenty years later, as Russell and he passed through the city, he was overwhelmed by a "confusion of recollections so various, so tender, so melancholy, so delicious, so painful . . . , so sweet, that, if I had been alone, I am sure I should have melted into tears." He would have liked to have stopped for a day or two, but "duty" beckoned, and he and Russell continued on through Rotterdam to a small town beyond, where they spent the night. The next afternoon they were in Antwerp, forced to wait until morning for the incoming high tide that would allow them to cross the River Scheldt.

The morning of June 24, St. John's Day, was cool and beautiful, a gentle introduction to summer, and Russell and Adams, recovered from their evening at the theater, where Adams had been mistaken for the father of a covey of French children, rose early and went quickly to the river. For more than an hour they were delayed at this crowded anchorage for British men-of-war, while petty officials bickered over their tolls, but by early afternoon they were halfway to Ghent. The road, bowered by leafing elms and poplars and oaks, carved through rich fields of grain and meticulous flower gardens. The thirty miles were traveled with ease and pleasure, and at four in the afternoon their carriage came to a halt in Ghent's Place d'Armes before the

Hôtel des Pays-Bas. Adams was gratified to find that they were the first commissioners to arrive.

While waiting for the others, Russell and Adams, Adams especially, met the local officials and inspected the city that for some unknown period would be their home. The mayor, Count de Lens, and his aide, both resplendently uniformed, came to call the day after the ministers' arrival and returned the following day to invite all members of the commission to a ball in honor of the Czar, who was expected to pass through Ghent on his return from England. The Czar, in fact, was the talk of the city, and each day crowds gathered and waited, unrewarded, for Alexander to make his appearance. It was not until the morning of the 29th that the bells rang and the drums beat and the troops and citizens lined the streets for the real thing. They stood patiently in a steady rain, and at eleven, when the skies loosed a torrential downpour, a group of simply dressed men on horseback rode by, their bodies bent forward to shield their faces from the lashing rain. Most of the crowd paid them no heed. They continued to stand in the puddles that wet their feet, not knowing the Emperor had come and gone.

Two days earlier Bayard had made his appearance, after an enjoyable trip from Paris, where Talleyrand, the man of many loyalties and voices, had assured him of France's friendship for the United States. Clay, complaining of an "excessively unpleasant" trip and bringing the rain with him, damply preceded the Czar by a day. By June 28 the American commission was assembled, with the exception of Gallatin, who remained away until July 6. Gallatin's delayed arrival made little difference, for there was neither sight nor sign of the British commission, and the Americans had no choice but to wait and seek other diversions.

With Clay's arrival Adams had more than a quorum, and on the last day of the month he summoned the members of the commission to an eleven o'clock meeting in his chamber. The decisions made—to obtain an English passport for the *John Adams* and send that ship home in the near future, to subscribe to two English newspapers, to hold "regular" meetings and record same in a journal—hardly concerned matters of international importance, and, when the meeting ended, Adams noted in his diary for the first but certainly not the last time that "conversation was desultory." More and sometimes more animated meetings were held in the ensuing weeks, but the topics continued to be relatively trivial. England controlled and had not disclosed the agenda. Consequently, serious deliberations would have to await the opening of the negotiation.

In addition, the commissioners were unwilling to reveal their innermost beliefs and doubts and fears to one another. No one wanted to play the fool. The future lay beyond heights of unknown proportions. All but Adams, however, anticipated a lengthy session that might possibly end to America's advantage, and even his somber expectations were as much a guard against disappointment as they were a calculated judgment of the possibilities.

He could not, nevertheless, discern any favorable omens. He quickly accepted the personal and, to some extent, the political advantages of Ghent, but he was convinced, especially when he discovered that the city was a British military camp, that the change in site had resulted in a British diplomatic victory, and he remained firm in his belief that if he had known sooner of the proposed change "none of us would ever have come to Ghent." The move, he thought, satisfied the British strategy of delay, and he foresaw a one-sided vigil in the Flemish city "until it shall please the mistress of the world, as she now fancies herself, to send her deputies for the purpose, as she imagines, of receiving our submission." Although the tentative expectations of his colleagues gave him moments of doubtful optimism, he feared— or so he tried to convince himself—that the peace talks would be catastrophic and short-lived. "Peace," he wrote to a friend at home, "at the present moment, and I fear for a long time to come, is absolutely hopeless."

Furthest from Adams in his opinions was Henry Clay, although his few months in Europe had taught him surprising humility. He respected British power as never before, and if an untimely end to the negotiation eventually seemed likely, he had decided to accept "the personal risk of a violation of instructions" if doing so would prevent a rupture. He did not agree with Adams, however, that the delayed opening of the talks was unfavorable to the United States; for his faith in the emergence of American military and administrative skills, while shaken, was unequivocal. Everyone, including his friend Crawford, disagreed with him, but Clay was prepared to wait patiently and without gloom.

Bayard and Russell, lacking firm convictions of their own, gravitated from one extreme to the other. Bayard, much recovered from but still sobered by his Russian nightmare, was receptive to signs that were favorable but kept an uneasy eye on those that were not. While all his experiences provided evidence to the contrary, he, along with the other members of the commission, looked to the Czar for some if not all of his country's salvation. A falling political barometer, Bayard found merit in the arguments of Clay—America was, after all, a rapidly growing country—but he could not logically dismiss the prophecy of doom exuded by Adams, and as time wore on and the British commission failed to materialize, his hopes of peace became "very slender."

Russell's beliefs, like Bayard's, were less matters of deep conviction than reactions to the opinions of the person with whom he was conversing or corresponding. After spending a month with Adams as his principal companion, he was an outspoken convert to pessimism and, soon after reaching Ghent, wrote to Monroe that "despotism & intolerance appear to be the order of the day." Restored to a sunnier and more welcome association with Clay, his outlook brightened. In his unique fashion, he began to regard the continued delay as a slight to the commission rather than as an indication of evils to come. "Our patience and our pride begin to be severely taxed," he wrote Beasley. He did not think the mission would long "consent to be trifled with in this way."

The American commission was complete with the arrival of Albert Gallatin, accompanied by his son James, on July 6. Gallatin, as was his habit, kept his thoughts to himself. His observations had been fully reported to Monroe, and he saw no value in engaging in conversational predictions. Whether the negotiation was abruptly severed or protracted mattered little compared to the essential fact that Americans at home must take the war more seriously than they had. He was annoyed to discover that the British commission had neither arrived nor been heard from, but he considered this primarily a breach of faith rather than an act of British policy. What the immediate future held he knew not, and, knowing not, refused to speculate.

Although the Americans were annoyed at the delay and uncertain as to what lay in store, they were not unhappy with

Ghent or with their reception in that city. In response to the mayor's invitation, they, with more than two hundred others, attended the ball in honor of the Czar at the Hôtel de Ville, and Adams, who occasionally evidenced an unexpected interest in such matters, commented that the ladies were "not remarkable either for beauty or elegance." Both Adams and Bayard, separately for the time being, pursued their principal diversion of walking. They stood reverently in the Cathedral of St. Bavon; they paused to observe the busy activity in the canals; they marveled at the paintings of the Van Eyck brothers.

Even Clay, whose stay in Gothenburg had turned him into a more critical traveler and a modest aesthete, declared Ghent "quite comfortable," and, when he was not playing cards or holding informal open house in his room, he joined the others on their brief excursions. One day he went with Adams to the Hôtel de Ville to see twenty couples joined in matrimony. Somewhat startled, the two Americans watched and heard the mayor's aide call off the prospective partners' names, ages, and characters, mumble a few cementing words, and clearly point out the brass collection box. Thus, and en masse, were twenty "ugly" brides (Adams's description) wedded to a like number of apparently younger bridegrooms.

A common pursuit of the ministers was the rental of a house. After lengthy discussion, Adams agreed to the others' persuasion to surrender their rooms at the Hôtel des Pays-Bas for common quarters, providing they could obtain a monthly lease. Adams was afraid of being stuck with a longer one if the negotiation were unpleasantly brief. With the mayor serving as real estate agent, the commissioners finally met their prospective landlord, a cook and wine merchant and owner of a shop which sold perfumes, millinery, prints, drawings, and secondhand furniture. There was much debate over assignment of rooms and harsh bargaining with the many-faceted landlord. The final hurdle devolved around "whether we should be obliged to take wine from him, or, if we supply ourselves from elsewhere, to pay him one franc a bottle for drawing the cork. We finally came to a compromise, and are to begin by taking wine from him. But they must be at his peril such as we shall relish; for if not, we shall look further, and draw the corks without paying him any tax or tribute for it at all." To be on the safe side and to keep the landlord on his toes Russell ordered a supply of wines from Paris. The messengers and secretaries, preferring the greater freedom of the transient hotel, declined to join their elders, and, without them, on the last day of July, the commissioners moved into their new home, the Hôtel d'Alcantara—later to be known as "Bachelors' Hall"—on the Rue des Champs.

Among five such individualistic and prominent men perfect accord was not to be expected, but, with the antagonisms of the Russian sojourn laid to rest and no important new frictions to replace them, the weeks of July unfolded in relatively placid fashion. Since each had been warned by his friends of the short-comings of the others, there was general surprise among the commissioners at the goodwill that existed. Adams, especially, pre-pared by experience and his mother to expect the worst, was delighted by the harmony that prevailed and was amazed by the transformation in Bayard. Not only did Bayard appear to be a new and friendlier human being, but Adams was both em-barrassed and flattered when on July 11, Adams's forty-seventh birthday, Bayard rose at dinner to propose a toast. It was Adams himself who upset the near-absolute equanimity. Not having sent couriers, he chastised the others for having done so and in the process having wasted the government's money. It was the daily communal dinners, however, starting at four and often not ending until six or seven, that did the most to tax Adams's precious supply of patience. "They sit after dinner and drink bad wine and smoke cigars," he wrote in his diary, "which neither suits my habits nor my health, and absorbs time which I cannot spare." One evening, having made up his mind, he abruptly rose from the table and announced to the assembled group that he would in the future dine alone. The next day, Clay pulled him aside to express "some regret," and that evening Adams appeared once more at the dinner table, "as I propose to do hereafter."

If Adams suffered daily purgatory at dinner, the others were equally disenchanted by the commission meetings which he called and presided over. For weeks after Gallatin's arrival Adams made them daily occurrences, and each noon the com-missioners met dispiritedly to be guided by Adams's agenda. For a while, they studied United States laws; they discussed renting a house; they argued over the sending of messengers; they labored for days to compose a joint note to Monroe, a dis-

patch which, as usual, completely satisfied none of them, so that
Monroe eventually received one joint letter and five private
ones. Also under Adams's leadership, each minister was assigned
the task of drawing up a paper on some part of the American
instructions, but, in time, even Adams became aware that this
was so much busy work, for nothing certain could be decided
until the British indicated their intentions. Of these intentions
nothing definite was known.

The only word came from Americans in London and Paris,
and the messages were not comforting. The British commissioners, wrote Beasley from London, "do not appear in a hurry to
leave this Country. . . . It is some times reported that they are
not going at all, at others, that they are waiting until intelligence
is received from the U. States." As July aged, the Americans in
Ghent began to fear that a negotiation might never take place.
On the 21st of that month Gallatin and Bayard marked the
anniversary of their arrival in St. Petersburg. They were, it
appeared, no closer to negotiation than they had been in Russia,
and peace seemed further away than ever.

The American commissioners were right in believing that
delay was part of Britain's strategy, but this tactic was as much
the result of indecision and neglect as of conscious intention.
The American war was by no means forgotten nor dismissed,
but the reshaping of Europe was of first and foremost importance, and it was not until the latter part of July that Castlereagh,
the man who was meant to be the architect of Anglo-American
peace and American defeat, found time and strength to consider
the proposals of other cabinet officers and subordinate members
of the Foreign Office.

From the first knowledge, however, of American acceptance
of Castlereagh's offer of direct negotiation, the British government gave careful, if intermittent, thought to the coming peace
talks. In February, as soon as Prime Minister Liverpool had
heard that the Americans had agreed to meet in Gothenburg, he
assembled the members of the cabinet to consider the subject of
a British commission. They decided "that a lawyer and especially a civilian, if a good one could be found, would be more
proper for this business than a diplomat. . . . What is wanted is
a man of legal mind and of a very accurate understanding." The

Americans had a distressing habit of resurrecting old treaties, agreements, and statements—of worrying and polishing seemingly insignificant details as if they were gold nuggets. Clever, gracious, philosophic men, schooled in the emotional generalizations of European diplomacy, would not do. To deal with Americans one needed a human composite of a bookkeeper, an army quartermaster, and a lawyer; and Bathurst, Colonial Secretary, was "exactly the man for such a business," but, wrote Liverpool to Castlereagh, who was busy on the Continent, "there is some objection to employing a Cabinet Minister in such a negotiation." The settlement of the contemptible uprising in the ex-colonies did not rate the services of a ranking member of the British government.

Guided by this restricted outlook, the British government, in the following months, considered and finally rejected a number of possibilities. It was not until May that the indifferent trio of Lord Gambier, Dr. Adams, and Mr. Goulburn, men who could be counted on to trifle with devotion, were selected. Anthony St. John Baker, former attaché of the British legation in Washington and anathema to Americans, was added as secretary. The real decisions would be made by the cabinet in London or by Castlereagh, wherever he was. The commission—the crusty old admiral, the pompous and garrulous maritime lawyer, and the young civil servant, eager to make his name—would take orders and embellish the details.

While the cabinet considered the composition of the commission, awaited the return of Castlereagh, and stocked its diplomatic armory, the Foreign Office added its considered opinion and kept track of the comings and goings of the American ministers. The five Americans may have felt neglected, but such was not truly the case. The Foreign Office was discussing the appointments of Clay and Russell long before these appointments were known to Adams, Bayard, and Gallatin. The British kept watch over Bayard and Gallatin in Amsterdam. They knew before Gallatin and Bayard that Clay and Russell had arrived in Gothenburg. When Gallatin and Bayard came to London the British refused to have any official conversations with the two visitors to their capital, but they observed their every move. "They both profess very amicable dispositions," reported Hamilton to Castlereagh, a little more than a week after Bayard and Gallatin had arrived in London, "and seem anxious to have unofficial conversations with the heads or seconds in the departments of State. They hope to get out of the war with a safe conscience, by saying that, the war in Europe having ceased, the causes of their quarrel with us have ceased also." The British government also received intelligence from sources within the United States, and they were better able to judge the extent of Federalist dissension than were the British public or the American commissioners. The privy council did not expect the Union to separate of its own accord, but they hoped, not without cause, that a strong dose of Wellington's veterans would provide the necessary wedge.

Troops were being assembled for operations in America even before Napoleon was far on his journey to Elba. In April and May, Wellington was directed to send thirteen thousand experienced soldiers to the Atlantic ports of France. He quickly responded, selecting "the best of the officers and troops for this service" and by June had exceeded his orders and parted with more than fifteen thousand. "The government have determined to give Jonathan a good drubbing," wrote Colonel Torrens of the Horse Guards, and his words were supported by the huge encampments that were springing up on the outskirts of Bordeaux. As quickly as transports and warships could be formed into convoys, the regiments were dispatched for service with General Prevost in Canada or to Bermuda to form an expeditionary force that would co-operate with Admiral Cochrane's fleet.

The only problem was choosing a commander for the latter army. Several generals considered service in the American war beneath their dignity, and it was some time before the assignment was given to Major General Robert Ross, a distinguished veteran of Wellington's Peninsular campaign. Near the end of July, as other troops in their transports approached or ascended the St. Lawrence, Ross and his force landed in Bermuda. So far as the British were concerned, Madison's administration was living out its last days.

The diplomatic offensive was launched with less efficiency and speed. For one thing, little could be finally determined until Castlereagh temporarily put aside his European obligations; for another, the extent to which demands could be made depended heavily on anticipated military successes, and these

could not take place until midsummer and not be known until a
month or more afterwards. The British public, however, was not
restrained by such considerations. In newspaper and pamphlet
the propaganda campaign budded in March and, like sumac,
grew to alarming proportions thereafter, as Gallatin and Bayard
well knew. To these diatribes and lists of grievances the Foreign
Office contributed behind the scenes, but, in the long run, it was
more recipient than giver. While Napoleon threatened, little was
heard or said of the American problem, but emotions had been
simmering, not slumbering, and with Bonaparte out of the way
the pot of vehemence came quickly to a boil, and the British
government, somewhat amazed, took heed.

Calling its enemy's conduct "so base, so loathsome, so hateful,"
the London *Times* of April 15 sounded the call to battle. "There
is no public feeling in the country stronger than that of indigna-
tion against the Americans . . ." continued the *Times*. "As we
urged the principle, No peace with Bonaparte! so we must maintain the doctrine of, No peace with James Madison!" America's
wrinkled little President rapidly became a kind of poor man's
Napoleon. Dozens of satirical prints caricatured his wizened
features and pictured him suffering a multitude of imagined indignities, and the British newspapers made him the symbol for
most of the sufferings of Englishmen and Americans alike. "He
must fall a victim to the just vengeance of the Federalists,"
announced the *Times* in May. "Let us persevere. . . . We shall
demand indemnity. . . . We shall insist on security for Canada.
. . . We shall inquire a little into the American title to Louisiana;
and we shall not permit the base attack on Florida to go unpun-
ished." A few weeks later, the *Times* spoke as bluntly and more
succinctly: "Our demands may be couched in a single word,—
Submission!"

While the *Times* was seldom outdone in the violence of its
opinions, it was not often specific in its demands. The *Courier*, a
rival paper and one that was closer to the ministry, and several
pamphlets were generally less abusive but more pointed in the
expression of their expectations. In March, one of the latter, the
Pamphleteer, appeared with an all-inclusive set of instructions
and demands that almost certainly drew inspiration from within
the Foreign Office. Probably intended merely as a trial balloon,
the tract set the pace for the months to come. It wasted little

time on maritime rights; they simply were not to be discussed. It insisted, however, that two major subjects be paramount in any negotiation: the importance of Canada was not to be underestimated, and that colony should be protected against future American ambitions; the errors made in the Treaty of 1783, that gave America her independence, must be rectified.

To satisfy one or the other of these aims, continued the *Pamphleteer*, the Americans would have to submit to a number of specific demands. The salient Maine boundary, that thrust like a fist into New Brunswick and Quebec, would have to be straightened, and the disputed Passamaquoddy Islands, mere specks of land between New Brunswick and the Massachusetts region of Maine, must be recognized once and for all as British territory, as the Treaty of 1783 meant them to be. The Great Lakes and Lake Champlain too were to become exclusively British. The Indians, cause of so much disagreement between the United States and Canada, and unfortunate sufferers from the inequities fashioned in 1783, must be granted inviolable territory to be bounded on the American side by the Ohio River, the Mississippi, and the Missouri to the latter's source in the Rockies. Whites in the area would simply become British subjects.

For some pages, "A Compressed View of the Points to Be Discussed in Treating with the United States of America" itemized the mistreatment of America's aborigines, but although the author lavished much energy on the subject he was by no means exhausted, and eventually put aside the White Man's transatlantic burden to demand similar security for North Atlantic fish. More precisely, he insisted that the Americans be excluded from their fishing and drying rights granted by the Treaty of 1783. The British, however, were to retain a corresponding right to navigate the Mississippi and should demand, in addition, the cession of New Orleans. Wandering a bit from the professed objectives of protecting Canada and undoing the mistakes of 1783, the pamphlet went on to call for a curtailment of American commerce with the West Indies and British possessions in Asia and, going even further afield, required the United States to give up the Floridas and perhaps Louisiana. Never for a moment did the author doubt that all demands were reasonable and obtainable.

The British government was surely in sympathy with the
statements and diplomatic dictates that found their way into
print, but they were more sensitive to the concomitant burdens
of taxation, European unrest, and waging war in the uncomfortable wilds of America. In any event, subordinates in the
Foreign Office and cabinet ministers could propose and discuss,
but final decisions awaited the attention of Castlereagh. He
finally concentrated his efforts on the American negotiation in
mid-July and on the 28th of that month issued the first official
instructions to the British commission, ordering them to Ghent,
"to which town you will repair with the least practicable delay."
It was not until August 2, though, that the British commissioners, armed with Castlereagh's instructions, completed their last-
minute preparation and farewells and left London for the city
in Flanders.

On Sunday, July 31, two days before Lord Gambier, Dr.
Adams, and Mr. Goulburn departed from London, the five
American commissioners moved into their supposedly haunted
house on the Rue des Champs. Although the eerie nature of the
place alarmed the servants, Adams brought his puritanical pur-
gation to bear and was soon able to announce that "the per-
turbed spirits have all forsaken the house since we entered it,
and we hope they are *laid* for ever." Unfortunately the more
solid British apparition could not be eradicated as easily, and as
the American ministers settled into their new rooms, they were
discouraged and incensed by the latest news from England.

Less than a week before, Peter Irving, brother of Washington,
had arrived with letters from his superior, Reuben Beasley. One
of these, to Jonathan Russell, described an exchange in the
House of Commons. Whitbread, a member of the opposition and
friend to the United States, had risen from his bench and demanded an explanation for the delay in the negotiation. In reply,
Mr. Vansittart, Chancellor of the Exchequer, angrily blurted out
"that the war with America was not likely to terminate speedily"
and, he added, might result in much expense. Dismayed and
caught off guard, Castlereagh leaped to his feet and assured
the Members of Parliament that there had been no "undue
delay" and that Albert Gallatin, in any case, was still in Paris.

Beasley further reported that Castlereagh had known for two weeks that Gallatin was in Ghent.

Gallatin, when he learned of this, was not startled by Castlereagh's ingenuity, but, like Russell, he had reached the point where he was more annoyed by British treatment than fearful of what it portended. He wrote to both Beasley and Alexander Baring the day after Irving's arrival in Ghent. He instructed Beasley to insert in the London newspapers the statement that the American commissioners had been completely assembled since July 6. To Baring he wrote an abrupt note that evidenced no pretence of politeness. "I have been here since the sixth instant. My colleagues had arrived on or before the 29th ult. But to our great astonishment the British Commissioners who were by us expected to depart from London on the 1st inst. have not appeared; nor have we any account of them." Gallatin in these and additional words, vented his spleen, but he knew, as did the others, that the American ministers had no choice but to wait and hope for the best.

August replaced July, but the daily activities of the American commissioners remained unchanged. The only British in evidence were uniformed members of His Majesty's Army, men who bore no instructions to treat for peace, and the Americans, biding their time, continued to tend their private interests. Gallatin's concern momentarily turned to his duties as guardian. John Payne Todd, Dolly Madison's son, had been in Paris for six weeks and appeared reluctant to leave. Various sources, including Hughes, the commission's secretary, who referred to the young man as "Monsieur Toad," hinted to Gallatin that Todd was enjoying the city and its feminine inhabitants altogether too much. Gallatin firmly advised Todd to come to Ghent and, from there, carry dispatches to the United States, where, thank God, thought Gallatin, Todd would again be his mother's problem. "Permit me therefore," he wrote, "to urge the propriety of your leaving Paris where you have remained long enough for every useful purpose. . . . I would be very sorry that either your property should be injured or your time improperly wasted by your trip to Europe." Todd, however, considering his time well spent, remained for some weeks where he was and continued to soak up this delightful form of culture so recently discovered.

Ghent had its own form of entertainment and culture but not

such as would capture a young man's fancy. Dinners, balls, and civic festivities abounded, and typical of these occasions was the presentation ceremony at the Academy of Fine Arts on the afternoon of August 1. The visiting American dignitaries were seated upon the stage, and, to the "flourish of horns and clarions," each, in turn, rose and handed prizes to young people for their accomplishments in painting, drawing, and architecture. Following the ceremony, each of the commissioners, somewhat abashed, was sent with a prizewinner to his home. With his young man of fifteen, Adams paraded self-consciously down the winner's street, filled with the boy's admiring neighbors and festooned as if for a carnival. That evening at dinnertime, the Society of St. Cecilia came by to serenade the ministers, who, dinner over, wearily trooped off to the Society of Fine Arts ball, beginning to wonder if there could be such a thing as too much hospitality.

In those early days of August a letter came from Beasley, saying the British commissioners were to leave London that week. The Americans hoped so but placed no faith in the information, and Russell doubted it so strongly that on Thursday, the 4th, he left on an excursion to Dunkirk, glad for any escape from "this dull hole." His less restless colleagues were not as disappointed in Ghent, and, accepting the modest diversions of the Flemish city, they ceased to speculate on the future and settled into a mildly pleasant lethargy. When they retired on the night of August 6 they knew not whether the British commissioners would arrive in a day or a month or ever, and, except that they were nearing the time when they might, in disgust, leave, they gave little thought to the matter. The delay had become absurd.

PART THREE

Negotiation and Invasion

Britain Makes Her Demands

Before going to bed on the night of August 6, a Saturday, James Bayard sat at his desk and in the dim candlelight completed a letter to his cousin, telling of the delay in the negotiation and the feeble chances for peace. When he had finished, Bayard put the letter aside and prepared to retire. Unknown to him, a party of Englishmen, a few blocks away, were checking into the Hôtel du Lion d'Or. The three British commissioners and their secretary and messengers had come to Ghent.

The next morning, a quiet summer Sunday, Anthony St. John Baker, secretary to the British mission, stepped quickly along the streets that lined the canals, strode through the Place d'Armes, and entered the lobby of the Hôtel des Pays-Bas. He asked for the American commission and was directed instead to Colonel Milligan, who greeted him and led him out again into the warm sun and to Milligan's master in the house on the Rue des Champs. Bayard listened respectfully to Baker's proposal for the commissions to meet at one on the following afternoon at the British hotel and promised to send a reply that evening, after he had talked to his colleagues. His task completed, Baker returned to the Lion d'Or.

Bayard quickly informed the others that the British had arrived, and at noon the commission, without the absent Russell, met to decide on their answer to Baker's proposal. That they would agree to meet with the British the next afternoon no one questioned, but all had some misgivings about what seemed almost a summons to the British quarters, and Adams, gesticulating fiercely, argued that the suggestion was "an offensive pretension to superiority." He referred the others to Marten's Summary, where, said he, such an act was described as a method of treating with "an inferior order." Clay, Bayard, and Gallatin were not as disturbed by the possible slight, but they acceded to Adams's demand that Hughes be sent with a message insisting on the neutral Hôtel des Pays-Bas as a meeting place. So instructed, Hughes went to the British that evening, and, at ten, Baker returned to say that the Pays-Bas was perfectly acceptable to his side. The stage was set.

It was Monday, August 8, fifteen months after Bayard and Gallatin had sailed from New Castle, Delaware, when four of the five American commissioners and Hughes, after a brief preparatory meeting, sallied forth from their house and went across town to meet representatives of the British government for the first time. When they got to the hotel they found the British commissioners already assembled. There were brief introductions and the exchange of official orders. Then all of them except Gambier sat down on opposite sides of a long table. The Admiral, clearing his throat and fingering the brass buttons that pocked his front from collar bone to navel, looked about him and formally opened the negotiation between His Britannic Majesty and the United States of America. His government, said Lord Gambier succinctly, was firmly desirous of peace. Adams replied in the same pious vein for his government, and, formalities over, Gambier sat down and motioned to Goulburn to take over.

For thirty-year-old Henry Goulburn, Member of Parliament and Under Secretary for War and the Colonies, the most important political moment of his life had arrived. He knew well —or thought he did—the nature of his assignment, and he meant to fulfill it with distinction and dispatch. Graciously, but never forgetting that he was to right the wrongs of several generations, he addressed himself to the Americans, stating at the outset "the most explicit declaration that nothing that had occurred since the first proposal for this negotiation would have the slightest effect on the disposition of Great Britain with regard to the terms upon which the pacification might be concluded." Having delivered himself of this grand pronouncement, he prepared to dictate terms that were in shocking contradiction.

He would, said Goulburn, recite the points of instruction from the British government, "which they supposed would naturally arise for discussion." When he was finished, he would ask the American commissioners if they were prepared to discuss these subjects and if they had any others of their own to add. Pausing for a moment in the dead silence, he allowed time for his words to penetrate. Then, pleasantly but firmly, he began.

If the Americans insisted, the British would discuss "the forcible seizure of mariners on board of American merchant vessels, and, connected with that subject, the claim of the King of Great Britain to the allegiance of all the native-born subjects of Great Britain," but *discussion* of impressment, suggested Goulburn, was about as far as the British commission was prepared to go. On their part, the British would require some revisions along the Canadian boundary. They would not, without a suitable equivalent, "candor" forced Goulburn to say, renew the privilege which allowed the Americans to dry fish on Canadian coasts. And most important, as an indispensable condition to be accepted before any other matters could be discussed, the treaty must embrace terms of peace and satisfactory boundaries for Britain's "Indian allies." On this latter point Goulburn did not elaborate. He announced bluntly that he was done and then sat back, awaiting the reply of the Americans.

At first no one spoke. Then Bayard asked if the proposed Indian boundaries meant acquisition of American territory by Great Britain. Goulburn said no. Again there was silence, until Goulburn, speaking softly and smiling pleasantly, said he did not mean to pry into the contents of the American commissioners' instructions, but were the gentlemen instructed on any of the British subjects? Adams replied that his mission must first confer and would report its answer at the next meeting. Goulburn said that he and his colleagues were instructed to obtain an *immediate* answer, but Adams, speaking forcefully and choosing his words with care, ignored him and proceeded to repeat the British points item by item as Goulburn had stated them, to make sure, said Adams, that the Americans thoroughly understood what the British were proposing. When he had completed his recital with a fidelity for detail that must have chilled the Englishmen, Adams asked if the Americans were to understand that the British desired to discuss impressment. Three British voices chorused a negative, and Adams, nodding his head dryly to indicate acknowledgment of the answer, emphatically repeated that his side would reply at the next meeting and not before. The British reluctantly acquiesced. After a brief discussion, the two commissions agreed to meet alternately at one another's quarters, with the next meeting to be held at the American house at eleven the following morning. In little more than an hour, the first meeting between the British and American commissioners came to an end.

Later that afternoon the Americans paid a courtesy call on the British. They arrived back home shortly before dinner, and before, during, and after their meal, they aired the proposals of the afternoon's meeting and, as well as they could, tried to determine a course of action. The British attitude on impressment seemed clear enough, but the other British points were obscured by the brevity with which they had been stated. What boundary revisions had the British in mind? How determined were they on the Indian *sine qua non?* Would a separate peace with the Indians, a fact which might have already occurred, satisfy this British demand? To none of these questions did the four Americans have answers. They knew only that on two British points, the Indian pacification and boundaries and the fisheries, they had no instructions whatever, other than to resist the latter, and that on the other two points, impressment and boundary revisions, their instructions were very likely the opposite of those given to, but not fully revealed by, the British commissioners.

Certainly the British demands were cause for serious concern, but even more troublesome were the dictates from their own government by which they were supposed to abide. The last instructions received from Monroe, those of April 4, merely reaffirmed those issued in the latter part of January, which, in turn, had simply expanded upon the theme so fully developed in the preceding year. Definitions of neutral rights and blockade, indemnities for spoliations, prohibition of British trade with the Indians, and freedom of United States operations on the Great Lakes—all must be pursued. In addition, Britain should be advised of the wisdom of giving up Canada before that colony was forcibly detached. But all of these aspirations paled in importance beside the one remaining cause cited as an inspiration for war. As a hot August sun warmed the Flemish canals, the abolition of impressment, that practice which mocked independence and human rights, was the primary goal the American commissioners were expected to achieve. "This degrading practice must cease," wrote the Secretary of State in January; "our flag must protect the crew, or the United States cannot consider themselves an independent nation." No end to impressment: no peace. Absurd as it might seem in mid-1814, the American commission was so charged to honor the promises of the administration.

After dinner, Adams, Clay, Bayard, and Gallatin sat in Adams's room, uncertain, hoping for inspiration, wondering, debating what they would say to the British in the morning. In the midst of their discussions, Hughes entered, bringing with him and introducing a Mr. Myers, courier from Crawford in Paris. In Myers's packet were letters from Crawford and Todd and dispatches from Monroe. Crawford wrote pessimistically of British strength and American debility. Todd, wounded by Gallatin's apparent distrust of his Parisian occupations, wrote nonsense and churlishly proclaimed his intention of staying for a time in the French capital. Clay and Bayard, expecting no new insights on Monroe's part and discouraged by Crawford's predictions, left the session for the sanctuaries of their own rooms. Adams, Gallatin, and Hughes remained and worked through the long, hushed evening, laboriously decoding Monroe's message, until, at one in the morning, the Secretary's dispatch was completely deciphered, and the three tired men read aloud the latest advice from their government.

Monroe wrote that his last word from the mission had been Gallatin's and Bayard's letter of May 6 from London. From this and other sources he was aware of Napoleon's downfall and Britain's rise and her nefarious plans for the peace conference. Britain, conceded Monroe, was stronger than ever. The other European Allies, America's warm-weather friends, were timid. Nevertheless, the United States would not give in to British demands. The American commissioners were to remain firm. As to the propriety of pushing the American stand on impressment, however, the ministers were to judge for themselves. "On mature consideration it has been decided that under all the circumstances above alluded to incident to a prosecution of the war, you may omit any stipulation on the subject of impressment, if found indispensably necessary to terminate" the negotiation. Adams and Gallatin and, when they had heard, Bayard, Clay, and Russell, needed no argument to convince them of the indispensable necessity. One of the principal causes of the war was to become an almost forgotten resolution.

Promptly at eleven on Tuesday morning the British commissioners were ushered into the American house, and, when all were seated, John Quincy Adams got down to business. He informed the British that the American mission was instructed on impressment and national boundaries, though not, however, on the fisheries or on Indian peace or Indian boundaries. In fact, there was no reason why they should have been instructed on the latter two subjects, as neither had been a matter in dispute between the two countries.

At this all three British commissioners tried to gain the floor, but Adams, paying them no heed, went on to recite the American points. The first item, he said, was to achieve a definition of blockade and, as far as possible, a companion definition of "other neutral and belligerent rights." Too, the Americans would submit "certain claims of indemnity to individuals for captures and seizures preceding and subsequent to the war." These were the principal demands of the United States, hardly fit offspring, as the American commissioners knew, of the great causes which had kindled hostilities in 1812. Adams went on to say that other points would be raised after peace had been negotiated, possibly during discussion of a commerce treaty. There were, he added, even more subjects which the American commissioners had discarded to facilitate progress toward peace. His words hinted at a condescending American restraint but fooled no one. It made scant difference what points the Americans raised or suppressed. The intiative was held by the triumphant British, and everyone present knew it.

As soon as Adams had finished speaking there was a general debate over the validity of Britain's interjecting the Indians and the fisheries into the negotiation. Clay, echoing Adams, pointed out that Castlereagh's letter proposing the negotiation had not mentioned either subject, that neither was germane to the war, and that no country had ever regarded the Indians as comprising nations. Goulburn and Dr. Adams brushed these objections aside, and Dr. Adams reminded the Americans that the Indian subject was a *sine qua non*. Were the commissioners from the United States prepared to reach any provisional arrangement?

It would be better, suggested the American Adams, if the British government, being closer to Ghent, were to modify its stand. Then the Indian problem and other points could be discussed. But the British would not hear of it.

Gallatin, occasionally interrupted by Goulburn, began a long defense of his country's treatment of the Indians. America's policy toward them, he insisted, was the "most liberal of any nation." Furthermore, the idea of including the Indians in an Anglo-American treaty was new and unprecedented.

Not so, replied Goulburn; both countries in fact had treaties with the Indians.

With them, yes, said Gallatin, but not about them. The Americans might be willing to discuss the subject, continued Gallatin, if the British explained more fully what they had in mind, but Dr. Adams quickly retorted that a discussion was useless unless the British were assured that the Americans were authorized to reach a provisional agreement.

Bayard, who, like his colleagues, was beginning to suspect that the British commissioners could not or would not discuss the Indian question and might, thereby, be hoping to delay or disrupt the peace talks, spoke for the first time that day. What, he wanted to know, did Great Britain intend by setting up boundaries for the Indians? Was it to keep the United States from making future treaties with them? or to keep his country from buying Indian lands? Looking in turn at each of the British ministers, Bayard continued to pepper them with questions, until Goulburn could no longer endure it. The Indian territory was meant to be a barrier, he blurted out, a barrier between the United States and Canada. The Americans nodded and looked at one another. Dr. Adams, hoping perhaps to make the statement more tolerable, added that neither side would be able to buy the Indian lands, but, not surprisingly, none of the Americans cheered his statement. Although the British had not outlined the proposed boundaries, the Indians in question were presumably American Indians living in American territory. It was scarcely an equivalent, thought the Americans, that both Great Britain and the United States should be prohibited from purchasing American real estate.

The British, deciding they had said enough, if not too much, then proposed an hour's adjournment so the American commissioners could decide if they would agree to a provisional article on Indian peace and boundaries, but each of the Americans rejected the idea, and Gallatin, summarizing the American position, said that it would be more honest to object now than to agree to a provisional understanding that would surely be rejected by the American government. Against such unanimity of opposition the British commissioners had neither pleas nor arguments. They suggested a suspension of the conference while they consulted London. The Americans readily agreed. After the conferees had settled on a session the next day, again at the American house, to draw up a protocol of the first two meetings, "the conference," wrote Goulburn to Bathurst, "broke up with mutual expressions of satisfaction at the candour shown by the other." More "candour," Bathurst was to decide, than was necessary.

The British commissioners returned to the American house on the morning of August 10, and proceedings began with a reading of the American draft of a protocol. As Adams read his skeletal repetition of the points presented by each commission during the first two meetings, the two commissions maintained absolute silence, but, toward the end of the American paper, Adams spelled out the American rendition of each side's explanations and arguments, especially those concerning the Indian question. "The British commissioners declined . . . discussion," said Adams, focusing intently on the paper in his hand, "unless the American commissioners would say that they considered it within their discretion to make a provisional arrangement on the subject . . . and proposed to adjourn the conferences, for the purpose of consulting their own government on this state of things."

At this there was acute restlessness on the British side of the table, but Adams droned on. To questions concerning the Indian boundary, continued Adams, the British "answered, that it was understood, that the Indian territories should be a barrier between the British possessions and those of the United States; that the United States and Great Britain should both be restricted from such purchases of lands; but that the Indians would not be restricted from selling them to any third party."

For a few moments, when Adams had finished his peroration,

the British commissioners interrupted one another in their haste to speak. They were incensed that the American draft protocol contained arguments and was not limited to the "dry facts." Goulburn complained that he had never heard such a protocol, and Dr. Adams, blustering and reddening, said that if the Americans gave reasons for not having instructions on Indians and fisheries there was no reason why the British should not give reasons for expecting the Americans to have such instructions. Precisely so, said John Quincy, but the British had failed to give any reasons. The Doctor quieted and shrank into his chair, and Goulburn replaced him. For a time, the exchange between Goulburn, Bayard, and Clay grew heated. Finally, one of the British spokesmen, excited beyond control, volunteered that the British could not now or probably even later give "the ultimate views and intentions of their Government." Temporarily, this stunned everyone into silence.

It was the still seething Dr. Adams who had the temerity to reopen the discussion. He objected to the use of the word "declined" in reference to discussion of the Indian matter. Clay, who was to some extent enjoying himself, reminded William Adams that the statement was a direct quote of his own words. But, protested the Doctor, he had spoken in "friendly discussion," never foreseeing that the Americans would repeat him. Goulburn came again to his defense, and after another vehement argument, the Americans, sensing that they had won something of a moral victory, backed down and accepted what was essentially the British draft of a protocol. The American government, after all, would receive the American version as originally written, and its propaganda effect at home was all that truly mattered. The British version of the protocol, so innocuously stated, was agreed upon, and the three English commissioners and their secretary left, only to return later that day, when tempers had cooled, to pay a social visit. With their second departure of the day the first round of events came to an end. What lay in store now rested in the hands of a small group of men in London.

The British statements at the meetings of the 8th, 9th, and 10th of August were too ambiguous to give the Americans any certain clues as to the British government's future demands. The magnitude of Great Britain's diplomatic campaign had yet to be disclosed at Ghent, and it was obvious that not even the British commissioners were fully informed about their superiors' intentions. Even the customary gloom of John Quincy Adams was speckled with patches of optimism. "You will now receive in the most exclusive confidence whatever I shall write you on this subject," he wrote to his wife after the second conference. "Say not a word of it to any human being, until the result shall be publicly known. At present I do not think that the negotiation will be of long continuance. At the same time I cannot yet speak on the subject with perfect certainty."

It fell to Adams, as head of the commission, to prepare an account of the initial proceedings for Secretary of State Monroe. Adams began to write the dispatch immediately after the meeting of August 10 and presented the finished draft at the noon session of the commission on the 11th. At that time it was agreed that each member would take the document in turn and enter his comments and additions. In the next few days, the paper went from Bayard to Gallatin, back to Bayard, and then to Russell, who had returned from Dunkirk in time to be a spectator at the arguments over the joint protocol. Russell, unable to find sufficient marginal space on the draft, passed on to John Quincy an additional sheet containing extensive changes in style and pointing out that until was spelled with but one "l." A day later, Adams was still sourly reflecting that changes made by one who was not present "are not very likely to improve its accuracy" when the commissioners assembled in his room for their daily meeting. Bayard, having given up on the original draft altogether, crushed Adams by submitting his own, "not one sentence of which," noted Adams, "agreed with mine." Adams sarcastically proposed that Bayard's version be substituted for his, which it was, but it was soon discovered that the Bayard account had its share of flaws, and Gallatin was assigned the delicate task of fusing the disparate elements into an acceptable whole. Gallatin struggled for more than three days before arriving at a compromise that all adopted, however reluctantly. The result, of course, was that Monroe was sent an official dispatch, which might easily have been written by Hughes in the first place, and a rash of private letters, in which each member expressed his favorite comments previously deleted by the others.

The official document contained little more than a detailed account of the three meetings between the two commissions. In his private communication Adams added his opinion that the British were seeking an immediate rupture in the negotiation and went on to repeat rumors of British troop sailings and to give the words of Lord Hill, possible commander of the British expedition, who, at a ceremonial dinner, had predicted that his nation would "humble the Yankees."

Of a different nature was the private epistle of Henry Clay. Less accustomed than the others to such extracurricular undertakings, Clay began his letter by apologizing for this "somewhat irregular" procedure but commented that it was necessary to help Monroe form "a correct opinion." Clay referred to the "well known arrogance of the British character" and admitted that the British had put forth "most extravagant pretensions" which might lead to an abrupt end in the negotiation. He was sure, however, that, at the moment, British plans were not entirely formulated and their strategy, such as it was, was intended to induce delay and fright. "I am inclined to think," he wrote, "that the Ministry has been attempting an experiment upon us, under the supposition that a panic has seized us, and that their policy is to consume as much time as possible before the termination of the negotiation, under the hope that they will strike some signal blow, during the present campaign." Unless the British did obtain a definite military advantage, however, Clay thought they would pause before breaking off "on the points in question."

The American commission, Clay told Monroe, was firmly united. It had no intention of giving in on the Indian question, and "we could have as little difficulty as to the surrender of any of our rights connected with the Fisheries." While no overt help could be expected from Continental Europe, America would, in the long run, Clay thought, benefit from Allied struggles over the spoils of the Napoleonic wars, which might result in a renewal of European hostilities. Great Britain would not speedily retreat from the formidable position she had taken in the Anglo-American negotiation, but stiff resistance by Americans on both continents, the scrutiny of the opposition party in England, and promise of further war in Europe gave Clay cause to hope that the faint taste of victory in Britain's mouth would eventually turn sour.

The American commissioners continued to write and receive numerous letters, argue with their landlord, and attend Flemish dinners and balls, but for more than a week they heard nothing official from the British. This is not to say that the Americans saw nothing of the British commissioners. Both commissions dined with the intendant, and in answer to an American invitation to dinner, Lord Gambier, his brother, Dr. Adams, and Mr. Baker accepted. Goulburn, who had "burst a blood-vessel, as they say, in the throat" and consequently lost his voice, sent his regrets, but in spite of his absence the evening was a success, with hosts and guests behaving in an "affable and courteous" manner. Admiral Gambier, in a mellow mood, recalled his visits to America—first as a boy of twelve, when his uncle was naval commander in Boston in 1770, and again in 1778, at age twenty, when he himself had returned to New York during the Revolution in command of a frigate. He had been pleased to encounter the senior Adams, he told John Quincy, and both he and the junior Adams discovered that they were, in their respective countries, pillars of the Bible Society.

It was also to John Quincy Adams that Dr. William Adams disclosed his family history and fortunes. Originally a prominent Welsh family, the Adamses now resided in Essex in declining circumstances. Relieved to discover that the American and British Adamses were probably not related, John Quincy later wrote to his mother: "I think we have neither Essex kindred, nor Welsh blood in our pedigree. His arms are a red cross. Ours I think are no other than the stripes and stars." Probably spared this chauvinistic comment at dinner, Dr. Adams enjoyed the party, talking freely to everyone and telling Bayard that while the American commissioners waited in Ghent, wondering at the British delay, the British commissioners rode at anchor, asking themselves the same question. The Britishers could not have been at anchor for long, and the remark was not an astonishing revelation, but it did reaffirm the American commissioners' belief that their British counterparts bore little responsibility for what took place in the negotiation.

Actually the British commissioners had already taken more responsibility for the details of the negotiation than was theirs to assume. A set of instructions intended for them, but never used or published, had been reduced by Castlereagh, in his orders of July 28, to a compilation of ambiguous but, it was hoped, frightening statements. The earlier instructions mentioned the necessity of the Indian territory to protect Canada from exposure to American invasion and outlined a boundary between the United States and the Indians that followed the Wabash and Miami Rivers. Castlereagh, in his draft of the instructions eventually used in Ghent, made no mention of the possible limits of an Indian territory, saying only that "a full and express recognition of their limits" was required, and, although he noted that "the best prospect of future peace appears to be that the two Governments should regard the Indian territory as a useful barrier between both States, to prevent collision," he emphasized the step as necessary protection for Britain's "allies" who were "entitled to claim at our hands."

In like manner, Castlereagh confined himself to generalities in the remainder of his instructions, hoping thereby to allow latitude for future British maneuvers and to force specific statements and concessions from the Americans. He did not foresee, however, that the British commissioners, by his own choice a lackluster trio, would be more questioned than questioning.

As Goulburn faithfully repeated at the conference on August 8, the first item in Castlereagh's instructions concerned the matter of maritime rights, "especially the undoubted right" of Great Britain to impressment. The British commissioners were to see if the Americans had any specific instructions on the subject, and, if American claims were not too "extravagant," the British threesome could suggest that something might be "devised." Under no circumstances were the British commissioners to stress the issue or commit their own government. "The right of search and of withdrawing our seamen from on board American merchant ships can never be given up . . . but, if the American negotiators have any regulations to propose tending to check abuse, the British Government will weigh them dispassionately, and with a desire to conciliate."

Next came the Indian matter, as both commissions now knew, and the third point was the "regulation of the frontier between the United States and Canada" to prevent "jealousy or collision." The unpublished, unused instructions specified this reconstituted border, but, for the moment, Castlereagh put aside details and stuck to pious reasons. Britain wished to revise this frontier, the Foreign Minister told his peace agents, "not in the spirit of conquest or dominion," but for purposes of defense and the best interests of both sides. The Treaty of 1783, that "hastily and improvidently framed" document that had recognized American independence, must now be reconsidered, particularly in light of the "avowed" intention of the United States to annex Canada and her illegal seizures of Louisiana and the Floridas. To an American moral dilemma, real or fancied, Britain had a solution.

The final subject, at least in the privy council's first official instructions, was the matter of the fisheries. Britain, wrote Castlereagh, had no objection to Americans fishing in open waters, but their privilege of conducting fishery operations in British waters and on British coasts was "annulled" by the war and would be renewed only for a chunk of American territory or some other equivalent. On this point the British commissioners were to be very explicit.

With one major exception, armaments on the Great Lakes, Castlereagh covered in general terms all the demands listed in the intended instructions—the ones that were superseded by his official directives. Other than the fact that attention was called to the Indian settlement as a *sine qua non*, the extent and relative importance of each of the British points was left purposely vague —even for the British commissioners. Their primary task, as Castlereagh more than once pointed out, was to "ascertain, as far as possible, the views of the American Commissioners, without committing your Government." When Castlereagh knew the "extent and nature" of the American commissioners' powers he would, he promised, send Lord Gambier, Dr. Adams, and Mr. Goulburn "more precise" orders. For the moment, however, they were to restrict discussion and probe.

As well as they could, the British ministers had adhered to their instructions. They reported to Castlereagh immediately after the second meeting on August 9, and on the following day they transmitted a copy of the official protocol. Their dispatches were not noteworthy for detailed attention to questions and answers, but the three men did make some effort to summarize American attitudes. "Nothing fell from them," read the section of their dispatch of August 9 concerning the Indian matter, "which induced us to believe that they considered it practicable to conclude any provisional arrangement which would be satisfactory to their Government." The report further noted the American desire for discussion prior to reaching *any* agreements, and the British commissioners commented that the Americans had made no issue of the fisheries question.

More revealing of the attitude and observations of the three Britishers was Goulburn's private account sent to Earl Bathurst. The Americans, Goulburn wrote to his immediate superior, had been awaiting the British commission's arrival "with some anxiety." Despite indications to the contrary, Goulburn was sure that the Americans earnestly desired peace. "They have conducted themselves with more candour and openness than I had expected to find from them, and I might say with as much as could have been expected by anyone." Where American "candour" was more grating than refreshing, the British, said Goulburn, behaved in a manner that was polite and discreet. He agreed with his colleagues that the representatives of the United States would not press their claim to the fisheries right, and he emphasized the vehemence of the American stand against an article calling for peace and neutral lands for the Indians. The American commissioners would not change in this attitude, thought Goulburn, unless they were instructed to do so by their government. Consequently, the decision for the British government, Goulburn told Bathurst, was whether to bypass the Indian question temporarily or to suspend the negotiation. He left little doubt that he preferred the latter solution.

Diminished Hopes of Peace

The accounts of the first meetings between the American and British peace commissioners reached London at the end of the second week in August, as Lord Castlereagh was preparing to depart for the Continent to attend sessions preliminary to the Congress of Vienna. The American war was not uppermost in his mind or in those of his fellow cabinet ministers, and consideration of the British commissioners' reports and the resultant instructions to those commissioners were undertaken in haste. The privy council did reflect on the unexpected perversity of the Americans, and Castlereagh took pains to make his second set of instructions more explicit and threatening than the first. If there arose any necessity to postpone the conferences so the American ministers might receive instructions from home, he wrote at the conclusion of his new dictates, "you will . . . declare to them, that the British Government, upon the resumption of the conferences, will not consider themselves bound by any thing which has hitherto passed, or precluded from regulating its conduct by the then state of the war."

Having constructed the framework of the next offensive in the Anglo-American negotiation, Castlereagh decided to add Ghent to his route and to deliver the new injunctions in person. Accompanied by his wife, her sister, and a considerable retinue, he set foot in the Flemish city on the evening of August 18, at an hour when John Quincy Adams was almost surely snug in his bed. Early the next morning, Anthony St. John Baker traveled across Ghent to the American house and alerted its inhabitants to a 3 P.M. meeting at the British residence. The peace parley was again in session.

At the appointed hour on that hot Friday afternoon the American commission was ushered into the British quarters. Greetings were brief and perfunctory, and, when all were settled in the room set aside for the purpose, Goulburn, without preface, began his frigid and forceful rendition of his government's requirements for peace. With Castlereagh's instructions on the table before him, he both read and paraphrased its contents.

His government, he said, was most "surprised" that the American commissioners were not instructed on the subject of Indian pacification and boundaries. Great Britain could not be expected to abandon her allies to a more powerful enemy, and the least that could be expected on the part of the American commissioners was agreement to a provisional article, "without which the negotiation could not proceed." Furthermore, if the government of the United States later rejected such an article all other treaty agreements would be nullified.

Since the American ministers had "complained of their [the British] want of explicitness" on the Indian proposal, Goulburn reminded the five solemn men across from him, the British government was now prepared to outline this necessary condition in detail. The Indians must be included in any Anglo-American peace treaty. Their security was to be insured by the establishment of a permanent buffer state between the United States and Canada, which territory neither present belligerent could purchase in part or in whole. Great Britain was willing—and Goulburn paused to emphasize his government's moderation—with necessary modifications, to accept the line of the 1795 Treaty of Greenville, an accord that had been concluded between the United States and the Indians, as the basis for setting the boundaries of the projected Indian state. If Goulburn realized it, he made no reference to the fact that said treaty had long since been canceled by agreements more favorable to the United States. Probably no one at the conference table could at that moment fully envision the extent of the territory—a parcel that would swallow most of the existing and future states of Ohio, Indiana, Illinois, Wisconsin, and Michigan—that would form this peaceful Indian preserve, but the Americans were painfully aware that the British meant to sever nearly a third of the Union. Not only that, the British hinted that the Indian utopia could, perhaps should, and, if the Americans were overly hesitant or stubborn, would be even larger.

With scarcely a pause, Goulburn moved to the next subject, the adjustment of the remaining frontier between the United States and Canada. Quoting from Castlereagh's dispatch, Goulburn stated that Great Britain, unlike the United States, had never attempted North American conquests, and, since her North American possessions were weaker than the United States, she felt herself "entitled to claim the use" of the Great Lakes for her exclusive military occupation. Ideally, Britain should demand full possession of the shores and waters of the lakes, but magnanimity prompted her to insist only that the United States maintain no warships on the Great Lakes or forts or posts on their shores. The Americans could, however, continue commercial navigation on these bodies of water.

Grimly devoted to his task, Goulburn continued his recital. The American commissioners were too numb with shock to interrupt. There was to be a revision of the boundary line from Lake Superior to the Mississippi River. Great Britain was to continue to exercise her right, granted in the Treaty of 1783, to navigate the Mississippi. Enough of Maine would have to be ceded to allow for a direct route from Halifax to Quebec. . . . Goulburn paused. Then, speaking more quietly and slowly, he announced that "these propositions must be considered as proofs of the moderation of Great Britain." She could have asked for more.

When Goulburn sat down, the Americans looked at their scribbled notes and at one another, as if questioning where one might begin in efforts to stem a flood. Gallatin spoke first. There must be, he said, at least 100,000 white settlers living in the area which Britain was insisting become an Indian buffer state. What would happen to them?

Goulburn, surprised by the question, admitted that the British had not thought of this. Perhaps this would be a reasonable basis for the United States to claim some modifications. Then again, the white settlers might simply have to move. Dr. Adams entertained no doubts on the matter. "They must shift for themselves," he said gruffly.

Bayard asked if the Indian demand was still a *sine qua non*.

He was told that it was. Was this also true, he continued, of the Great Lakes proposition? Dr. Adams, perhaps pleased with the chilling impact of his first statement, volunteered to answer Bayard. "One *sine qua non* at a time is enough," he replied. "It will be time enough to answer your question when you have disposed of what we have given you." Bayard was silenced.

Changing the subject, Gallatin recalled a newspaper account of the British occupation of Moose Island, one of the Passamaquoddy Islands off the coast of Maine. According to the news item Britain meant to keep the island. Was this so?

Quite so, said the British commissioners. The islands unquestionably belonged to Nova Scotia. They were as much a part of Great Britain as Northamptonshire. The matter was not open for discussion.

For a time the questions continued, as did the abrupt, uncompromising answers. Finally, John Quincy Adams intervened and requested a written statement of the British demands, to which the Americans would reply before the holding of another conference. Dr. Adams, recalling Castlereagh's admonition to restrict proceedings to verbal exchanges, objected violently, but Gambier and Goulburn overruled him. The British impressed upon the Americans, however, that if the latter did not soon agree to sign provisional articles Great Britain would not consider herself bound by the present terms and, if war progress warranted it, would enlarge those demands as she saw fit. With this menacing valediction ringing in their ears, the Americans departed and, in funereal procession, made their way through the sunny streets of Ghent to their house on the Rue des Champs. They had just been ordered to surrender American territory that exceeded the land mass of the British Isles. Their sovereignty was to be circumscribed, their honor trampled underfoot. Such terms were, noted Bayard, those of a conqueror to the conquered. The rumors and threats of spring had achieved grotesque fulfillment.

Not displeased with the results of their afternoon's labors, the British commissioners immediately set about preparing the note which the Americans had requested. The result, an abbreviated and somewhat more arrogant restatement of Castlereagh's instructions, approved by him but not entirely to his liking, was delivered to the American commissioners the following morning. Castlereagh, apparently convinced that matters were progressing satisfactorily, left Ghent and continued on his journey.

Neither in the joint conference nor in their written communication to the Americans had the British commissioners mentioned any of the American points. The Foreign Minister had granted his agents the discretion to ignore the fisheries and impressment if they were certain the American ministers thoroughly understood the British position on both matters and would not revive them as subjects for debate. As to claims of indemnity for British captures and seizures Castlereagh was adamant in his opposition. "You cannot be too peremptory," he urged the British commissioners, "in discouraging, at the outset, the smallest expectation of any restitution of captures made under the Orders in Council." Again the British commissioners judged that the Americans would not press the claims, and Castlereagh acquiesced in their decision to remain silent. It evidently did not occur to Lord Gambier, Mr. Goulburn, and Dr. Adams that the Americans made no fuss about impressment, fisheries, and claims to indemnity largely because the British demands for relinquishment of American sovereignty and territory made all other issues seem parenthetical by comparison.

After the meeting on August 19 the contrast between the dispositions of the two commissions was marked. The Americans retreated to the Hôtel d'Alcantara, stunned, angered, and in despair. In a much happier mood, the British composed their official note with genuine enthusiasm. They were not engaged in a vendetta against the American commissioners, whom they respected, but their hatred for the United States was not to be denied. The three of them truly felt that their government had been exceedingly modest in its demands and overly patient with the questions and niggling arguments of the five Americans. Not privy to the complex diplomatic and financial dilemmas that faced the more highly placed members of their government, they were obsessed by the restricted belief that they were to demand and receive America's submission.

Goulburn, especially, was impatient to accomplish the task with utmost speed and efficiency. He and his colleagues were, he wrote to Bathurst, waiting for an answer from the Americans, an answer that would, he hoped and believed, cause the rupture

of the negotiation. When the answer, a negative one, came four
days later, Goulburn wrote to Bathurst again. He noted that the
American rejection of a provisional article was not covered by
Castlereagh's instructions, "though we have little doubt that the
spirit of them would warrant us in declining to proceed in the
negotiation unless that basis was admitted." For fear that Bathurst and his fellow cabinet ministers might not fully grasp what
America was up to, Goulburn pointed out that she "is saying
that although America declared war for the sake of annexing
our dominions, yet she will cede nothing which can contribute
to increase their security." This attitude, said Henry Goulburn,
gave Downing Street a simple choice: to break or not to break.
And though he paraphrased the Dane, Goulburn was not in
Hamlet's quandary; his was merely a poetic, not a genuine,
option.

Confident that things were going well for them, the British
commissioners were sympathetic to the plight of the Americans,
and being sympathetic they tended to be condescending. Both
commissions were invited for dinner at the home of the intendant on Tuesday, August 23. At the dinner table, Clay took his
place next to Goulburn and immediately introduced the subject of the negotiation. The British demands, said Clay, were
the same as asking for the cession of Boston or New York. As
the conversation continued, Clay, it seemed to Goulburn, was
more sorrowful than angry, and Goulburn got the impression
that the American commission, doubtful what course to take,
was referring home for new instructions. This was two days
before the British received the American answer to their note
of the 19th. After dinner, Goulburn was taken aside by Bayard
for a "private and confidential conversation," during which
Bayard said that Britain's present stand would mean continua-
tion of the war and the demise of the Federalist Party. It was,
suggested Bayard, to Great Britain's interest to support the
Federalists, and the pursuance of peace was the policy best
calculated to accomplish this. Had the Federalists been in
power, he hinted, the problem of impressment would never
have reached such frightening proportions. Goulburn listened
in bored silence. "I did not think it necessary," he told Bathurst,
"to make much reply." Before the two groups parted, Clay promised that the American answer would be forthcoming tomorrow

or the day after, confessing, by way of explanation for the delay, that with so many on the commission it was "not easy to compose an answer." Without true understanding, the British expressed their tolerance. They felt sorry for the Americans. They also felt superior.

Four days later, following the transmittal of the American answer, the commissioners of the United States were invited to dine at the British house. Although they were still feeling superior, the British were no longer—after receiving the American note—either so sympathetic or condescending. The talk was polite but occasionally cutting. Again, Bayard drew Goulburn aside and earnestly discussed the British territorial demands, and once more Goulburn held his ground. Concluding their discussion, Bayard asked if the Americans could soon expect another note from the British, which, he presumed, "would terminate the negotiation." Goulburn readily agreed that this would be the likely result and assured Bayard that the British would not delay matters.

The British cabinet, however, was not so punctual or, apparently, so eager to end the peace talks; for days of silence followed the receipt of the American note. Reporting to Bathurst on September 2, Goulburn wrote that one or the other of the Americans had dropped in nearly every day, and that whenever members of the two commissions met, the Americans sought "unofficial discussions" which the British commissioners discouraged. The Americans' "only anxiety," said Goulburn, "appears to be to get back to America."

The day before, John Quincy Adams had called and, finding Goulburn the sole British minister at home, had for several hours engaged him in heated discussion. Adams emerged from the verbal fracas convinced that he had put Goulburn on the spot and laid bare the rotten motives that Britain was attempting to cover with pious proposals concerning the Indians and Canadian security. "In the whole tenor of his discourse," he later wrote of Goulburn, "I perceived not only a spirit of inflexible adherence to the terms which we have rejected, but . . . a cancorous [sic] animosity against America, which disclosed that there was nothing like Peace at the heart." Goulburn concluded only that Adams "is a very bad arguer."

.   .   .

The American commissioners could not claim that they had not been forewarned of the dreadful terms which Goulburn announced on August 19, but it is human nature to resist omens of death or destruction or dismemberment. Though the British press had time and again shouted of penalties more oppressive than those which Castlereagh had dictated at Ghent, even Henry Clay, the happy cynic, was surprised by the extent and apparent gravity of the British mandate. "The prospect of peace," he wrote to Monroe, "has vanished." Clay, however, could never entirely forsake his gambler's wisdom, and to Crawford and among his colleagues he expressed what Adams called the "inconceivable idea, that they [the British] will finish by receding from the ground they have taken."

Hesitating between despair and hope, Clay stood alone among the American ministers. The others were certain that the British had ruled out all possibility of successful peace talks. Russell immediately made plans to return to Sweden. Bayard wrote to his friends and relatives to prepare them for the long, desperate war which would ensue. Adams, apparently the proven prophet of catastrophe, maintained that the demands of the English were exactly what he had anticipated. He advised his wife, Louisa, that he would soon return to St. Petersburg, after he and his fellow commissioners had fulfilled their roles in the great "tragedy." To Crawford he wrote of the alternative of a "long, expensive, sanguinary war" or submission. "But if our countrymen are not all bastards, if there is a drop of the blood flowing in their veins that carried their fathers through the Revolutionary war" the lengthening of the war would mean only greater triumph in the end. "Bastards" was a harsh word for a proper Adams to utter but these were harsh times.

Gallatin, like Adams, was more dismayed than startled by the turn of events. In only one respect, he told Monroe, was he mistaken about British intentions: he had thought that the British ministry was continuing the war as a sop to the people, but now he believed that they were pursuing the more serious and dangerous goal of territorial acquisition. He did not waste his words on a recapitulation of the negotiation. Instead, he advanced his considered judgment concerning the probable objects of British military movements. Retracting his earlier statements, he predicted that coastal attacks would be relatively minor and made mostly for diversionary purposes. He expected a major push in the area of Lakes Erie and Ontario, but, he warned Monroe, the "true and immediate object is New Orleans." Waiting for the outcome of her war operations, Great Britain would attempt to delay the negotiation, although the opposition of the American commission, Gallatin thought, would terminate the business in Ghent within two to three weeks. He concluded his letter by assuring Monroe that he would soon see him in Washington.

If the pursuit of peace was to suffer the deplorable conclusion which the British promised, the American commissioners, who, it would seem, could not alter events, were resolved at least to make their final acts serve as historic evidence of American courage and determination. They returned from the conference of August 19 to an early dinner and soon afterward went into session. It was decided that Gallatin would prepare the draft of a dispatch to Monroe and that Adams would, when the British note was received, devise an answer to it.

With more serious problems facing them, the ministers repressed their usual differences over the report to the Secretary of State and accepted Gallatin's version without argument. The answer to the British was another matter altogether. Sure of the probable contents of the British document, Adams had begun his task before the note was delivered. Doing with much less sleep than he was accustomed to, he had a ponderous reply ready for the 2 p.m. meeting on the 21st. The draft dealt with the Indian question grandly and at inordinate length, ending the discussion of the subject with a statement that the idea of a buffer state was "a concession so pernicious and so degrading" as to be utterly unacceptable.

Unfortunately, the handiwork of Adams was not much more acceptable to his fellow ministers than was the British Indian proposal. Clay came to the meeting with his own sketchy outline of a possible answer to the British, and from his pocket Gallatin pulled a stack of notes. The debate soon raged. Adams, engaging in a bit of understatement, later confided to his diary: "I found, as usual, that the draft was not satisfactory to my colleagues." Gallatin thought some of his expressions were "offensive"; Clay was sarcastic about his "figurative" eighteenth-century language; Russell set about improving John Quincy's grammar; and Bayard thought everything should be stated somewhat differently. They all agreed that John Quincy had gone overboard on the Indians. Although he complained bitterly that the others were better critics than creators, Adams ended by taking the shredded remains of his masterpiece back to his room for another night of work and revision.

By the next morning Adams had completed a new draft answer which he turned over to Gallatin. The following morning, August 23, the commission held another meeting. Gallatin, having added copious amendments, brought Adams's paper. Clay submitted several paragraphs of his own devising, and Bayard exhibited his unfinished manuscript. Confusion and disagreement reigned supreme. It was only after hours of wrangling that a decision was reached to turn the mess over to Hughes, in hopes that he could reconstruct an entire document from the emaciated bits that remained.

The final session was set for the morning of the 24th, but Bayard, busy with a new version, failed to appear, and Russell, critic at large and extraordinary, decided he needed more time for consideration of yesterday's compromise. The commissioners did not convene again until after dinner, and then they remained closeted, amid fearsome cacophony, until eleven that night. The result was a note that none of them really liked but that, out of desperation, all of them acceded to.

The note began by pointing out that "the novel pretensions" of the British Indian proposal "could no more have been anticipated by the government of the United States, in forming instructions for this Negotiation, than they seem to have been contemplated by that of Great Britain, in November last in proposing it." In a war over maritime affairs, said the Americans, the Indian boundary had never been a subject of controversy. Not only was the proposed agreement unique in the annals of diplomatic history but it was unnecessary for the object which England "professes to have in view." Amicable relations with the Indians could be restored by each belligerent independently. "To a provisional article, similar to what has been stipulated in some former treaties," concluded the statement,

> engaging that each party will treat for the Indians within its territories, include them in the peace, and use its best endeavors to pre-

vent them from committing hostilities against the citizens or subjects
of the other party, the undersigned might assent, and rely on the
approbation and ratificaion of their government. They would also
. . . propose a stipulation which should preclude the subjects or
citizens of each nation respectively from trading with the Indians
residing in the territory of the other. But to surrender both the rights
of sovereignty and of soil over nearly one-third of the territorial
dominions of the United States to a number of Indians, not probably exceeding twenty thousand . . . would be instantaneously rejected by their Government.

In response to the British terms on the Great Lakes and
on rectifications of the northern frontier, the note of August
24 was equally firm. "It must be perfectly immaterial to
the United States," stated the American commissioners, "whether
the object of the British Government in demanding the dismemberment of the United States, is to acquire territory as
such, or for purposes less liable in the eyes of the world to
be ascribed to the desire of aggrandizement." In short, the British proposals were completely dishonorable to the United States
and would at best result in a mere armistice between wars. Such
terms were utterly unacceptable. Weary and frightened though
they were, disunited and weak as was their country, the five
Americans in Ghent refused extensive compromise or surrender.

Their refusal, Adams predicted, would "bring the negotiation
very shortly to a close," and exhausted, sick at heart, fearful for
his country's future, he stumbled into his bed on that August
24 as the chimes of Ghent tolled the strokes of midnight. It was
still early evening in Washington. Neither Adams nor his colleagues had any way of knowing that Dolly Madison would be
spending the night fleeing through the countryside; that her
husband, leader of the American people, would be ignominiously
riding through most of the darkness along a Virginia road
choked with refugees; that when dawn came to Washington, the
Capitol, symbol of American majesty and dreams, would be
hardly more than smoldering ruins at the feet of her enemy.

The Rape of a City

To predict death is not so difficult a thing to do, for as a climax it is inevitable, and its foretelling requires an excess of neither courage nor wisdom. But to warn of destruction and shame and the unnecessary agonies of ignorance and misplaced faith— though in retrospect these destinies were obvious—requires perception and strength that transcend the ordinary limitations of humanity. Even men of stature sometimes embrace deceptively simple truths and causes.

Thus it was not easy for Albert Gallatin to write to his government so ominously from London in May and June and from Ghent in July and August, for he was much a part of the administration he addressed, and, however distinct his own beliefs, he shared to some degree the innocent faith that was the majority's passion. That his words of warning were not altogether ridiculed and scorned was not so much out of respect for him but more the result of leisurely communication. His and Bayard's first letters from England arrived in Washington in late June, when the news of impending disaster was beginning to impress even the devoutly stubborn and the simpleminded. His later admonitions, arriving as they did with the British army and navy, found few unbelievers, and his reports from Ghent were gratuitous and, for the most part, arrived after the events they warned of.

In May, 1814, however, when Gallatin and Bayard stood mute in the happy, noisy streets of London, the American government, after two seasons of premonitory poverty, was busily polishing its vision of hope. Even the first notes of the crescendo of doom

were thought to be encouraging. "The turn of recent events in
Europe," wrote Madison to Jefferson, "if truly represented, must
strengthen the motives [of the British] to get rid of the war with
us; and their hopes, by a continuance of it, to break down our
government, must be more and more damped by occurrences
here as they become known there." In Allied victory Madison insisted on seeing signs of transatlantic British fatigue, and, despite a crushing succession of Hulls and Wilkinsons and frightened, ineffective militia, he was confident that fresh incompetence
and further ranks of raw citizen soldiers would bring victory. It
was a faith that could be born only in the spring of the year
and one that was not likely to survive a summer.

It was not that warning signs were not in evidence; it was
largely that Madison and his cabinet preferred not to heed
them. In the same letter to Jefferson in which he expostulated
his unique view of British motives, Madison remarked that the
Republican victory in New York State had destroyed the Federalist faction in New England and thus Britain's dependence on
the excesses of this faction. This was, to say the least, a char-
itable view of the situation. It ignored Federalist victories in
Massachusetts and New Hampshire; it turned a deaf ear to the
violent speeches of Massachusetts' Federalist Governor Strong;
it paid no attention to the seditious tone of New England's town
meeting addresses for an end—almost any end—"to this hopeless
war"; it was in happy defiance of the threats of Senator Pickering
of Massachusetts, who was openly suggesting a New England
convention to consider that section's relationship to the rest of
the Union.

The only concern that Madison admitted to Jefferson was
over the state of the nation's finances. Here again New England
played a vital if not a salutary role. Her industries replaced those
of Great Britain in supplying the predominantly agricultural
remainder of the country, and by selling foodstuffs and goods
to the King's forces in Canada, with no commitment of men or
money to one belligerent and scandalously little to the other,
she was able to enjoy the lucrative status of a neutral nation.
As a result, New England benefited from an exceedingly favorable balance of trade, but, as specie poured into her plump
coffers, the rest of the nation, including the National Treasury,
staggered toward bankruptcy. It was all Secretary of the Treas-

ury Campbell could do to raise a heavily discounted loan of ten million dollars, and that sum was only a quarter of the total needed to fulfill the country's financial obligations for the year.

If one cared to look, there were numerous other indications of trouble ahead. The British blockade had been extended and tightened, sealing off the American coastline from Maine to the Mississippi. Almost no American ships, commercial or military, were able to penetrate Britain's floating canvas fence. As a partial answer to this, the United States government made new plans to invade Canada, but in response to a call for volunteers for the regular army less than six thousand recruits showed up in the first three months of 1814. In this reluctant fashion Americans rallied to arms as thousands of British veterans were preparing to cross the Atlantic and shortly before raiding parties ravaged the American coast and British troops occupied Maine to the Penobscot. Even Republican Governor Shelby of Kentucky, a staunch supporter of the administration, grew nervous. "There is but one way to cure this evil [faction]," said he, "and that is an awful and desperate one; and in the choice of evils we had better take the least. Were we unanimous I should feel it less humiliating to be conquered, as I verily believe that the Administration will be driven to peace *on any terms* by the opposition to the war."

The administration shared the country's desire for peace but not "on any terms," and until the end of June it anticipated happy news from the brief negotiation it assumed was taking place in Gothenburg. Near the last of May, Dolly Madison wrote to Hannah Gallatin, predicting that husband Albert would be home in July or August. Little more than two weeks later the cabinet met to make the most of the limited time left before the expected peace and to arrange its plans for new operations against Canada.

That campaign was already taking direction, although as usual not the direction intended by the administration, and, though the results did not seriously threaten Canadian security, they did prove to Americans that trained and well-led native troops could oppose British veterans with distinction. In the late afternoon of July 5, three miles above the falls on the Canadian side of the Niagara River, Generals Jacob Brown and Winfield Scott led American forces to a stirring victory over the enemy on the plain that flanked the Chippewa River. Less than three weeks after the Battle of Chippewa, under adverse conditions, the two generals, at Lundy's Lane, a path overlooking Niagara Falls, nearly repeated their earlier success. Both battles were hard-fought tributes to American courage and military ability, but neither engagement materially changed the course of the war. Furthermore, by July 25, the day of the bloody meeting at Lundy's Lane, Washington and its citizenry lay under an evil and worrisome cloud that admitted few rays of promise or hope.

More than a month before American and British forces clashed within sight and sound of the Niagara River's great plunge, Monroe received Bayard's letter of March 18 from Amsterdam, and three days later the Secretary pondered the import of the contents of Bayard's and Gallatin's dispatch of May 6 from London. Neither letter contained information that was altogether new, but the authoritative nature of the one from London threw a cold splash on the dying embers of once impending glory. Even with this frightening document before them, the members of the cabinet were not overly exercised, but after days of discussion they finally gave up their *sine qua non* on impressment (as the American commissioners, following their first conference with the representatives of Great Britain, learned on the night of August 8). More difficult for Madison and his advisers to achieve was a realization of the military threat that faced them, and another week passed before, on July 2, they established the Tenth Military District for the purpose of defending Baltimore and Washington and the surrounding territory.

Having taken this step, the leaders of the American government still moved with consummate reluctance and delay. Gallatin and Bayard had warned of the great forces that were sailing for America, and the government they addressed had no reason to doubt the warning. It already knew that troop transports were plying the St. Lawrence. On July 11 a small detachment of British troops seized Moose Island off the coast of Maine, setting a precedent for the larger invasion to come, and in that summer of 1814, as they had the previous year, British naval forces cruised the Chesapeake, making soundings, charting, occasionally raiding.

Now and then, Commodore Joshua Barney, an intrepid veteran of the Revolution and privateering, used his flotilla of small gunboats to annoy the British in the Chesapeake, as a fly bedevils a horse. The British were not amused. On June 9 they chased Barney into the shallow reaches of a creek feeding into the Patuxent River and bottled him there until the 26th, when Barney and a body of militia succeeded in prying the enemy from his position—allowing Barney to retreat safely upriver. The American government was pleased with Barney's escapade. They seemed not to realize that, with troops and small ships of their own, the British could go up the river as easily as Barney, at which time they would be approximately sixteen miles from Washington and no more than twice that distance from Baltimore.

Although few in the administration feared the British would move inland from the waters of the Chesapeake, it was to discourage and defend against such an attempt that the Tenth Military District was created. Madison passed over several competent officers before selecting Brigadier General William Winder to command the district. For more than a year Winder's only military experience had been service as a prisoner of war. A thirty-nine-year-old Baltimore lawyer, he had been appointed a Lieutenant Colonel in the regular army in July, 1812, and had been elevated to Brigadier General in March, 1813. His knowledge of the art of warfare was not extensive. His most impressive credential was his relationship to Levi Winder, his cousin and the Federalist Governor of Maryland, from which state most of the manpower for the district would have to come.

Winder may have posed no threat to Wellington's reputation, in fact to none save his own, but his task was made more difficult by the muddled and divided attitudes of the cabinet. As early as mid-June Madison had begun to worry about the great forces that were crossing the Atlantic, but he wrote to Governor James Barbour of Virginia that the states would have to defend themselves, and he had no more idea than a roulette player where the British would strike. Only Monroe considered the situation truly dangerous and tried to annoy his colleagues into a spirit of greater urgency. They, however, always wondering whether Monroe's motives were more political than patriotic, refused to be moved. Secretary of the Treasury Campbell foresaw no imminent threat, especially since he was convinced that peace was likely to come soon. Secretary of War John Armstrong, onetime minister to France and a strong rival and enemy of Monroe, treated the possibility of a British invasion of Washington as nonsense. If, thought Armstrong, the British landed and marched anywhere they would certainly go after the richer prize of Baltimore. If the British did venture toward Washington, the Secretary believed that local militia would provide a sufficient deterrance; "that bayonets are known to form the most efficient barriers; and that there was no reason in this case to doubt beforehand the willingness of the country to defend itself. . . ."

On paper, at least, the administration took impressive action, outlining for the Tenth Military District a corps of 93,500 men. Of this shadow army, a force of about fifteen thousand could, with difficulty, actually be mustered, but Armstrong warned Winder that he should call up only part of his quota, that he was "to avoid unnecessary calls and to proportion the call to the exigency." Coming from a man who did not perceive any exigency, this advice left Winder with little more to command than himself and his horse, and, combining these forces, Winder set out on July 5 to scout the extensive area that so much depended on him. For nearly a month he rode upriver and down, sloshed through meandering creeks, clopped along dusty roads and across rough fields, and on August 1, in a state of near exhaustion, returned to Washington. He had, from his tedious journey, discovered what almost everyone already knew: the Tenth Military District was practically without defenses.

While Winder studied the needs of his command, rumors sprang up like toadstools in the rain and were rejected or accepted as they suited the convictions of the hearers. John Jacob Astor, the wealthy New York merchant, wrote to Monroe of every dismal report he received from Europe, and, offering the government one of his own fast sailing ships as a courier, suggested that the American commissioners should be given unlimited freedom to alter their instructions. Astor, besides nourishing a businessman's concern for his investments, was to some extent influenced by the moderate Federalists, such as Rufus King, who, while they did not openly toy with disunion, saw nothing but calamity ahead if the administration continued on its dead-end course. Most of the cabinet, however, remained unmoved by the signs of danger. Campbell assumed blandly that the imminence of peace would solve the nation's financial problems. Armstrong sneered at the paltry defense preparations, so belatedly undertaken, and treated Winder like a disinherited son— to be restrained but not encouraged. In lonely impotence, Monroe fumed and fretted and felt sorry for himself.

Between the opposing factions of his cabinet Madison was torn in his emotions and beliefs. Even when he was under the sway of Monroe, Madison did not know what effort to make that was not already being made. Dolly reflected her husband's divided feelings and growing concern. Near the end of July she scolded her Washington neighbors for being overly apprehensive about the city's defenses and preoccupied with plans to flee their homes. A few days later she asked Hannah Gallatin if arrangements had been made to remove the belongings from the Gallatin residence and, offering to take care of the Gallatin possessions herself, advised Hannah to burn the letter. She hurriedly wrote again two weeks later, August 17, to inform Hannah that the Gallatins' personal things were to be moved. It was the last she was to write for some time. The next day excited messengers rode into the city with news that a large British fleet had appeared off the mouth of the Patuxent. Washington fell into a swirl of activity.

On the second day of June, the 4th, 44th, and 85th regiments, 2,500 seasoned members of His Majesty's Army, had sailed from Bayonne, France, under the command of Major General Robert Ross, a veteran aide of the Duke of Wellington. By July 24 the transports had reached Bermuda, and a few days later the forces were augmented by the arrival of the 21st regiment. Not long afterward, the expanded armada, led by Ross and Vice Admiral Cochrane, set sail once more, and at dawn of August 15 the low cloud of canvas passed between Capes Charles and Henry and "stood in gallant style up the Chesapeake." The force was shortly joined by Rear Admiral Cockburn, his battle fleet, troops, and marines, forming a sight "as grand and imposing as any . . . ever beheld; because one could not help remembering that this powerful fleet was sailing in an enemy's bay, and was filled with troops for the invasion of that enemy's country."

The fleet moved up the bay slowly but purposefully, anchoring each night to avoid running aground on hidden shoals. On the 18th the British were within the banks of the Patuxent, and the next morning they moved up the river, coming to anchor a few miles below the town of Benedict and less than fifty miles distant from Washington. Late that afternoon the troops were loaded into boats and rowed ashore. Prepared for a fight, the British met not a single American in opposition, and by evening an army of more than four thousand men had been safely landed. In the seemingly hospitable land of the enemy the British army bedded down to spend a tranquil night.

Ross's orders called for him to "effect a diversion" without occupying or destroying private property. Cochrane and Cockburn, owing allegiance to other superiors, were not so restricted in their aims. Sir George Prevost, Governor-General of Canada, had written to Cochrane of American raids across the border and the resulting devastation of Canadian settlements. That the American government had disowned the raids and the raiders influenced neither British commander in the least, and on the 18th, as the British fleet entered the Patuxent, Cochrane issued an order for the retaliatory destruction of American coastal areas.

From the beginning of their excursion Cochrane and Cockburn included an attack on Washington in their plans, but Ross, upon whom most of the burden would fall, doubted the wisdom of such a project and worried for the safety of his army. The first order of business, in any case, was to do away with Commodore Barney's flotilla, which had withdrawn about twenty-five miles up the river above a place called Pig Point. As Admiral Cochrane later partially reported to the Admiralty, the three British leaders reached a tentative decision, Ross postponing final commitment until he had tested American defenses. "Information from Rear-Admiral Cockburn," wrote Cochrane after the fact, "that Commodore Barney, with the Potomac flotilla, had taken shelter at the head of the Patuxent, afforded a pretext for ascending that river to attack him . . . , while the ultimate destination of the combined force was Washington, should it be found that the attempt might be made with any prospect of success."

Through indecision or caution, the British forces did not move with haste. On the 20th three naval groups parted from the main force. The largest tacked up the Patuxent in pursuit of Barney. Another headed for the Potomac to ascend that river and bombard Fort Washington, some ten miles below the capital. A third body of ships sailed through Chesapeake Bay to divert American attention to Baltimore. The army lolled through the morning and part of the afternoon, not moving until evening drew near and then proceeding only six miles toward the village of Nottingham before it again pitched camp. No American was to be seen.

At dawn of the 21st the British army set off again and, respecting the August heat and the possibilities of ambush, marched slowly through forests of giant trees until it reached Nottingham, about twelve miles from the previous night's camp. This day finally produced some Americans. Several careless scouts were seized by the British, and just outside Nottingham some shots were exchanged with a small and rapidly retreating party. Yet nothing, not even the laying of roadblocks, was done to hinder the British advance, and the village of Nottingham itself was devoid of people though well stocked with harvest.

The advance continued on Monday, August 22, toward Upper Marlboro, about seven miles away. Most of the march was through the cool shade of thick woods, and only when an occasional clearing was passed did the British force catch glimpses of distant small groups of Americans. The forest eventually opened upon the beautiful, fertile valley that sheltered Upper Marlboro, and as the British lines poured down the road into town they could see what appeared to be the train of an army retreating to the west. At the same time, from the northeast, came the sounds of muffled explosions that marked the end of Barney's flotilla. Marlboro was empty, and the British settled down for a rest that lasted through the night and a good part of the next day.

It was the next morning that Ross fully determined to assault Washington, but it was not until the afternoon of the 23rd that the splendidly uniformed regiments moved off in perfect order down the road that led directly to Washington via the bridge over the Eastern Branch of the Potomac and indirectly to that city through the village of Bladensburg. The British had not gone far before the advance units were engaged in a brief skirmish, and after six miles of marching, as they approached Battalion Old Fields, near the three-pronged fork to Alexandria, Washington, and Bladensburg, the British came in sight of an American army in battle formation on the heights above. Recovering from momentary surprise, the mass of the British army proceeded around the American right flank down the road that led to

Alexandria. At the same time, the British advance guard set out to storm the heights. The Americans above them fired several deadly rounds before quickly vanishing in the direction of Washington. The British did not pursue. Instead, they returned about two miles to a place called the Woodyard and settled down for the night where the Americans had camped the night before. Throughout the hours of darkness the British slept undisturbed.

The night was not nearly so peaceful in the city that lay but ten miles distant from the British campsite. Since the 18th the residents of the American capital had been frantically, if not very profitably, busy. Private citizens and government clerks fought one another for wagons to carry their belongings or documents into the rural safety of the Virginia hills. Families boarded up their homes, hiding whatever valuables they could not remove. By Tuesday evening, when the British posted their pickets on the outskirts of the Woodyard, most of the women and children had been evacuated, and late arriving militia from Maryland and Virginia were seeking campsites on government grounds. Haggard from worry and lack of sleep, General Winder was riding at breakneck speed from the Navy Yard to the White House, while to his rear, at the naval station he had just left, his ragged troops slumped to the ground, completely exhausted from their running retreat of nearly eight miles from Battalion Old Fields.

When news of the arrival of the British fleet reached Washington on Thursday, the 18th, preparations for defense were not much further advanced than they had been on July 2 when the Tenth Military District had been created. Since destruction of bridges would thwart British entry into the city at other points, the obvious place to arm and fortify was the village of Bladensburg. Yet on the 18th there were but 250 troops in Bladensburg, manning entrenchments that had voluntarily been dug by the exasperated citizens of Washington. Madison immediately sent out a call for more militia.

Until the eve of battle, however, the majority of the cabinet remained impassive before the threat that faced them. Only at the last moment did Armstrong concede that Washington was in danger, and only then did he take an active interest in the frantic movements that eddied around him. Monroe, however, sensed disaster from the beginning, and, feeling useless and uncomfortable in Washington and having offered his service as a scout, he rode off toward Benedict on the evening of the 18th. He arrived there on the morning of the 20th, counted the British ships, determined that their army was not on the move, but was unable to ascertain the size of the force. This scout, one of the highest ranking in his country's history, remained on the fringe of the British expedition for the better part of two days before riding off to join Winder and his gathering army.

Winder had joined his men, now about two thousand strong, at the Woodyard on the evening of the 21st, just a few hours before the weary Secretary of State rode into camp. Whatever may be said of Winder, he cannot be accused of having lacked energy, however misplaced. For four days and three nights he had carried on as if possessed by demons. "The innumerably multiplied orders, letters, consultations, and demands which crowded upon me at the moment of such an alarm can more easily be conceived than described, and occupied me nearly day and night, from Thursday the 18th of August till Sunday the 21st, and had nearly broken down myself and assistants in preparing, dispensing, and attending to them." Winder might have been more rested and less emotionally upset, however, if he had not served as his own clerk, scout, quartermaster, and aide de camp. Like Monroe, he insisted on performing the duties of a corporal when his nation badly needed a general. As the British approached, Washington was full of amateur strategists and high level advisers, but no one actually undertook to assemble and lead an army.

On Monday, the 22nd, Winder, at the head of his cavalry, led part of his force toward the British camp at Nottingham. He arrived to discover that the enemy army was on its way to Upper Marlboro, and for an hour or more, from a safe distance, the Americans watched the colorful legions weave their way through Maryland forest and field. By noon, at about the time Commodore Barney was scuttling his gunboats, Winder was back at the Woodyard. Evidently feeling that the British were too close for comfort, Winder ordered his own army to retreat to Battalion Old Fields where, joined by Barney's sailors and marines, it spent the night—leaving the quiet and bountiful hamlet of Upper Marlboro to the placid occupation of the enemy.

That evening Madison and his cabinet rode out from Washington, and the next morning, the 23rd, the troops, now about 2,500 in number, passed in grand review before their President, who uttered some words of inspiration and then sensibly returned to the capital. At noon Winder once more rode forth to scout the British, whom he found still at rest in Upper Marlboro. Apparently convinced that the enemy would not move from this position that day, Winder turned toward Bladensburg, intending to bring militia from there to join his force at Battalion Old Fields. He had not gone far when a breathless messenger caught up with him and announced that the British were on the march toward the army Winder had left. Riding almost parallel to the British, Winder arrived at Battalion Old Fields in time to see the greater part of the enemy force going by his right flank down the road to Alexandria, and the remaining enemy regiments ascending the hill in his center. Not many volleys had been fired before Winder decided to retreat; his army turned tail and, spurred on by its general, ran for Washington. It was then that the British, evidently startled by such tactics, retraced their steps to the Woodyard.

Throughout Tuesday night, August 23, Washington was fearfully alive with rumor and frenzied activity. Men raced through the streets, pounding on doors, telling the awakened residents that British invasion was imminent. Most of the remaining women and children fled to the Virginia hills. Colonel George Minor, leader of more than six hundred Virginia militia who had arrived that day, spent the moonlit hours vainly searching for an officer who would issue him ammunition. Madison met briefly with his cabinet and listened to the entreaties of Secretaries Jones of the Navy and Campbell of the Treasury to appoint Armstrong field commander. Madison said he would think about it, and after he had received the gasping report of Winder, the general whom part of the cabinet wished to replace, he went to bed. Winder, almost intoxicated with responsibility and lack of sleep, labored until nearly dawn, collecting his troops and personally supervising plans for the destruction of the bridge that spanned the Eastern Branch from Maryland to Washington.

On Wednesday morning, as a hot sun rose steadily over the hills of Maryland, the members of Madison's administration hurried to Winder's camp at the Navy Yard. Most of them were assembled at seven and were still engaged in fruitless discussion at ten when a scout came pounding across the bridge to announce that the British army had marched at dawn for Bladensburg. Monroe was off toward that village in a flash. Winder followed soon after, and the rest of the cabinet and the army trailed behind.

As the opposing forces raced one another to the probable field of battle, General Tobias Stansbury of the Baltimore brigade worked to deploy some two to three thousand Maryland militia and regulars—who had been dribbling in for some days—on the high ground west of Bladensburg and the Eastern Branch. Stansbury had pulled his troops out of their positions that morning and headed for Washington to join Winder. Told, soon after his march had begun, that the British were headed for the place he had vacated, Stansbury hurriedly reversed his direction. He placed most of his force behind and above a deep ravine that crossed the Washington turnpike nearly at right angles, less than a third of a mile from the bridge over the Eastern Branch. From their stations, the troops looked across the ravine, an orchard that lay just beyond, and a marshy area that skirted the river, to the village on the other side of the river. The road to Washington came out from Bladensburg, crossed the Eastern Branch bridge, ran level through the marsh, rose slightly through the orchard, bridged the ravine, and ascended gradually through the hills. This was the route the British would have to take.

Sometime after eleven Monroe came galloping down the hill from Washington, and, without consulting Stansbury, altered the disposition of the troops. The rest of the cabinet, some of whom had to be restrained from inadvertently riding past the American lines, straggled in not long afterward. Winder got there about twelve. He arrived just in time to see the long, redcoated columns of British, six abreast, winding down the road across the river, almost parallel to the American position and approximately a mile away. His army came streaming down the hillside as the first of the British reached Bladensburg.

Winder had no alternative but to approve Stansbury's placement and Monroe's replacement of the American army, which probably numbered somewhere between 5,500 and 7,000. The American force was deployed, after a fashion, in three lines, each more or less flanking the Washington turnpike. The first line had been hastily placed behind the marsh, at least that section of the marsh that was north of the turnpike. Part of the second line was behind the orchard, and the rest was beyond the ravine. The third line was somewhat randomly scattered in the hills. Few portions of the army had any clear notion of their geographic relation to other regiments. Some were in an admirable position to fire on their own comrades. Others had an obstructed view of the enemy. Nearly all were tired and confused, and most had never been exposed to enemy fire.

The two armies were still on the move—the tail of the British army stretched out along the road across the Eastern Branch, the last of the American force running down the road from Washington—when some American cannon opened up on the British in Bladensburg. The redcoats dodged behind the buildings, and there was a moment of hesitation. Then, with Colonel Thornton in the lead, the light brigade streamed across the bridge and through the marsh. Congreve rockets shrieked over their heads and thudded into the ranks opposite them. The first line of American pickets on the edge of the marsh fired and folded. As fast as they ran they could not catch up to the raw militia behind them who had fled at first sight of the rockets. The light brigade pressed forward through the orchard to the lip of the ravine. Only then were they met and turned by a devastating barrage, but by this time other British regiments were swarming across the bridge, fording the river, and sweeping both right and left.

From their hilltop position the cabinet looked down on the debacle. America's citizen soldiers streamed past and refused to be influenced by the screams of Monroe to get back into line. Winder was everywhere, moving those regiments that were still intact, and shouting orders, many of which were misunderstood or contradictory. Many of the militia did not even retreat toward Washington, where they might have been of some use, but headed instead for Georgetown or for their homes in Maryland. When the British 4th and 44th regiments and the 1st brigade joined forces with the light brigade the rout became certain, and Madison and Armstrong agreed that it would be wise for the cabinet "to take a position less exposed."

Nevertheless, it was with difficulty that the British made their way through the ravine, and it was after doing so that they faced the most formidable obstacle of the day. Blocking their path was Commodore Barney, who had belatedly come out from Washington, where he had been directed to stay by General Winder in case the British navy came up the Potomac. What Barney could have done to the British navy had it appeared is a matter for speculation. Barney protested to Secretary of the Navy Jones and was finally allowed to take his cannon, sailors, and marines to Bladensburg.

With the battle already under way, Barney placed his cannon directly in the road about a mile from the Bladensburg bridge, the sailors and marines flanking the battery on either side. For a time there were some American troops on his left, and Colonel William Beall's regiment of Maryland militia occupied a strong position on a knoll to his right. Barney allowed the first line of British to come forward until they were nearly staring down the muzzles of his guns, "when I ordered an eighteen-pounder to be fired, which completely cleared the road. . . ." Twice more the British advanced and twice more Barney wiped them out. The enemy then tried to approach through a field on Barney's right, but Captain Samuel Miller and his marines and cannon shifted with them and decimated the lines of redcoats that tried to come on. It was not until the British swung far to Barney's right and threatened Beall's regiment that the tide was turned. The militia broke and scattered, and the British flocked around and came down on Barney from behind. Even then Barney held fast for as long as he could. His men were bayoneted as they stood trying to load and fire their guns. The little force did not surrender until Barney himself lay on the ground in a pool of his own blood. It was four in the afternoon. Save for the moans of the wounded and dying, the field was quiet. The battle was over. Only then, and slowly, did the British officers come up to the wounded naval officer, to pay their respects to him—to the one who had almost done what an entire army had sadly failed to do.

The savage defense put up by Commodore Barney had cost the British dearly, and it took them two hours to remove their wounded and reunite their regiments. Reports on the respective numbers of dead and wounded were conflicting and never fully authenticated. The British listed 64 dead and 185 wounded, but the Americans, especially those who later tramped over the battlefield, claimed the British loss was between three- and five hundred. The Americans reported no more than 25 killed and 41 wounded, most of them Barney's sailors and marines. Whatever the precise figures, it was clear that of the troops actually engaged the British lost a far higher proportion. Most of the frightened American militia escaped without a scratch.

No concerted effort was made to establish a last-ditch stand closer to Washington, even with those regiments that retreated in fairly good order or with the ones that never reached Bladensburg, such as Colonel Minor's group which finally received its ammunition—counted out box by box—just before the battle took place. What remained of the army fled to Washington, withdrew from there to Georgetown, and continued running northwesterly until the men dropped. The President and his advisers left the field about 2 P.M. and rode slowly over the hot, dusty road back to Washington. For the sixty-three-year-old Madison it was a grim and fatiguing journey. He was on the second leg of a sixteen-mile round trip to and from Bladensburg, and he was to be in the saddle for many more hours before the day was over.

Before the cabinet members reached Washington, excited messengers swept into the city with exaggerated tidings of an event that would soon seem pathetic enough. Mordecai Booth, a naval clerk who had sweated for days to transport powder and records to Virginia, was just finishing his dinner when the first of the sprinting militia came darting down the street, yelling that the British were right behind. The British, as Booth shortly discovered, were still eight miles away, but the flying militia's report decided those who had been waiting until the last minute that the time had come. Dolly Madison left the White House, taking the portrait of George Washington with her, and joined the crowd heading for Virginia. Remaining behind, Booth rode through the city's streets which were "covered with the fugitive soldiery of our army—running, hobbling, creeping, and apparently panic-struck." The President arrived, spent a few hours in the White House, and then, before six, crossed the Potomac in a boat. As the sun went down over the knotted, frightened groups that kicked up the dust of the Virginia roads, the capital was nearly deserted.

Earlier, while American citizens and soldiers scattered like ants before the threatening toe of a boot, Mordecai Booth continued his lonely tour of the city. Seeing no signs of the British, Booth began to hope the reports of defeat were untrue, and, hearing the thunking sounds of the American demolition of the Eastern Branch or Navy Yard bridge, he rode in that direction to consult with Commodore Thomas Tingey. As he approached Tingey in the Navy Yard, he found an excited army officer telling the Commodore that the British were nearing the Capitol. Having just ridden by that building, Booth angrily denied the report and offered to find out where the British really were. Tingey, who bore the responsibility of firing the Navy Yard before the British captured it, accepted the offer, and Booth spurred his horse in the direction of Bladensburg. At about the time Madison was rowed across the Potomac, Booth located the British army still near Barney's gun emplacements but beginning their march to Washington. Booth hurried back to Tingey, who reluctantly turned the Navy Yard into an inferno. With no more need for his services, the naval clerk rode across the Potomac Bridge to Virginia. After riding awhile he paused on the summit of a hill and turned toward the capital. What he saw "almost palsied my faculties."

The British did not reach the city proper until nearly eight o'clock, and, leaving the bulk of the army above the burning Navy Yard, about a quarter of a mile from the Capitol, General Ross and Admiral Cockburn with two or three hundred troops rode off to complete the day's work. Passing Albert Gallatin's house, Ross had his horse shot from under him, and to that dwelling came the unhappy distinction of being the first to receive the torch. The Capitol was next, and around 11 P.M. Ross himself was seen helping the soldiers pile the President's furniture for the kindling of the White House. To the members of the light brigade, first to enter battle but only then marching toward the scene of the gruesome festivities, the sight was impressive indeed. "The sky was brilliantly illumined by the different conflagrations," Lieutenant Gleig wrote afterwards, "and a dark red light was thrown upon the road, sufficient to permit each man to view distinctly his comrade's face. Except the burning of St. Sebastian's, I do not recollect to have witnessed, at any period of my life, a scene more striking or more sublime."

In the early hours of the morning a violent thunderstorm served to dampen the flames and strike terror in the hearts of the incendiaries, but as soon as the sun rose the British were back at work, destroying most public buildings and sparing most private ones. One of the last tasks was to destroy the type of the *National Intelligencer*, a paper particularly obnoxious to Admiral Cockburn, who supervised the undertaking while inanely seated atop a white mare whose foal hugged her side. The rape of the city was barely completed when, soon after noon, a second storm, described by some as a hurricane, by others as a tornado, descended upon the conquerors. It moved cannon from their mounts, tore roofs from houses, and sent the British scurrying for shelter. It raged for two hours, bringing further havoc to a city that was already in ruins. Ross apparently accepted it as an evil omen. With reports filtering in of an enormous American army collecting in Georgetown, he prepared his troops for a night march, and about nine, with their campfires left burning, the British sneaked away in the darkness. In the moonlight, they negotiated the site of the previous day's battle, stepping carefully over the dead. They did not pause to rest until seven in the morning, when they were well past Bladensburg. What was left of Washington again belonged to the Americans.

Uncertainty in London

If the tragedy that befell Washington was fated to occur it was well for the United States that it happened when it did—after the commencement of the negotiation. News of the capture of the American capital did not reach London until September 27 and was not revealed to the American ministers in Ghent until October 1. By the time word of the deplorable event was known in Europe two more rounds of notes had passed between the American and British commissioners, and other incidents had taken place on both sides of the Atlantic, which, although they did not diminish the appalling emotional impact of the exploit at Washington, served to dull the political consequences of the deed.

The American commissioners completed their first formal note to the British on August 24, as the village of Bladensburg was assuming its dubious niche in history. Hughes delivered the document to the British commissioners on the following day, and they, after drafting an answer, submitted both note and answer to Castlereagh in Paris and the American note alone to Liverpool and Bathurst in London. In separate letters the British commissioners pointed out to their superiors where the Americans were at fault and how the negotiation could be brought to a swift and dramatic close.

The proposals and words of advice of the three negotiators did not have the effect they anticipated. As confusion and fear sullied the fields near Bladensburg, Castlereagh, passing through Brussels on his way to Paris, wrote to Goulburn: "Your report of the approaching rupture of your negotiations does not surprise me."

But a few days later, with the American statement and the proposed answer of the British commissioners before him, he was anything but delighted. He thought—or at least he now professed to believe—that the British commissioners had badly misjudged matters and had, furthermore, misled him into believing that the Americans "were disposed both to treat and sign on the frontier and Indian arrangements." This, as the American commissioners had made abundantly clear, was not the case, and Castlereagh feared that the American note, "evidently intended to rouse their people upon the question of their independence," would succeed in its efforts. The Foreign Minister, again deeply involved in European political questions, did not undertake to write a reply to the Americans, but he suggested that the Indian proposal should be reconsidered, and he noted that the substance of the problem facing the British government was whether it wished to continue the war to gain territorial adjustments or make peace soon, "saving all our rights and retaining the fisheries, which they do not appear to question."

Liverpool was already acutely aware of the problems outlined by Castlereagh, and for a few days he and Bathurst, who had received the American note but not the suggested answer of the British commissioners, lived with the fear that their agents in Ghent had, without bothering to consult their superiors, made known their opinions to the Americans. Bathurst received the American note and letters from the British commissioners while on his way from Dover to London. As soon as he got back to Downing Street, he dashed off a frantic letter to Goulburn. Readily admitting that some answer to the American note was imperative, Bathurst, however, emphasized that "Liverpool & I are of opinion that there are reasons why the answer should not be construed as *necessarily* closing the negotiations." If an extreme reply had been composed but not sent, "we are anxious you should not deliver it, even if Lord Castlereagh should have approved of it, and instructed you to deliver it." The British commissioners were to "suspend all further proceedings until you hear from us." Bathurst did not draw an easy breath until the next morning, when a dispatch came from Castlereagh in Paris, enclosing the British commissioners' "too conclusive" answer which Bathurst was "happy to find" had not gone to the Americans.

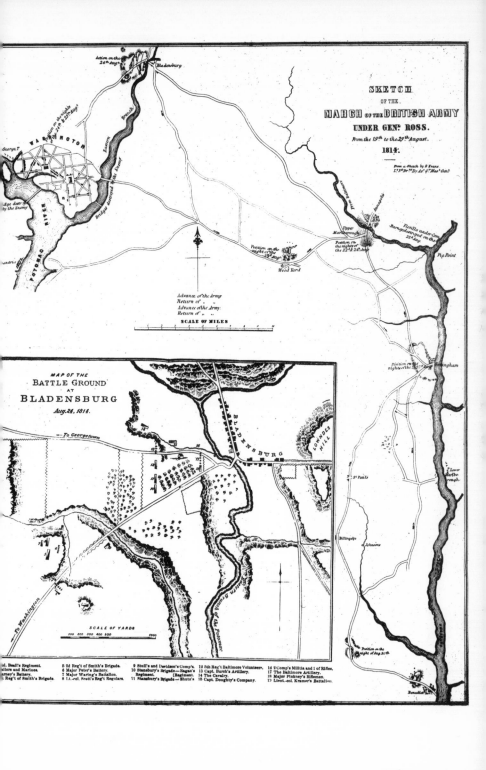

SKETCH
OF THE
MARCH OF THE BRITISH ARMY
UNDER GEN? ROSS.
From the 19th to the 29th August.
1814.

From a Sketch by B. Evans
Lt. Sd Dr. Dy As? Qr. Mas? Gen?

MAP OF THE
BATTLE GROUND
AT
BLADENSBURG
Aug. 24, 1814.

Advance of the Army
Return of ʺ
Advance of the Army
Return of ʺ

SCALE OF MILES

SCALE OF YARDS
100 200 300 400 500   1000

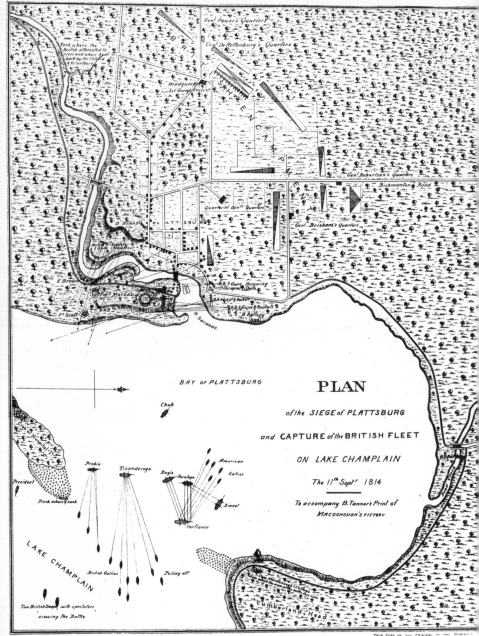

Ford where the
British attempted to
cross and where beat
back by the Militia
& Volunteers

Road to Chazy

B R I S B A N E

Gen.l Power's Quarters

Gen.l De Rottenburg's Quarters

Headquarters
Sir George Prevost

S P E N C E

Gen.l Robertson's Quarters

Dickmanton Road

Quarter.r Gen.l Quarters

Gen.l Brisbane's Quarters

Rocket
& Bomb Battery

P L A T T S B U R G

British Shells
& Shot thrown
British
Hot Shot thrown

E. Brown

Fort Moreau

F.t Scott

B.B.3 Guns throwing
Shrapnel & Shells

Shrapnel & Rockets

R. Saranac

B.B 3 Guns & Rockets

B Battery

BAY OF PLATTSBURG

Chub

PLAN

of the SIEGE of PLATTSBURG

and CAPTURE of the BRITISH FLEET

ON LAKE CHAMPLAIN

The 11.th Sept.r 1814

To accompany B. Tanner's Print of
MACDONOUGH'S VICTORY

Hospital

President

Preble

Finch ashore & sunk

Ticonderoga

Eagle

Saratoga

American
Gallies

Linnet

Confiance

L A K E   C H A M P L A I N

British Gallies

Pulling off

Two British Sloops with spectators
viewing the Battle

Cumberland Head

MAP N.º 8.

0   500   1000   1500   2000   2500 Yards

TRUE COPY OF THE ORIGINAL IN THE DOMINION
ARCHIVES OF CANADA ENLARGED BY H. ALBS. OTTAWA

Macdonough's victory on Lake Champlain, a romanticized version of the battle of Plattsburgh. Ships in foreground: *Confiance* (Br.), *Saratoga* (Amer.), *Linnet* (Br.). British gunboats, left; American, right.

The signing of the Treaty of Ghent, 1814. From left to right, as identified at the National Collection of Fine Arts: Anthony St. John Baker, Henry Goulburn, William Adams, Lord Gambier, John Quincy Adams, Albert Gallatin, Christopher Hughes, James Bayard, Henry Clay, Jonathan Russell, unidentified.

Bruin become MEDIATOR or Negociation for PEACE.

An American caricature, presenting a quaint view of international affairs. It was Russia, not Great Britain, that proposed mediation, and Great Britain, not the United States, that rejected the offer.

The Hartford Convention or LEAP NO LEAP.

A Republican caricature of Federalist New England's tendency toward disunion. It glosses over serious internal political differences, and emphasizes the rest of the country's fear of the outcome of the Hartford Convention.

In Walmer Castle, his country home, Liverpool had been sharing Bathurst's apprehension and attending diligently to the message transmitted by the five Americans. He considered the American statement "a most impudent one" that was "capable of an irresistible answer," but he agreed with Castlereagh that the British commissioners, in the document that had called forth the American tirade, had "certainly taken an erroneous view of the line to be adopted." A break then would almost surely be to the benefit of the United States. On the other hand, Liverpool did not believe that his government was faced with an immediate decision between peace and a long, bitter war. With few changes, basically the same demands could once more be presented to the American ministers, in such a way that "our reasoning on the subject of the avowed intentions of the American government to conquer and annex Canada can hardly fail to make a considerable impression on the reasonable people in the United States."

Liverpool thought it likely that the representatives of the United States would be forced to consult with their own government. By the time the negotiation could be resumed the results of the American campaign should be known. "If our commander does his duty, I am persuaded we shall have acquired by our arms every point on the Canadian frontier which we ought to insist on keeping." He did not count on the destruction of Washington. Its capture would be icing on the territorial cake.

The new note for the British commissioners to deliver to the Americans, its parts assembled while Ross was retracing his steps to Benedict, was the joint effort of Liverpool, Castlereagh, Cooke of the Foreign Office, and Henry Bathurst—the latter composing the final draft of what was largely his creation. Bathurst gave the commissioners permission to alter the style of the message, "particularly my part of the dispatch, . . . but the substance, & the disposition manifested throughout not to consider our first project as our Ultimatum, from whence we could not depart, must be preserved." After conveying more instructions and a brief review of British military intentions, Bathurst concluded: "I do not think you can flatter yourself to be clear of Ghent for some days at least—a reference home for further Instructions will however relieve you."

The communiqué was received in Ghent on September 3, and the British commissioners, flattered by Bathurst's apparent indulgence of their stylistic judgment and not yet aware of the cabinet's opinion of their previous editorial labors, proceeded "to render the Note more consistent with what we had previously expressed." Whatever was conciliatory or at least not unreasonable was changed so that the Americans would not misunderstand the meaning. The conquest of Canada as "the avowed object of the American government," for instance, became "the declared object of the American government," providing the American commissioners with an opportunity to state that their government had disavowed the declarations. The revised version was delivered by Baker to Gallatin on the morning of September 5.

Despite the shifting and uncertain attitudes of the British cabinet and the contrasting resoluteness of the British commission, the document which the British commissioners revised and dated on September 4 did not differ drastically from the first British note of August 20. The second note went to greater lengths, especially after Goulburn and company had finished with it, to chide the United States for its expansionist tendencies, which, as the British commissioners worded it, were "too clearly manifested by their progressive occupation of the Indian Territories," Louisiana, the Floridas, and Canada. The note repeated all the former demands for unilateral disarmament on the Great Lakes, revision of the Maine boundary, and settlement of the northwestern frontier—adding some new arguments but offering "amicably to discuss the details of them with a view to the adoption of any modifications which the American Plenipotentiaries or their Government may have to suggest, if they are not incompatible with the object itself." As to the American attitude on the Indian proposal, the British viewed it with "equal astonishment and regret," and said they could not honorably alter their stand. This did not mean, however, "unwillingness to discuss any other proposition or any modification." The last phrase was almost lost in the surrounding jungle of irritating verbiage. It was a sign, nevertheless, if ever so slight, that the British had taken a step away from their Indian ultimatum.

It was a sign, though, that completely escaped the eyes of the American commissioners, although they grasped the rest of the contents of the British note quickly enough and were even more responsive to its language. Bayard called the note a "very stupid production." Clay said a half-page rejection would be sufficient answer. Adams and Gallatin did not disagree with the others' opinions, but they thought the statement could not be curtly dismissed, and they prevailed upon their colleagues to consider a detailed reply. All of them, however, continued firm in their belief—Clay even asked the British commissioners for his passport—that the rupture of the negotiation was imminent.

By common consent, the task of initial creation of an answering note passed from Adams to Gallatin, although Adams continued to write and submit lengthy paragraphs until eventually he had his own complete draft. For five days the commissioners wrote, rewrote, met, and argued. Adams's insistence on the inclusion of his pet Indian paragraphs became almost intolerable to the others, and finally, in despair or, as Adams saw it, having taken the "true and strong ground," they adopted the "substance" of one of his favorite statements. Adams, in turn, thought that Bayard and Gallatin "manifested symptoms" of concession, and he and Clay stood together to oppose the dangerous tendency. The commission's differences were not composed until the morning of September 9. That afternoon Hughes took the answer to the British.

The American note attacked the British proposals item by item, phrase by phrase. It pointed out that the boundary revisions, put forth with such apparent reasonableness by the British, involved territory that was exclusively American—that the Indian buffer state, however it was presented, still applied to "Indians residing within the dominions of the United States." The British, said the American commissioners, discussed everything but the real issues between the two countries and made mention of completely unrelated subjects in an effort to support their claims. They attempted to justify unilateral disarmament on the Great Lakes by dragging in American relations with Spain, the purchase of Louisiana, treaties with the Indians, and the purported attempt to annex Canada. In accusing the United States of harboring a spirit of conquest, the British were simply trying to justify their own lust for territory. Even if British arms were successful, said the Americans (fearing such success might be in the offing), the American rejection of the British terms would not be altered.

The American note was more emotional than logical, and it

raved on endlessly about the Indians, citing American justice
toward them and British misuse of them in warfare, "itself a
departure from the principles of humanity. . . ." But, whatever
its shortcomings, it was excellent potential propaganda, and it
showed a clearer understanding of Britain's ultimate aims than
was possessed by the British commissioners. After stating that
the Great Lakes and Indian proposals "are both inadmissible,"
the American commissioners concluded firmly but hopefully
that they "cannot subscribe to, and would deem it useless to
refer to their government, any arrangement, even provisional,
containing either of those propositions. With this understanding,
the undersigned are now ready to continue the negotiation, and,
as they have already expressed, to discuss all the points of difference, or what might hereafter tend in any degree to interrupt
the harmony of the two countries."

We have left "to be or not to be" up to the British, Adams
wrote his wife the day the note was sent, and he was convinced
the British choice would be continued warfare. Goulburn fully
shared Adams's convictions. "He had no doubt," he told Clay
later in the week, that his government's answer "would terminate
our business, and . . . we must fight it out." The sixteen-page
American document erased any lingering doubts the British
commissioners had about the outcome of the negotiation. In submitting the note to London, they asked "to be favoured with
Instructions as to the line of conduct which it may be proper to
adopt with respect to the continuance of the negotiation." In
other words, how soon should they break off? Again the decision
rested with the privy council.

On the day Hughes delivered the American note to the British
commissioners in Ghent, Castlereagh was writing to Liverpool
from Munich. The further the Foreign Minister got from the
American problem the more he regretted the stand Great Britain
had taken, and his concern over the difficulties he would face
in Vienna increased as he moved closer to that city. He did not,
he told Liverpool, anticipate a short or pleasant stay in the
Austrian capital. Consequently, it might be well, he thought, to
call Parliament soon, before there was much grist for the opposition mill to grind, especially on the American question,
"which I hope you may contrive to leave sufficiently open for

this purpose." Castlereagh was sure the American ministers had sent or shortly would send a detailed history of the negotiation to the administration in Washington, which, in turn, would release the information to Congress and the world at large; so "it will be difficult for us not to be exposed to a question before Christmas on the line taken." If things went well, however, Parliament might have met and disbanded before American propaganda crossed the Atlantic.

Liverpool did not need to be reminded that his government's handling of the negotiation invited criticism. He was, as Castlereagh and the American commissioners worked in their own ways to trouble him, engaged in an extended discussion of the matter with Bathurst. Bathurst, perhaps swayed by the frequent epistles of Goulburn, was insisting on no major retreat from the Indian proposal. Liverpool agreed on the *"absolute necessity"* of including the Indians in an Anglo-American peace treaty and restoring them to such privileges as they held before the war, but he felt the British could no longer make a *sine qua non* of more, not "when we cannot well avoid explaining ourselves on this question."

The Prime Minister also was beginning to fear that the British position on the Great Lakes was untenable. This latter point should not be given up until the Americans had accepted some ultimatum on the Indians and, then, it should not be so much surrendered as exchanged for more defensible territorial demands based on the results of the campaign. The British would ask for more than they expected to get and force the Americans to sacrifice something to reduce the total penalty. "We might thus be naturally brought by degrees to our ultimatum, and during the time occupied by the discussion we might hear what had been the progress of our arms. I confess I cannot believe that with the prospect of bankruptcy before them, the American government would not wish to make peace, if they can make it upon terms which would not give a triumph to their enemies."

It was Liverpool's view of the negotiation which prevailed, and, before the American note of September 9 had been received in London, Bathurst wrote to the British commissioners to inform them of the cabinet's latest diplomatic position. Perhaps inadvisedly, he began his letter to Goulburn by complimenting him and his colleagues on their changes which had "improved" the

British note of September 4. He next spoke of the government's plans and fears, and his words were revealing:

> We are certainly anxious to make Peace before this next Campaign. We do not think the Continental Powers will continue in good humour with our Blockade of the whole Coast of America beyond that Period; and the prosecution of the War will not be popular here much longer.

When he wrote of the "next Campaign" Bathurst was referring to the winter and particularly the summer that lay ahead. He assumed that the dividends of the current campaign—when "we will have cleared our Territory of the Enemy" and when Britain would possess some negotiable pieces of American soil—would be declared before the first of autumn's frosts. Then Great Britain would bargain on the basis of acreage for proposition, "which under the circumstances they would not I think refuse, & with which we might be willing to conclude, keeping a fair Boundary for our Indians."

Nothing, however, would be gained if the Americans left Ghent, armed with a cause that would incite their countrymen and infuriate Parliament, and Bathurst undertook to explain the concerns of Liverpool to the British commissioners.

> Our first object certainly is to make a good Peace now, or to get their Commissioners to sign a Provisional Article, the War continuing until it be ratified. A secondary Object with us is not to let the Treaty be so broken off, as to require us to lay the Papers before the H of Commons & have them debated. . . . By getting the Commissioners to refer the Question home for further Instructions, we should obtain this end. I once thought that the continuing the Negotiation would be advantageous to them, by enabling them to borrow money with greater facility; but I think it appears quite clear that nothing will give them facility in this particular except their being able to show that they cannot obtain Peace on what they will call honourable terms. I do not think that the breaking off on the Indian Question would have this effect. Our Demand to have the Lakes to ourselves would on the contrary raise a great Clamour, if we had permitted the Question to end without much qualification.

For the three Britishers in Ghent, who had been led to believe that Indians and lakes were the hooks on which war or peace would be suspended, the words of the Colonial Secretary were bound to be a sobering revelation. Perhaps aware of this, Bathurst next proceeded to commend the commissioners on their behavior in private conversations with the Americans. Evidently lumping Clay, of all people, with Bayard in the opposition party, Bathurst told Goulburn that he and his colleagues were to continue "not to encourage much confidential communication with the Federalists; if you cannot get them to talk, without talking confidentially yourself. I make no doubt they hate us, but their hate to the opposite party may lead them, very unintentionally, to give us some assistance." Although he may have been unique in his assessment of Clay, Bathurst shared the cabinet's distorted view of American politics.

Bathurst concluded his private epistle to Goulburn by making some suppositions on the American note, which, unknown to him, was then on its way to London. He did not expect a reply soon, and he assumed that when it came it would call on the British to state their terms in detail. To this, ventured Bathurst, the British would respond "that we cannot do so, unless they will assure us that they are prepared to sign on the Questions of Boundary for the Indians & for Canada. . . ." While the American commissioners contemplated this answer, news might arrive from Admiral Cochrane or General Prevost that would change the course of the war and the negotiation.

The next news came not from America but from Ghent, in the sixteen pages of the second American note. It arrived at the Foreign Office, where it was received by William Hamilton, who promptly wrote to Goulburn: "It seems your diplomatic Career is drawing to a close. . . ." From London the American note went to the pastoral retreat at Walmer Castle. Liverpool had just finished writing to Bathurst, telling him that he was much satisfied with the way the British commissioners had edited the last British note. While not by any means pleased with the progress of the negotiation, he thought that matters were improving, and he anticipated a more reasonable attitude on the part of the Americans. His reading of the defiant American response quickly reversed his growing optimism. Momentarily he was tempted to break off the negotiation, and for a day he wandered about the castle in a state of anguish and anger.

It was the thought of the further problems a rupture would

bring that eventually cooled Liverpool's emotions and restored him to the course he had already largely selected. In time, he was even able to admit that in the second exchange of notes the Americans had the better argument and, what was worse, the more popular one. If the negotiation ceased over the Indian proposition, Britain would forever after be stuck with it and unable to retreat from it. More tenable would be the fruits that victory would bring. Slowly, perhaps, but surely the Indian demand would have to be whittled down, and the lakes proposition would have to be abandoned as such and merged into the larger question of the readjustment of the Canadian boundary.

While Liverpool routed Indian spirits from the nooks and crannies of Walmer Castle, Bathurst tended to the task of devising a new set of instructions for the British commissioners. The results, when Bathurst had finished, were not quite what Liverpool had expected. Bathurst, although he agreed with his superior in principle on the Indians, had not been so successful in exorcising them from his thoughts and feelings. His statement on the Indians differed from earlier ones but not by much. Liverpool finally acquiesced, but he feared the reworded Indian demand would only start new arguments. He was not to be disappointed.

The third draft note of the British government was sent to the British commissioners on September 16, accompanied by a personal letter from Bathurst to Goulburn. Again the British commissioners were "authorized to make any alterations which may strike you to be necessary, provided they are in conformity with the spirit of the draft . . . ," and again the three ministers accepted the permission with alacrity. Bathurst had little else to say to his charges. He did not foresee any violent reaction to the note by the Americans, but, lest the British commissioners feel no restrictions, he warned them that "there are many political reasons to make us anxious to conclude a Peace if we can do it on proper terms."

The Indian utopia seemed doomed, but as it neared its unlamented death its shape barely appeared to differ from what it had been in full bloom. The question still accounted for a major portion of the British note, and paragraph after paragraph was devoted to answering the American stand. This mound of prolixity was topped by a restatement of the Indian proposal—really two proposals. The first, or first part, made a *sine qua non* of including the Indians in the treaty and restoring them to their rights and territory as these existed in 1811. The second, that to which Liverpool and the Americans, in turn, objected, called for an article in which both sides would bind themselves not to buy lands occupied by the Indians within their own respective national territories, according to certain boundaries which could be revised at the end of a stated period. The British commissioners did not alter the proposals, but they offered the observation that the Indians were no longer, contrary to American beliefs, under United States "protection (whatever may be the import of that term)." It was an addition calculated to bring out John Quincy Adams's finest rhetoric.

As to unilateral control of the lakes and their shores, the British note protested that this had never been a *sine qua non*, an objection that was as interesting to the British commissioners as to the American. Without referring further to the lakes themselves, the British note stated that when the Indian question was settled Great Britain would make a final proposition on the Canadian boundary, so just "it cannot be rejected."

It was about boundaries that the rest of the note, actually the first part, concerned itself. No specific proposals were made, but a sarcastic attack was launched on the American tendency to expand "on any side," as the British commissioners phrased it. The American purchase of Louisiana and her forays into the Floridas were mentioned, as was the American commissioners' refusal to discuss the Passamaquoddy Islands off the coast of Maine. But it was the American hunger for Canada that was given prominence. If the American commissioners insisted that Canada was not the "declared object" of the United States they were badly uninformed. To convince the American ministers that such declarations did exist the British enclosed proclamations of Generals William Hull and Alexander Smythe as evidence.

The proclamations of the two American generals were of the same unfortunate character as was their conduct of military operations. Hull, before going into an emotional coma and surrendering Detroit, called upon the Canadians to surrender, threating that *"this war will be a war of extermination."* Smythe, the man who crossed and recrossed the Niagara River

without once doing damage to the enemy, had preceded his little
excursions with a call to his troops that astounded if it did not
excite them. "Companions in Arms!" shouted Smythe to the men
who were sometimes behind him:

> The time is at hand when you will cross the stream of Niagara to
> conquer Canada and to secure the peace of the American Frontier.
>   You will enter a Country that is to be one of the United States.
> You will arrive among a People who are to become your fellow
> Citizens. . . .
>   Soldiers! You are amply provided for War. You are superior in
> Number to the Enemy. Your personal strength and activity are
> greater. Your weapons are longer. The regular Soldiers of the
> Enemy are generally old men—whose best years have been spent
> in the silky climate of the West Indies. They will not be able to
> stand before you when you charge with the Bayonet.

Unfortunately, Smythe's words lived longer than his deeds. It is
to be hoped that someone in the Foreign Office had the grace to
smile as he read them.

Certainly the American commissioners were not amused when
reminded of the gauche pronouncements of their posturing generals, and before Bathurst's note with the enclosed proclamations arrived, the British commissioners had lost what remained
of their limited sense of humor. Bathurst's letter of September 12
to Goulburn was delivered but a day before the draft instructions,
and neither Goulburn nor his colleagues found solace or cheer
in what the Secretary had to say. Suddenly the Indian and lakes
propositions were matters of the past, and the negotiation was
to be preserved at almost any cost. Goulburn, with bitterness in
his soul, wrote to Bathurst that he could not thank him enough
"for so clearly explaining what are the views and objects of the
government. . . ." He readily admitted that he had not previously
been aware of the government's intentions. He complained that
a peace that left the Indians to the mercy of the Americans would
not be a good peace. He argued that a continuance of the negotiation would give more ammunition than would a rupture to the
opposition in Parliament. He raved about the stubbornness of the
American commissioners. But, after all was said and done, he,
Gambier, and Adams bent to their editorial labors and, on
September 19, sent the third British note to the representatives
of the United States. Only Goulburn's dedicated patriotism kept

him from expressing aloud his hope that the Americans would reject the note and go home.

A week later, on Monday afternoon, September 26, Christopher Hughes brought the American answer, their third note, to the British commissioners. That evening, Henry Goulburn, Lord Gambier, and William Adams read what their adversaries had wrought. It did not take them long, nor did it require a careful reading, to discover that the Americans were not going home; that they flatly rejected both Indian propositions; that they stoutly defended the activities of the United States in Louisiana and the Floridas; that they renounced responsibility on the part of the American government for the absurd statements of Generals Hull and Smythe. To the three Britishers the American note demonstrated that its authors were as unreasonable, vindictive, and preposterous as ever.

The American document tended first to the matters of Louisiana and the Floridas. These concerns, bluntly stated the American commissioners, involved the United States and other independent nations and were not the business of Great Britain. The problem of the Maine boundary was dismissed with equal finality. After discussing the partial settlement of that border in the Treaty of 1783, the American commissioners proposed the appointment of a commission that would extend and once and for all determine that boundary. What Britain was proposing, said the Americans, was cession, not alteration, and this they had refused in the past and would continue to refuse in the future.

Apart from a few sentences that ejected Hull and Smythe from the official American family, the remainder of the American note was rife with ringing phrases on the subject of the Indians, their treatment, and their boundaries. Out of this forensic forest emerged enough pith to make clear to anyone that the American commissioners were not entranced by Britain's watered-down Indian proposals. The United States would not, said her representatives, preserve "a perpetual desert for savages." The American commissioners could not consent to include United States Indians in a peace with Great Britain. They would not recognize the Indian tribes as independent nations. They would not surrender their nation's land or sovereignty, no matter how ingeniously Great Britain phrased the deed of cession. In thus rejecting Britain's demands, said the American commissioners, they were following the precedents of the British themselves, set in earlier negotiations.

The American ministers did agree "to go as far as possible in securing the benefit of the peace to the Indians, now the only object professed by the British Government in their present *sine qua non*. . . ." In a counterproposition the Americans stated "that no person or persons, whether subjects, citizens, or Indians, residing within the dominions of either party, shall be molested or annoyed, either in their persons or their property" for any part in the war, "but shall retain all the rights, privileges, and possessions which they respectively had at the commencement of the war. . . . " Goulburn, when he read this, was not sure what it meant, but he was convinced that it was not what his government had in mind.

On the other hand, Goulburn and his colleagues were no longer certain what the government did have in mind. When the youngest member of the British commission wrote to Bathurst, he pointed out that the cabinet, if it accepted the American Indian proposal, would be flouting its own principles. He also added, more for the benefit of his superiors than the Americans, that it should be made clear to the enemy commissioners that in her desire for peace Great Britain was "reducing [her] original demands at a moment when the success of [her] arms might have authorized an opposite line of conduct." But Goulburn, no matter how or how much he advised the privy council, no longer entertained the expectation of a break in the negotiation. Neither understanding nor quite resigned to the inscrutable doings of the men in London, Goulburn, Adams, and Gambier sent their letters and the American note westward across the Channel —wondering and almost afraid to discover what would happen next.

CHAPTER

→» 12 «←

An American Dilemma

For the American commissioners, the month—August 25 to September 26—that spanned the completion of their first and third notes was as unreal as it was unpleasant. The five ministers had come to Ghent to seek peace and some recognition of the rights of a sovereign and usually neutral nation, but, instead, they found themselves violently debating the rights and property of Indians and defending their nation against dismemberment by diplomacy.

At that, their plight was not as unpleasant as it might have been. The war they endeavored to end was an ocean and seemingly an age away. Many of its encounters, when the commissioners heard of them, which they did for the most part through the English press, seemed little more current than those which had been waged in the Revolution. Although the commissioners took heart or lost hope as news of the war was belatedly revealed to them, the distance in time and space tended to reduce the poignancy of what was occurring and allowed the Americans in Ghent to assure themselves that if another year of war was necessary it was also possible. They knew that the federal patient was badly hurt and, being part of that patient, felt pain, but through the end of September, at least, they were spared the symptoms of possible mortality.

It was the insanity of debating points that were alien to the war and its causes—so far as the five Americans were concerned —and the endless wait for the real negotiation to commence that slowly eroded the Americans' spirits. As the British expected them to break off the talks, to send for instructions, or go home, the American ministers daily awaited dismissal by the British. Yet no one went home. The exchange of notes went on; the rumors and confusing bits of news continued to pour in from London and Paris; the dinners, balls, and teas were given and attended; and little changed that really mattered. It began to seem as if the American commissioners might grow old in Ghent.

Had they been able to determine where the British government was headed the Americans might have achieved the peace of mind of the damned or the delivered, but, though they knew little for certain, they already sensed more than did the British commission, and they could not, after all, fathom that of which the British cabinet itself was not sure. Information arrived from nearly all the principal cities of Europe—Harris wrote from St. Petersburg, John M. Forbes from Copenhagen, John L. Lawrence from Stockholm, Crawford from Paris—but the accounts were composed largely of conjecture and stale news. The most faithful reporter was Reuben Beasley. His informants, however, were growing few in number, and those that remained were probably more confused than he. Consequently he was forced to content himself with wild rumors, with following the newspapers, and with keeping track of the pulse of the stock market.

He wrote on August 19, for instance, of the rumor that the British had proposed a neutral Indian territory and the Americans had responded by writing home for instructions. He was soon disabused by Russell of the latter part of the rumor, but on the 30th Beasley wrote again to say he had heard that the American commissioners had broken off the negotiation and were leaving Ghent. He reported also that there was much speculation in cotton, enhanced, if not initiated, by the arrival in London of Bayard's secretary, Colonel Milligan, and an American friend who knew little but said much of the course of the negotiation. Although he did not mention it at the time, Beasley dabbled a little in the market himself, a venture he was later to regret.

Beasley began September by passing on a report that the British commissioners were about to come home, a misunderstanding he shared with Goulburn. He repeated the tale a few days later and became certain of it when he heard from Paris that the American commissioners were expected there. Even though mail kept arriving from the commissioners in Ghent, Beasley never tired of the rumor, and throughout September his letters were obsessed with the imminence of a rupture. He was not alone in his expectation. In Paris, Crawford, the American minister, and other Americans heard the same rumor. Lafayette even journeyed to the French capital expressly to greet the American commissioners when they arrived. Nearly everyone in Europe had the two commissions moving faster and further than the respective armies, but in Ghent neither commission budged, save to take occasional excursions to enjoy what John Quincy Adams—who did not go—hinted were the sinful delights of Brussels.

Certainly the possibilities for sin in Ghent were circumscribed, and it took an Adams to recognize that they existed at all. For the most part, time was divided between answering British notes and waiting, with some apprehension, for a new one to arrive. In periods between American answers and British overtures the American commissioners attended to the collateral details that accompanied their mission. They answered their correspondents in Europe and America. They listened with growing impatience to the selfish requests of Americans in and out of Ghent for advice, for inside information that could be translated into speculative profit, for a berth home. Adrian Bentzon, son-in-law of John Jacob Astor, clung to the ministers as a tick does to a dog. He dined with them; he was ever within sight and sound; he roomed with and was inseparable companion to the secretaries and messengers—persistently waiting for a definite omen of peace or rupture that he could transmit to his father-in-law and employer. The Smith brothers, Charles and Jacob, traveling in Europe for Jacob's health, pestered Beasley and then the American commissioners from their comfortable nest near the beach in Brighton, within the shadow of the Prince Regent's establishment. They sought passage home—not on just any vessel, but on the *Neptune* itself, the ministers' ship, and they demanded the best berths aboard her. Beasley secretly hoped they would drown in the Channel.

When not answering friend, enemy, or pest the American ministers were guests of and hosts to the socially prominent of Ghent. As they did not represent a country whose troops pounded the Flemish streets, painfully reminding the citizens of the source of power and money, the American commissioners were far more popular than the British. To the teas, card parties, and balls given by the elite of Ghent, the Americans responded with galas of their own, lasting from dinner to midnight. They would string the garden with varicolored lanterns, hire a band, and award a multiplicity of prizes indiscriminately. After dinner, as the band swung into a Viennese waltz, John Quincy Adams would approach one of the ladies, lead her on to the dance floor, and inaugurate the dancing. As the evening waned, the assemblage would gather about the card tables, where Henry Clay would take on all who were willing or foolish enough to accept his challenge and would almost invariably win back the prizes that had been given earlier.

Not all, however, was play. When Anthony St. John Baker came down the Rue des Champs with note in hand the American commission was once more reminded of its serious and perhaps hopeless purpose, and until the note was answered the days were full of work and anguish. It took the American commissioners the better part of five days to answer the second British note and a week to answer the third. The composing of an answer to the second British note, like that to the first, knew its moments of heated argument, but no difference of opinion was so great or so lasting that John Quincy Adams could not write to his wife, after the American note had been sent, that the American commission was "still perfectly unanimous. . . . We are . . . severe judges upon one another, and setting aside your correspondent, everyone of his four associates is, to say the least, a match for the brightest of our opponents." But by the time the third British note arrived, the pressure exerted by the British and the monotony of waiting were beginning to take their toll, and divisions of more enduring consequence began to appear.

Adams was working at his desk when Baker was ushered in with the third of the British messages on the morning of September 20. The minister read the dispatch that was handed to him, noted suspiciously that the lakes demand seemed to have been dropped and the Indian *sine qua non* altered, and, commenting that the note was "overbearing and insulting in its tone," took it to Gallatin, who was now acknowledged by all as the principal architect of each answer.

The commission met early that afternoon, after each of its members had scanned the contents of the British document. At first the discussion was vague and tentative, but the little that

was said was enough to stoke the fire of anger in John Quincy
Adams. It seemed to him that Gallatin and Bayard were preparing themselves and their colleagues to accept Britain's modified
Indian demand. The American commissioners, like the British
cabinet, thought that the point was a bad one to break upon—
a conformity of belief which would have surprised the men in
London—and Gallatin and Bayard maintained that a break
should come on a point which would unite their country. Adams
agreed, but argued with some warmth that a good point for a
rupture might never arise.

Gallatin repeated, with "a very earnest look, that it was a bad
point to break upon."

"Then," said Adams heatedly, "it is a good point to admit the
British as the sovereigns and protectors of our Indians!"

Gallatin laughed and told John Quincy he made a *non sequi-
tur,* and even Adams shared in the general laughter that followed. He had made his point, however, and before the meeting
ended he suggested, for the nth time, that the mission propose
an Indian amnesty to replace the British *sine qua non.* No one
answered him, but the silence alone assured Clay, who shared
Adams's feelings if not their intensity, that the commission would
once more oppose the British demand.

By the next afternoon all were unanimous in their opposition
to the British proposals, and, coming home from a party that
evening, Clay and Adams convinced one another that things
were going well. For three days Bayard, Gallatin, and Adams
worked on their own versions of an American answer. It was
not until the afternoon of the 23rd that the drafts of the latter
two were exposed to their colleagues. While none of them was
completely satisfied with the production of Gallatin, all of them,
save the author himself, objected to nearly everything that had
been written by Adams. His long section attacking the tone of
the British note and his paragraphs on the "moral and religious
duty of the American nation to cultivate their territory" stirred
up nothing but distaste among his colleagues. They finally
agreed to adopt his Indian amnesty proposal but only after they
had rewritten "almost every word" in it.

There were no serious outbursts at the meeting, but the van-
quished author retreated to his room in misery and with a touch
of hatred in his heart. "This is a severity with which I alone am

treated in our discussions by all my colleagues," he told his
diary, which already was well aware of it. "Almost everything
written by any of the rest is rejected or agreed to with very little
criticism. . . . But every line that I write passes a gauntlet of
objections by everyone of my colleagues. . . . " Adams blamed
himself for this state of affairs and resolved to try to "correct
the general fault from which it proceeds," but his tolerance was
in fact very nearly exhausted.

For a time the hurts and differences of the commissioners
were largely contained and were revealed only in petty acts of
annoyance. The final meeting on the American note was to have
taken place on the morning of the 25th, but when the ministers
came together they discovered that Adams was still editing and
rewriting the "miscellaneous draft" that had been completed by
Gallatin. Gallatin was annoyed with Adams, as the latter hoped
he would be. The meeting was postponed until noon, but when
the group assembled at that time it was learned that Russell had
gone out for "breakfast." It was not until one o'clock that Russell
returned from his leisurely brunch and the meeting commenced.

For more than four hours the final details of the American
note were hammered out. For several of those hours Gallatin
and Adams locked horns on the issue of the Floridas. Adams,
who knew almost nothing of the history of American encroach-
ment on the Spanish territory, demanded a long and strong
answer to the British attack on America's policy. Gallatin, who
was acutely aware that the administration's hands were not entirely clean, thought the commission would do best to ignore the
matter. Bayard sided with Gallatin. Clay and Russell agreed
with Adams, but Clay, fearing the British might disinter his old
"war hawk" speeches if too much was made of the subject, held
his tongue, and his shadow, Russell, joined in the silence. The
debate was eventually resolved by the continued obstinacy of
Adams, who refused to sign the American document until it contained a paragraph justifying the American stand. A statement,
much amended, was consequently included.

With the Florida question thus momentarily disposed of, the
discussion turned once again to the British Indian proposal. No
one argued against rejection of the demand, but Adams, much
to the others' displeasure, had reintroduced his pet words and
phrases—"moral and religious duty," "God," "Providence,"

"Heaven"—all intended to impress Britain and the world with the nobility of America's treatment of the Indians. Bayard thought some of Adams's statements might be left in the note, but Gallatin expressed the fear that the American commission would be letting itself in for ridicule if it allowed any of Adams's incantations to stand. Clay brought matters to a head. To the accompaniment of Russell's guffaws, he sonorously read excerpts from the vivid prose that Adams had created. When he was done, he turned to the man from Quincy and, in his offhand way, said that what he had just read was sheer cant. Humiliated, Adams mumbled something about the commission losing the "best argument" it had, but the skirmish was over and the remaining statements were given to Hughes to copy and deliver to the British.

With the completion of an answer, the relations among the American commissioners returned to some semblance of tranquillity, but the new scars did not heal with the rapidity of earlier ones. Adams attempted to unburden himself in a long, rambling letter to his wife. He fully described the editorial torture that his writings received, and, although he accepted responsibility for this, his anguished account of his colleagues' behavior would leave Louisa in no doubt as to her husband's malice. One man, however, could not anger or discourage him for long. "Mr. Gallatin," he wrote, "keeps and increases his influence over us all. It would have been an irreparable loss if our country had been deprived of the benefits of his talents. . . . "

John Quincy Adams was not the only commissioner nursing a hurt. Of a somewhat different nature were the seldom-displayed sufferings of Jonathan Russell. He was convinced that most of his colleagues did not regard him as an equal member of the mission. Only Clay, the man, Russell believed, in whom "all the nobler passions have found their home," appeared to appreciate Russell's true worth. Clay became his idol, but Adams, Gallatin, and Bayard received—in Russell's imagination and in his letters at least—the same animosity or indifference which he believed they dealt him. Adams he hated. Gallatin he suspected. Bayard he dismissed. His outbursts were rare, but he could be as sulky as a small boy and as delinquent in the fulfillment of his obligations. With each day his ire and grievances grew, until at the end of the month he moved away from his

condescending peers, back to the more appreciative companion-
ship of the secretaries and messengers at the Hôtel des Pays-Bas.
His colleagues were not sure what caused him to take the step,
but, on the other hand, they scarcely noted his departure.

Before Russell had transferred his belongings from the house
on the Rue des Champs to the hotel on the Place d'Armes and
while Adams was still dissecting the reasons for the unpopularity
of his literary and philosophical efforts, news came from the
United States that prompted that nation's commissioners to
consider another attempt to enlighten the British commission
and that commission's government. Early on the morning of
Thursday, the 29th, Adams, while writing at his desk, was surprised by the unexpected arrival of his brother-in-law, George
Boyd, who brought news and dispatches from Washington. A
lesser item in his packet, although not so to Henry Clay, was
word that that gentleman had been re-elected to Congress. More
important than the indication of the fidelity of Clay's constituents were clippings from the *National Intelligencer,* announcing
a new Treaty of Greenville and the shift of a large bloc of Indian
tribes from the British to the American cause. The United States,
it seemed, now had her peace with many of the Indians whose
rights and boundaries so troubled the British. It was the latter
nation that had yet to come to terms with the red men.

Clay, buoyed perhaps by the new evidence of his continued
political popularity, insisted that word of the Treaty of Greenville be transmitted to the British. Gallatin and Adams were not
sure that mere newspaper clippings would be sufficiently authoritative, but Clay pressed for a note, and on the 30th it was
drafted and sent. In addition to mentioning the Indian peace,
the note told of the necessity for Boyd to sail without a passport,
since Admiral Cockburn had refused to issue one until an
American courier ship had returned from Europe. Monroe did
not think this was in the spirit of things, and copies of the correspondence between him and Cockburn were sent to the American commissioners and by them, in turn, appended to the note
to the British commissioners for their edification.

Shortly after the message had been sent to the British, Russell
moved out of his quarters in "Bachelors' Hall," and later that
afternoon he, Clay, and Hughes departed "upon a party of pleasure" to Brussels, leaving Gallatin, Adams, and Bayard to keep

house in Ghent. No sooner were the excursionists gone than William Shaler, one of the commission's messengers, arrived with British newspapers telling of British military operations in the Chesapeake. Reading the papers alone in the cold of his room, Adams shuddered at what the news presaged. He could not believe that the British would ignore the enticing proximity of Washington and Baltimore, and he crawled into bed, as chilled from fear as from the icy touch of the last day of that September —a month that ended with the same lack of promise with which it had begun.

The morning of October 1 crisply signaled the approach of winter, and when Adams arose from his bed, just before dawn, he hurried to light a fire and warm his numbed fingers so that he might write by the light of a candle. When the temperature was bearable he sat at his desk and for a few hours worked on his papers and letters, but the cold would not leave him, and he finally put his things away and went for a brisk walk about the city. He returned before noon and was met by Gallatin, whose face expressed pain and sorrow. Gallatin spoke quickly and softly. Washington had fallen. The Capitol and the White House were in ashes. This, said Adams, is "only the beginning of sorrows. . . ." October had arrived bearing misery.

The travelers to Brussels heard the news en route, and Clay returned to find a bundle of English newspapers and a note from Goulburn awaiting him, saying that he hoped Clay would enjoy the enclosed reading material, that it would perhaps make up for the dullness of his trip. Goulburn's crude jest only caused anger, and details of the sacking itself resulted in emotions of increased defiance and the belief that Great Britain, in the long run, would be damned as a nation of savages and suffer accordingly. There was no denying, however, that fear moved in with a substantial lease. The war, that had for a time seemed so distant, was now immediate and frightening in its implications. Hope was more difficult than ever to muster.

To add to the ministers' uncertainty there was no official word from the British. The delay in England's answer to the last American note was not appreciably greater than it ever had been, but to the Americans each additional day's wait seemed eternal and sinister in purpose. Outwardly the five of them

maintained their composure. They attended parties and the theater, visited country estates, talked to the citizens of Ghent as if
no crisis had occurred. Trepidation, exasperation, like clothed
boils, erupted only in the privacy of the house on Rue des
Champs, but there the poison of defeat and despair manifested
itself in adolescent acts of spite and obstinacy. Discord, at least
that which arose in the first few days after the terrible news had
been received, came not over great issues but over the trifling
one of which messenger would be sent to Vienna, and John
Quincy Adams became the *enfant terrible* of the commission.

For some time, the ministers had idly discussed following
Monroe's suggestion that they keep the supposedly friendly nations of Europe informed of the course of the negotiation. The
assignment, which had for so long seemed unimportant, came to
the fore with word of the fate of Washington. It was decided
that Adams should compose a document to be presented to the
Czar, then in Vienna, and Clay draft a paper for Crawford to
present to the French government. Adams labored diligently on
his assignment and on Thursday morning, October 6, showed
his creation to Gallatin and suggested that William Smith, his
nephew and secretary, serve as messenger. Gallatin agreed, and
later that day the commission approved Adams's draft, although
Clay hinted that he thought Adams had been his usual windy
self.

The next morning Clay brought his note into Adams's room,
where he found Adams and William Shaler. Despite Adams's
objections to Shaler's overhearing the details of Clay's draft,
Clay, noting that Shaler was "one of us," read it aloud. Adams
said no more, and at the commission's meeting that afternoon
Clay's note was adopted. All was going well until Russell asked
Adams how he proposed sending his letter. Adams mentioned
Smith. Russell said that Shaler had expected to get the assignment. Clay, sensing the approach of a dark cloud, diplomatically
proposed that Smith be sent to Vienna and Shaler to Paris. It
was a waste of Clay's talents for compromise. Adams was shaking with anger. He said he was not even sure a letter should be
sent to Vienna, but that he would do whatever he was directed
to do by the commission's written authorization. Clay, no longer
the man of sweet reason, declared that this was nonsense. Adams
repeated himself. He said that when he "received the letter from

the mission advising me to send to Vienna, I should take my measures accordingly; that if they gave me no advice, I should communicate . . . to the Russian Government in the regular form, and after my return to St. Petersburg." He added that none of this was his idea, that both countries already knew what was going on. The others, incredulous, argued and pleaded with him, but to no avail. Russell, finding it difficult to believe his own words, finally proposed that Gallatin write a letter to Adams authorizing him to send his dispatch to Vienna. It was so agreed, and the strange case of Shaler versus Smith and Adams versus all was momentarily at rest.

The final episode of the week, but not, unfortunately, of the debate, took place the following afternoon. The ministers assembled at two, four of them, at least, anticipating a brief and not unpleasant session. Gallatin presented Adams with the letter of authorization. John Quincy read it carefully and without haste. When he finally looked up at the expectant faces before him he slowly and determinedly shook his head. It would not do. Gallatin had failed to name a messenger and to state who would be charged with the messenger's expenses.

Clay and Russell, much agitated, simultaneously hastened to point out to Adams that he, as minister to Russia, should pick his own courier. Then, said Adams, he thought Smith was the better man, but it would still be necessary to have the commission's approval. Again in near unison, Clay and Russell told Adams that if he really wanted a recommendation theirs would be Shaler. Gallatin spoke in favor of Smith but again, with all the reasonableness of tone he could muster, suggested that the decision was really up to Adams.

But Adams, in his wondrous perversity, had reached a new solution. He would *mail* the dispatch. The response of utter disbelief was a chorus of furious "no's." In that case, said the man from Quincy, he would write to the ministers asking *them* to name a messenger. A frenzy of argument ensued. Russell had to restrain himself from using force. Clay threatened to report the matter to Monroe and advised Adams that he should be ashamed of himself. Adams was nothing of the sort. Telling himself that "a soft answer turneth away wrath," he remained unmoved throughout the afternoon, at the end of which he left the others to take one of his daily strolls about town. Unresolved was the

petty dispute of such pretentious proportions and such potential
for permanent harm. Because of it, the political and social animosity that already existed between Clay and Russell on one
side and Adams on the other was heightened and made more
lasting. In so strange a manner did the fall of Washington take
part of its toll.

It was that evening, Saturday, October 8, while the commissioners sat morosely at dinner, that the fourth British note was
delivered—a fitting climax to a trying day. The ministers read it
at once. The note began with the assertion that the continuance
of the negotiation depended on a solution to the Indian question.
Saying no more then about that subject, it turned abruptly to
America's interests in Louisiana and the Floridas, once more
berating the Americans for a display of bad faith and the practice of international immorality. Next, in the illogical order of
the document, came the Massachusetts district of Maine. Great
Britain, said her representatives, only wanted a small portion of
that section of Massachusetts, a part that might already legally
be hers. Maine gave way to a re-exhumation of the proclamations of Generals Hull and Smythe and by this route to another
attack on American designs on Canada. Not until much was
said, although nothing was specifically proposed, did the Indians
again emerge from the forest of words.

A lengthy section re-examined the relations of the United
States with her continent's initial inhabitants. The point of the
diatribe, in fact the principal justification for the note itself, followed. It was a new and final Indian proposal. The United
States was to make peace with the Indians right after the ratification of an Anglo-American treaty and restore to them all rights,
possessions, and privileges that they had held in 1811—providing the Indians ceased their own hostilities. The same terms of
Indian treatment were to be binding on Great Britain. Gone was
the threat of a permanent Indian territory. All that remained was
the demand that an Indian peace be an integral part of any larger
settlement reached between Great Britain and the United States.
The demand was annoying. To accept it might amount to acceptance of a dangerous precedent. But a serious menace to
American territory and expansion no longer existed—not, at
least, in the guise of an Indian article.

The British government made plain, and the British commissioners even plainer, that the possibility of peace hinged on the American answer. "Whatever may be the result of the proposition thus offered," read the note, "the Undersigned deliver it as their Ultimatum, and now await with anxiety the answer of the American Plenipotentiaries, on which their continuance in this place will depend." There was no room for evasion of the issue or for substitution of another proposal. At last, the British really intended to go home if they did not get their way.

The British note of October 8, wrote Adams, "is by far the most labored, the best written, and the most deserving of a complete and solid answer, of any one that we have received from them." His colleagues could agree that the British statement was sharply executed, although no one save Adams favored an extended answer to it. None of the ministers, however, harbored the belief that the British ultimatum could be rejected. Coming after the news of Washington, as it did, couched in moderate terms, as the most important sections of it were, it would be political suicide to break over it. The problem was *how* to accept the proposition, how to suffer with grace and without appearance of submission the accompanying threat of a rupture. Independently, Gallatin and Adams undertook to provide a reply that would save the negotiation and American honor besides.

While the two men were laboring over their drafts, Adams made known to the other ministers that he thought the British Indian demand should not be accepted without protest. The others kept their peace and hoped that Gallatin would come forth with something that would satisfy all of them. Their silence, though, was mute testimony that for once Adams was not completely alone in his opinion. With the possible exception of Adams, the prevailing emotion was one of uncertainty.

Gallatin did not complete his efforts until Wednesday, the 12th, and although Adams was still in the process of revising his text, the commissioners met that afternoon. Gallatin read his draft and Adams parts of his. Both drafts assented to the British ultimatum. Beyond that they differed as a handshake differs from a clenched fist. Adams, decrying Gallatin's answer as too defensive, too cautious, had set out to respond to British "arrogance" with a similar show of American insolence. So far as his fellow ministers were concerned, he had succeeded all too well. What astounded them was that Adams had resurrected Monroe's ancient and presumably dead suggestion that Great Britain be told the benefits of ceding Canada. The others thought this preposterous and said so. Adams defended his stand, especially on the ground that when the instructions were published, the fact that this one had not been pressed would be both obvious and embarrassing,* but he was most obstinate on the tone the American note should take, and the afternoon aged in argument without conclusion. The meeting did not end until Clay, who was not unsympathetic to Adams's beliefs, volunteered to take both drafts and work them into a common dispatch. When the ministers went to dinner, none was yet certain what approach to take in their reply, and four of them were apprehensive over what else to expect from the fifth, John Quincy Adams.

It was Bayard who paved the road to unity. For a week he had avoided sharing in the general recriminations. He was the only one of the group who could still approach Adams, his old nemesis of St. Petersburg, without having that gentleman stiffen at sight of him, and the moment had come for Bayard to bring peace and reasonableness to the scene. After dinner he invited Adams to his room. There, for more than four hours, the two men shared a bottle of Chambertin and held a conversation that was "perfectly friendly and confidential." Before the dawn of a new day, a thorn in the commission's side had been removed. Adams, though still angry and ill at ease, was no longer adamant in his position. Bayard had served the group well.

Such, at times, did not seem the case on the following afternoon when Clay presented his revised version of Adams's and Gallatin's offerings. Adams objected to nearly every sentence, but he did not protest further when the others voted adoption of most of it.

As finally stated, the note was relatively modest in length. It began by commenting on British allusions that previous American arguments on the imputed expansionist aims of the United States had seemed defensive. They did not fear, said the American commissioners, that the rest of the world could be persuaded "that the Government of the United States was liable to

* The instructions on the cession of Canada have never been published.

any well grounded imputation of a spirit of conquest. . . ." Consequently, any explanations of America's behavior and aims "were actuated by the sole motive of removing erroneous impressions"—presumably those held by the English.

This preamble served to launch another long explanation of the validity of American expansion. Why, asked the American commissioners, did the British question the Louisiana Purchase now, long after the fact, when they had failed to do so at the time the purchase was consummated? The American commissioners had hoped, their note continued, that their statement of August 9—that the United States had never sought territorial gains—would be believed by the British government, thus nipping a wasteful discussion at the beginning. The Americans concluded their self-righteous, if not altogether accurate, denial of aggrandizement by again disclaiming the mouthings and writings of Hull and Smythe and by refusing, to John Quincy Adams's annoyance, to acknowledge American interest in Canada.

The British had to wade through all this before coming to an answer to their Indian ultimatum. Even then, they were subjected to a rebuttal of their stand on the Indians. Only at the very end of the note were the British told that their last Indian proposal was so similar to the repeated suggestions of the ministers of the United States that those commissioners could "agree to admit it in substance as a provisional article, subject, in the manner originally proposed by the British Government, to the approbation or rejection of the Government of the United States. . . . " If an Anglo-American peace did not result from this negotiation, however, the article would have no effect and was not to be used as a precedent in any future negotiation. Having thus accepted Britain's "indispensable preliminary," the Americans requested their adversaries to turn to the real business of the negotiation and submit their project of a treaty, including *all* their points. When they received this, the American ministers would give a counterproject and peace talks could begin in earnest.

The note was conveyed to the British commissioners by Hughes on the afternoon of October 14. At almost the same time, and not quite by accident, the British commissioners sent the Americans newspaper accounts of British victories. The papers reported more towns seized in the Passamaquoddy Islands, the destruction of the United States frigate *Adams,* the reversal of an American attack on Michilimackinac, and, with more conceit than accuracy, predicted a British victory at Plattsburgh on Lake Champlain, a town which was, according to last reports, occupied by their forces. Clay, apparently regretting the statements in the note he had edited and just signed, was furious and, despite his fury, was fearful of what new terms the British would try to impose. If possible, his colleagues were even more apprehensive and dejected. "May it please God," intoned Adams, "to forgive our enemies, and to turn their hearts!"

What the Lord did to British hearts will remain a celestial mystery, but it is a matter of human record that the British attitude toward the negotiation was hardening during the last weeks of September and the first weeks of October. Though their strategy was but slowly devised and only partially specified, it was, as autumn settled over London, receiving impetus from favorable military prospects. Nothing, however, in the way of territorial changes could or would be broached to the American commissioners until those ministers had acceded to the Indian ultimatum, a subject to which British prestige was now intimately attached. Goulburn, after he had read the American note of October 14, was not sure whether the Americans had fully accepted the demand, but, leaving that decision to his superiors, he confined himself to the comment that the American commissioners had, as usual, evidenced their dislike of giving "a distinct answer to a distinct proposition." Distinct or not, it would prove, under the circumstances, to be an answer that relieved the privy council.

The American commissioners' acknowledgement of the Indian proposition was to be most gratifying to the Prime Minister, for although confidence grew as the history of the American summer unraveled, it flourished unevenly among the cabinet members and knew moments of blight among all of them, especially Liverpool. To him, more than to others, the American war was but part of an international dilemma and that part which was frequently most annoying. "I confess on many accounts," he wrote to Castlereagh in the latter part of September, before he knew of the capture of Washington, "I wish we were well out of it. . . ." He was mystified as to how the American commissioners could be so "unreasonable" when their administration was in such dire straits, and he could only believe that this stubbornness was born more of absurdity and ignorance than of courage and would vanish when the day came, as it almost surely must, that the Republicans were no longer "permitted to administer the affairs of the country. . . ."

Liverpool was in much better spirits a few days later when he sent tidings of the downfall of Washington to Wellington and Castlereagh. He was so pleased, in fact, that he outlined plans to occupy Rhode Island, "destroy Baltimore," take parts of Georgia and the Carolinas, and seize Mobile and New Orleans. In addition, he now felt certain of victories that would secure the northern frontier. All this, he claimed, would not alter "our anxious desire to put an end to the war," assuming that it could be done "upon such terms as we are fairly entitled to expect." Even these terms might, Liverpool thought, be insufficient to please the British people, "but I feel too strongly the inconvenience of a continuance of the war not to make me desirous of concluding it at the expense of some popularity."

If Liverpool's optimism seemed perforated with hesitancy it was not so much because of the American situation itself as it was a product of the problems posed by France and the Czar of Russia. From Wellington's reports it appeared that the government of Louis XVIII was anything but wise and stable and that it continued to live under the intimidating shadow and spirit of Bonaparte. In September and early October, however, political upset in France, while worrisome, still seemed almost comfortably remote, but Castlereagh's controversy with the Czar in Vienna, over Alexander's continuing interest in Poland, was authentic, current, and obviously dangerous, and since the Emperor's American sympathies were well known and a new European outbreak was not altogether unlikely, developments in Vienna affected and were, in turn, affected by the commitment of funds and troops in America. Liverpool admitted to Castlereagh that he was "apprehensive" over the course of the negotiations the Foreign Minister was pursuing with the Czar, and he requested Castlereagh to attempt to correct Alexander's and Count Nesselrode's "prejudices," for "I fear the Emperor of Russia is half an American."

As the events at Washington became better known and more

intoxicating in their effect and the indications of further triumphs
in America grew more plentiful, Liverpool lost some of his
timidity toward the negotiation at Ghent. This development was
sustained by the "inadmissible" American note of September 26.
The Prime Minister, recognizing the futility of further pursuing
an Indian boundary, ordered Bathurst to frame a "distinct and
specific" Indian demand based on the *status quo* of 1811, but he
was sufficiently annoyed and, at the same time, confident to tell
the Colonial Secretary to compose at leisure, letting the Americans "feast in the meantime upon Washington. . . ." If the
Americans could not agree to this final and milder Indian proposal, "we might as well suspend or break off the negotiations
at Ghent, and settle our instructions to Sir G. Prevost in the
course of the week after next."

Although not in complete agreement with the Prime Minister
over giving up the efforts to obtain territory for the Indians,
Bathurst was cheered by Liverpool's resolve to be firm about
the rest of the ultimatum, and he was excited by the demands
which were to be made. Less perceptive than other members
of the cabinet and, therefore, less bothered by events in Paris
or Vienna or the remote possibility of a setback in America,
Bathurst had already advised the trio in Ghent of the probable
nature of their future instructions. When the Indian matter was
settled, Bathurst informed Goulburn, the government would insist on retaining Forts Niagara and Michilimackinac and, without
needing to mention it because it was rightfully British, Moose
Island; and of possessing all the islands in Lake Ontario and a
strip of land running from Fort Niagara to Buffalo on the American side of the Niagara River. At the time, Bathurst made no
mention of demanding cession of enough of Maine to allow for
a direct road from Quebec to Halifax or of the discontinuance
of the American fisheries privilege, possibly because these terms
had long been known to both commissions. Other demands,
Bathurst stated, would depend on the extent of British military
successes.

This much had been conveyed to the three ministers before
Bathurst knew of Washington. When he heard of the feats of
Ross, Cochrane, and Cockburn he could scarcely contain himself. "I hope," he wrote to Goulburn, "you will be able to put on
a face of compress'd joy at least, in communicating this News

to the American Ministers. The federal party will I believe consider this Event as advantageous to them, & will not therefore
be much unnerved at it. It will I think be fatal to the present
Members of the Government."

Bathurst quickly and avidly completed his assignment to draw
up the fourth British note, that which contained the Indian ultimatum, and, while awaiting but also assuming the Prime Minister's approval, sent a preview of the document to the British
commissioners, bidding them to warn the United States ministers
that the ultimatum was on its way. "You will take care to impress them as much as possible that you are prepared to depart,
if the Proposition is not accepted." The Americans were to be
assured, of course, that the British government was still anxious
for peace, but they were to be told also "that we are aware it
will be more easy to conclude it now, than in a later stage of the
War: as our advantages may then have taken a more decided
turn, which would oblige us to require terms, now unnecessary to
be insisted upon: . . . that considering the force now directed
against them their affairs are more likely to become worse than
better."

The British commissioners were to raise the subject of Washington at every opportunity. If they held any private conversations with a Federalist, "you may very truly represent to him
how very desirable it must be to that party that a Peace should
now be signed. That the late Events, unless corrected by some
unexpected success, must overturn their Opponents. . . ." Naturally, the first step to peace and reason, for Federalists and Republicans alike, was to accept the Indian ultimatum, and this,
Bathurst again suggested, was to be made clear, while the
Americans considered their answer, by the obvious preparations
of the British commissioners to return home.

The actual draft note, accepted by Liverpool without criticism,
was sent to Ghent on October 5, with more words of advice from
Bathurst. The British commissioners refrained from giving the
Americans advance notice of the ultimatum, deciding that such
an act "might betray an improper degree of exultation on our
part," but in most other respects they followed Bathurst's coun-
sel, for which they received the government's praise. In London,
meanwhile, the cabinet settled down to await the answer from

Ghent and the next mail pouch from the commanders in America, with hope and confidence that what they were about to learn would justify turning the peace treaty into a real estate deed—involving a touch of Maine, a bit of New York, an island, a fort, a port here and there.

⫸ PART FOUR ⫷

Victory, Trouble, and Peace

CHAPTER

13

Plattsburgh, September 11, 1814

The news the British government was expecting from America was nearing London from one direction as the American commissioners' note of October 14 made its way to that city from Ghent, and Lord Liverpool left London on Saturday, the 15th, for his country home, Walmer Castle, with more than a passing desire for positive information from both sources.

If and when the Indian matter was settled the peace talks could progress—progressing to British advantage insofar as the military situation warranted. The reports of the summer's campaign—the invasion of Maine, the seizure of the Passamaquoddy Islands, the capture of Washington—had been highly encouraging, but what was needed to put Britain in a condition of indisputable mastery was word of one or more decisive victories: not of penetration into an area of semiwilderness or of hit-and-run conquests but rather of the taking of the rich port of Baltimore, of the seizure of Sackett's Harbor and the attendant control of Lake Ontario, of the occupation of the waters and shores of Lake Champlain—the latter an accomplishment that would menace New York and greatly stimulate the divisive tendencies of New England. Partial news of such subjects had already been disclosed. According to recent reports, a British army was at Plattsburgh on Lake Champlain, and another was at or nearing Baltimore. Liverpool would learn more of these matters when he returned to London on Monday.

The events of which the British cabinet was waiting to hear had spun out their destinies in September, as the American government struggled to find itself and prepare, as well as it could, for what seemed a dismal future. Madison had not returned to his scorched capital until August 27, two days after the British had departed. For a few days most of the administration's energies were poured into preparations for withstanding a new attack, which appeared to be approaching up the Potomac, and into finding places in which to live and set up shop. What political matters were settled largely resolved themselves. Secretary of War Armstrong returned, was set upon by a mob, talked to Madison, and left town within a day. He wrote out his resignation while passing through Baltimore on his way back to New York City. Monroe, first by self-appointment, later on a pro-tem basis, and then with full consent, acceded to Armstrong's duties and worked mightily to rouse and strengthen the surrounding areas. No one, however, in those first few weeks after Bladensburg, paid much heed to the further reaches of the demoralized country. Probably little could have been done if anyone had. The cabinet, in any event, was still poking about the ruins of its once fair city when a formidable British army and a British flotilla crossed the Canadian border and started down the western shore of Lake Champlain.

The redcoated force that moved south into northern New York State on the last day of August probably numbered eleven thousand men, perhaps more. It was an army of vast proportions compared to the groups of several hundred or a few thousand that had fought in most of the war's engagements. Its immediate destination was Plattsburgh, where it knew the American defenders lay in wait on land and water. Its eventual goal was not certain, but if the British host succeeded in leaving Plattsburgh in its wake and took control of Lake Champlain, there was little to stop its descent into the valley of the Hudson. As it was, no one contested the army's right to trespass across the boundary, and by September 4 the long, orderly columns, after a leisurely and unopposed stroll through the enemy's territory, had reached the village of Chazy, less than twenty miles from Plattsburgh.

At the head of this imposing horde was none other than the Governor-General of Canada, Sir George Prevost. Not one to make haste, especially where danger to his forces and his reputation was involved, Prevost had delayed his invasion until the optimum season for warfare had almost reached its end. Adventurous, Sir George was not. Throughout previous campaigns he had been content—in fact quite worried by the responsibility of doing so—merely to defend Canada against the generally feeble attacks of the unskilled, undisciplined, poorly led American troops. He excused the lack of offensive operations on his part by bemoaning his shortage of manpower and complaining of British naval inferiority on the lakes. About the latter the government did little, but after Napoleon's downfall the cabinet could and did supply seasoned troops; so that by the end of the second week of August Prevost had about thirty thousand men under his command in or near Montreal, most of them and their officers veterans of long and distinguished service with Wellington.

Even then the Governor-General was not propelled into action. The British army, wrote a young lady of Montreal to her cousin in England, was constantly training and marching, "and a most moving scene it is, but I think if I commanded, I would move it a *little nearer the enemy.*" Prevost finally moved nearer when the pressure from London became too intense to ignore. Bathurst presented him with the near ultimatum of venturing against Sackett's Harbor or the American forces on Lake Champlain or, preferably, both. In August, while not altogether ruling out Sackett's Harbor but, on the other hand, not seriously considering this seemingly more venturesome and less promising undertaking, Sir George decided on the Lake Champlain alternative, selecting to move down the western shore, partly because that was where the American forces were gathered and partly because the roads on the eastern side were choked with cattle and supplies for his army—offered for sale by enterprising if not entirely patriotic Americans. His army assembled not far from the border during the third and fourth weeks of August, and, as the great mass moved forward, an American army, just across the boundary, vanished from sight.

Although the fading away of an American army before the enemy was not an unusual occurrence, it was in this case owing to unique circumstances. The British invasion was not unexpected, and preparations to meet it had been under way for more than a year and had been accelerated since May. In June Major General George Izard had moved enough troops to the border to annoy the British. By August he and his subordinate, Brigadier General Alexander Macomb, had about 4,500 men five miles from Canada, intending to beat the British to the punch or at

least slow the British thrust when it came. Izard was not long
established in his threatening position, however, when he received a communiqué from Secretary of War Armstrong, suggesting that the general take most of his troops and go west to assist
the forces at Niagara. Izard replied that he would do so, but he
protested that "I shall do it . . . with the certainty that everything
in this vicinity but the lately erected works at Plattsburgh and
Cumberland Head will, in less than three days after my departure, be in the possession of the enemy." Armstrong was either
sorely ignorant of affairs both at Fort Erie and Lake Champlain
or he was playing a dangerous and irresponsible finesse. Izard
nevertheless regarded the Secretary's messages as constituting
an order, and on August 29, with Prevost's legions almost within
earshot, the general started westward through the Adirondack
wilderness with four thousand men who were desperately needed
at the place they had left. Shouldering the burden that had thus
been thrust upon him, General Macomb returned to Plattsburgh,
added his to Izard's frantic calls for militia, and, with the three
thousand men remaining, only half of whom were in fit condition
for battle, began earnestly to strengthen his defenses.

The British army moved southward from Chazy on September
5. Though the way was encumbered by felled trees and destroyed
bridges, the regiments made good progress and were by nightfall in Beekmantown, the van of the army only eight miles from
Plattsburgh. At dawn on the 6th the British were again on the
move, splitting into two massive columns: one pursuing the more
direct, inland route of the Beekmantown Road, the other branch-
ing east nearer the lake on a course that eventually wound along
Plattsburgh (or Cumberland) Bay and into the town.

The right column, under command of Generals Robinson and
Power, had not gone far before it was surprised by an American
force of about seven hundred New York militia under General
Benjamin Mooers and less than three hundred regulars led by
Major John Wool. The Americans opened fire from behind stone
walls and clumps of trees, but the advancing ranks of British,
like a flow of crimson lava, moved inexorably forward, and the
militia, overwhelmed by the sight, broke and fled. The regulars
were less easily discouraged, and though they too retreated they
did so with a semblance of order, skirmishing as they fell back.

At Halsey's Corners the Americans were reinforced by Captain

Leonard with his artillerymen and two field pieces. When the first lines of British troops appeared in the road the cannon were fired. The initial shot struck "near the center of the front platoon, about breast high and ploughed its way through, sweeping all before it, the whole length of the column; opening a space apparently several feet wide, which, however, was immediately closed as if by magic." The oncoming waves, the pride of Wellington, did not falter. Not until they had absorbed three volleys did the British lower bayonets and sweep the nuisance from before them. By three in the afternoon the right column was in possession of the deserted village of Plattsburgh.

The left column, with a longer route to cover, took longer but traversed the better part of its course virtually unmolested. A small group of Americans had been stationed at the site of Dead Creek bridge, where the road the British were following made an abrupt right turn and then curved southwesterly around the bay, but Macomb, fearing this detachment would find itself outflanked by the more rapidly advancing British right, then only a mile from Plattsburgh, recalled the group, ordering them, as they retreated, to add their efforts to those of the regulars and remaining militia who continued to annoy the right column. The little band did as it was told, barely getting across the lower Saranac bridge before the British blocked the way. The militia had already raced across the upper bridge. Beating off British attempts to cross both bridges, the Americans stripped them of their planking and dug in to await attack. As they were doing so, the British left approached along the shore road, under heavy fire from American gunboats. By evening the British army, somewhat battered but largely intact, was firmly in control of that part of the village north of the Saranac River.

It was thus on September 6 that Sir George Prevost became at least temporary master of a northern New York State hamlet that possessed a church, a jail, an inn, and a courthouse and which normally housed 1,500 people. He found the "Enemy in the occupation of an Elevated Ridge of Land on the South Branch of the Saranac crowned with three Strong Redoubts and other Field Works, and Block Houses armed with heavy Ordnance, with their flotilla at Anchor, out of Shot from the Shore, consisting of a Ship, a Brig, a Schooner, a Sloop and Ten Gun Boats." Whether the little American fleet was or was not out of gunshot later became a matter for considerable debate. It was, in any case, anchored across and somewhat inside the entrance to the bay, and it was to become Prevost's crutch and curse.

Sir George apparently gave some thought to attacking the American position early that evening, but he was easily dissuaded by General Robinson, an old Wellingtonian, who pointed out that they knew little of the disposition of the American defenses nor where they could ford the river. Robinson's further suggestion that the army could well use the co-operation of the British navy perfectly matched Prevost's own belief, and the Governor-General settled down to wait and prepare, agreeing to attack on land when the navy opened up on water.

When Prevost made, or more properly reaffirmed, his decision not to attack without the help of the navy, the principal ship and the commander of that flotilla were still in Canada. Coming from duty on Lake Ontario, Captain George Downie did not reach Isle aux Noix, the British naval base on the Richelieu River, until September 1, the day after the British army had commenced its American invasion. Downie found much to do, not the least of which was to outfit, arm, and man his flagship, the *Confiance*, which had been launched just a week earlier. For days he exhausted himself begging for parts and manpower that would turn what was little more than a barren hull into Lake Champlain's most intimidating man-of-war.

The *Confiance* did not begin its journey until September 7, and then, for two days, it had to be hauled by boats through the narrows of the Richelieu and Lake Champlain. At Ash Island, still north of the border, the *Confiance* paired with the *Linnet*, the second largest of the British vessels, and together the two of them moved to Chazy where most of the rest of the British flotilla had been supporting the army and waiting.

Most of the ships and crews, particularly the *Confiance*, which was still recruiting, needed extensive preparation, and at dawn on the 9th, amid rumors that an attack would be put in motion that night, work and practice were pushed forward with grim resolve. What inspired such feverish activity, aside from devotion to duty, were the impatient notes of Sir George Prevost. The Governor-General had written to Downie on the morning of the 7th, stating that the American flagship was "inferior to the Confiance" and that when the American gunboats were manned the "remaining craft appear to have but few men left on board." As if this report of American deficiencies was not enough to encourage the captain, Prevost added rather vaguely that Downie would "find the present moment offers many advantages which may not again occur. . . . As my ulterior movements depend on your decision, you will have the goodness to favor me with it, with all possible promptitude."

Although still north of the boundary, his capital ship attached to tow lines, Downie received and replied to the letter the same day. Faced not so much with a decision as a multitude of details, he kept his patience and wrote to Sir George that he was "aware of [the] Comparative force of the Enemy" and would be able to meet the American squadron in a day or two when, he assumed, the *Confiance* would be ready for action.

Prevost received Downie's letter on the 8th, and, displeased by what he thought was sluggishness on the captain's part, wrote back immediately. It is "of the highest importance," he told Downie, as if that gentleman did not realize it, that the fleet "should commence a cooperation with the division of the Army now occupying Plattsburg." With the letter went Major Coore, Prevost's aide, who was ostensibly to give the captain information on the position of the American fleet. Downie, who had yet to reach Chazy, was not fooled by Coore's role as a bearer of intelligence, and, with ebbing patience, he answered Prevost that he was coming "as fast as the wind and weather will allow." He repeated his statement of the day before that he could not enter battle until the *Confiance* was ready, adding "it is my duty not to hazard the Squadron before an Enemy who will be superior in Force," a judgment of relative strength opposed to that held by Prevost.

The following morning, the 9th, Major Coore along with Captain Watson, a new messenger who was to stay with the flotilla until it was ready to fight, arrived with the Governor-General's latest dispatch. Prevost complained that as a result of Downie's letter of the preceding day the army had been forced to postpone its attack. Sarcastically, Prevost went on to say that he need not elaborate on the evils facing both of them if the delay continued. He concluded by saying that the American ships

were undermanned and, at that, had been compelled to draw
on prisoners to obtain such as they had.

With both Watson and Coore standing at his elbow, the captain read the letter and gave vent to his anger. His annoyance
had the effect of diluting his caution and wisdom. He wrote to
Prevost that he expected to sail at midnight and round Cumberland Head about dawn. He briefly mentioned the problems that
still confronted him and, when done, told the general: "I have
the honour of Your Excellency's letter of this morning, to which
the preceding is a full answer."

The last of the crew, soldiers of the 39th regiment, joined the
Confiance that evening, and, with carpenters and mechanics still
going about their work, the fleet belatedly got under way at
dawn. It had scarcely budged, however, before the wind
changed, and midday of the 10th found the ships again secure
in their anchorage. Prevost was furious, or pretended to be. "I
ascribe the disappointment I have experienced," he wrote to
Downie, "to the unfortunate change of wind, and shall rejoice to
learn that my reasonable expectations have been frustrated by
no other cause." "The letter," said Downie to Coore, "does not
require an Answer, and I have nothing further to state to the
Commander of the Forces than you can tell him." Nonetheless,
Downie redoubled his efforts, and before another sunrise the
British fleet, with "a smart breeze" at its tail, was coming down
Cumberland Head.

Patiently waiting for them, not far within the brow of Cumberland Head, were the vessels of Commodore Thomas Macdonough. Tugging lightly at their anchors deep within the
jeweled waters of the bay, the larger of the vessels sat like
sections of a bobbing gate, extending from a point about 1,500
yards southeast of Cumberland Head to within about 200–500
yards of the shoals off Crab Island—all more than a mile from
the shore of the village. Behind them, closer to Plattsburgh, were
the gunboats, ten of them, each about seventy-five feet in
length. The picture the entire squadron formed as it waited
quietly in place did not altogether discourage the illusion that
this was an ordinary, pleasant Sunday morning of that wartime
summer.

The ships had been gathered in the bay since May and holding to their anchorages for days. For Macdonough the next few hours were to be the test of his endeavors since the fall of 1812. Born a doctor's son in New Castle, Delaware, he had joined the navy in 1800, served under Decatur in the Tripolitan War, and assumed independent command with the coming of hostilities in 1812. Ordered to Champlain in September of that year, he had been forced to build, buy, and convert a fleet. Two of his principal efforts sailed up the Richelieu in July, 1813, and did not return until May of the following year—under British flag. Undaunted, Macdonough retired up Otter Creek, near Vergennes, Vermont, and began to build anew. Lieutenant Pring, first Downie's predecessor and then his subordinate, ventured forth in May, 1814, to do away with Macdonough's flotilla as it lay at dock and in stocks, but Pring was driven off, and a few days later Macdonough sailed down the lake to Plattsburgh, prepared, or nearly so, to meet the British challenge. He was then thirty years of age.

Macdonough knew that as long as his fleet existed on Champlain the British could not enjoy unqualified control of the area, whatever their success on land. While American warships remained afloat off Plattsburgh no British supply line could safely extend beyond that point. It was thus Macdonough's plan to give himself the advantage of position and to force the British fleet to come after him. Consequently, by anchoring his vessels in line across the entrance of Plattsburgh Bay and beyond the range of accurate gunfire from shore (that which could distinguish between his ships and those of the enemy), he hoped to make his opponents come up the lake with the wind, come about against it, and beat a way to their own anchorages under his broadside. Furthermore, his larger craft had cables, "springs," attached to the anchor lines, so that each ship, when its starboard broadside had been damaged, could, like a floating carousel, rotate and bring its port guns to bear.

On that Sunday morning, September 11, the American fleet was so placed. Leading the line and nearest Cumberland Head was the brig *Eagle*, slightly superior in guns to her counterpart, the British *Linnet*. Next came the *Saratoga*, Macdonough's flagship. In number of guns and in firepower she was possibly superior to the *Confiance* at short range but decidedly inferior at a distance. If Macdonough's intentions were fulfilled, however, the capital ships would engage one another at close quarters and at anchor and not do battle in open water.

Completing the American line were the schooner *Ticonderoga*, originally intended to be a steamboat, and the sloop *Preble*, neither of which had a comparable opponent in the British sloops *Chub* and *Finch*, the repaired and renamed vessels that the summer before had belonged to the Americans. The British, on the other hand, had twelve gunboats to the American ten, giving Downie a faint but undependable edge in firepower among galleys. On the whole, the British flotilla had a few more guns, but the Americans had a shade more firepower. In a running fight on the lake the *Confiance* probably would have reigned supreme. At anchor and at close quarters the two fleets promised to be a close match.

That the success of his strategy would soon be challenged was obvious to Macdonough shortly after five on that Sunday morning when the distant thunder of the guns of the British fleet, a signal to Prevost, announced its coming to those on land and lake. Macdonough promptly sent out boats to scout beyond the entrance to the bay. Before 7:30 the boats returned, and not long after, the British flotilla, sixteen vessels strong, came into view and halted to the east of Cumberland Head.

The moment was "silent as death." Downie had himself lowered in a small boat and rowed toward the American ships, so that he could better examine their placement. Macdonough called his crew together on deck and led them in prayer. When Downie returned to his ship, he reported that things were as expected: that the *Linnet* and the *Chub* were still to concentrate on the *Eagle;* the *Confiance* was to sail past the *Saratoga* and the *Eagle*—blasting the latter in passing—come about, and anchor with her starboard broadside to the *Saratoga* and nearly within boarding range; that the *Finch* and the gunboats were to attack the *Ticonderoga* and the *Preble*. He promised his crew that "at the same moment we attack the Ships our Army are to storm the Batteries." He then wished his men well and gave the order to "bear up and sail large!" Starting with the crew of the *Confiance*, three loud cheers swept down the line of the British fleet, rending the Sabbath calm, and to a roaring reply from the decks of the American vessels, the *Confiance* hoisted her sails and "went into Action, hauling close round Cumberland Head with the wind on the Starboard beam."

It was not long before the wind, what there was of it, became capricious, and the British ships struggled to make headway. Impatient, the American crews, starting with that of the *Eagle*, poured shot harmlessly into the bay, but minutes later their metal was smashing through the rigging and into the woodwork of the *Linnet*, the *Chub*, and the *Confiance*, as the three leaders came closer. The British held their fire and inched onward. Finally, however, with the breeze almost nonexistent, the punishment became unendurable. Balls traveled the length of the flagship's deck, sweeping all before them, and Downie, still more than 300 yards from the *Saratoga* and unable to come about, threw over his anchors, furled his sails, and signaled his gunners to discharge their pieces. The entire port broadside of the *Confiance* spoke at once. The effect was awesome. "The *Saratoga* was nearly blown out of the water. She shivered from truck to keel and nearly every man on deck was knocked down by the concussion."

As a result of that single, booming blast forty men on the *Saratoga* lost either their lives or their ability to fight on. But the *Saratoga* was by no means stilled. Macdonough scrambled back to his feet, and, leaping from gun to gun, sidestepping maimed bodies and pools of blood, he roused his crew who, answering with a cheer, sent ball after ball thudding into the *Confiance*. The *Confiance* rumbled back. Spars and masts splintered into kindling; chunks, needles of shivered wood and metal hurtled through the air, smashing, piercing human bodies; sails were reduced to urchins' rags. To the north, sometimes hidden from the others in belches of acrid smoke, the *Eagle*, the *Linnet*, and the *Chub* plied the same desperate work of destruction.

The southern end of the line, that nearest Crab Island, was slower to erupt. Misjudging the vagaries of the wind, the *Finch* shuffled fitfully toward her assigned place, drifting downwind from the *Ticonderoga* to the *Preble*. With the *Finch* went four of the British gunboats, their crews straining to the oars or manning the guns that crashed their burdens against the two American ships. To the rear, the other British gunboats, hanging back like small, frightened children asked to play in a game for bigger boys, exercised their guns but crept forward gingerly. For their commander, Lieutenant Raynham, the responsibility, the sight of devastation were soon more than he could bear, and, taking himself to the hospital ship, he hid there, without spirit among men without arms and legs and life itself.

By contrast, the four leading gunboats and their crews fought to near self-destruction, although the *Finch,* their supposed leader, garnered no laurels. Altogether, the floating posse gave the *Ticonderoga* some moments of fright, but the wind and that ship's ability to lash back urged the five British vessels to converge on the *Preble* instead. The attack soon became too much for the little sloop. Crippled within an hour, she cut her cables and fled shoreward to shelter under the guns of the American army.

Done with that quarry, the four gunboats, without the aid of their companion sloop, bravely resumed their persecution of the *Ticonderoga.* The British sloop, the *Finch,* drifting out of control toward the shoals off Crab Island, as a result of both human and structural collapse, no longer figured in the engagement. She was holed beyond the mending capacity of her carpenter; her pilot had to be beaten from his preferred spot behind the pump to his rightful place at the helm; and her captain, Lieutenant Hicks, though he later convinced a court martial that he was no coward, could not be said to have displayed conspicuous courage. Listing and luffing, the *Finch* soon ran aground and for the remainder of the morning engaged in a private war of her own with the American invalids on Crab Island, who, answering the challenge, limped about their two cannon, returning shot for shot.

The British fleet suffered its first casualties at the two exteremes of the line. The *Chub,* though handled more resolutely than the *Finch,* suffered a similar fate. Heading for her northernmost position, she was badly mauled by both the *Saratoga* and the *Eagle.* For some minutes she repaid the *Eagle* in kind, but, unable to anchor and becoming uncontrollable, the *Chub* drifted astern of the *Linnet,* between the *Confiance* and the *Eagle*—forcing those two ships into a temporary and unwanted truce—and became prisoner of the Americans. Thus, with the *Ticonderoga* distant from the main scene of battle and plagued by the British gunboats, the struggle for supremacy was largely confined to the four largest ships—the American *Saratoga* and *Eagle* and the British *Confiance* and *Linnet.*

First of these to give way was the *Eagle*. For the *Linnet* alone she was more than a match, but the *Confiance* was so placed that several of her forward guns were used to better advantage on the smaller ship than on the *Saratoga*. At last, with many of her cables cut and most of her starboard guns out of commission, the *Eagle* pulled up her anchors, nosed around past the *Saratoga* on the inland side, and anchored again between the flagship and the *Ticonderoga*. With her largely undamaged larboard guns now toward the enemy, she played a destructive fire on the *Confiance*, while generally out of harm's way herself. The movement saved the *Eagle* and hurt the *Confiance*, but it left the *Saratoga* at the mercy not only of the *Confiance* but now of the *Linnet* as well.

After close to two hours of unremitting devastation, both capital ships were approaching prostration. Almost every starboard gun on the *Saratoga* had been silenced. On the exposed side nearly all above deck and much below had been battered beyond recognition. In the wreckage men groaned, cursed, and died. The ship's complement of officers had been decimated. Ultimately, as her crew sought shelter from the rain of metal, the *Saratoga* went mute, every starboard gun beyond use.

Across the water, the *Confiance*, though still able to fire, was in a condition not much better than that of the *Saratoga*. Water sloshed above the gun-room deck, and the wounded lying there had to be shifted from place to place to keep them from drowning. The open deck was hell. Bodies were dumped overboard so the living might have a place to stand and walk and work the guns that could still operate. But the greatest calamity for the *Confiance* had come but fifteen minutes after she had anchored. One of her own gun muzzles, jarred from its base by an American shot, had been flung against the groin of her captain, flattening him in the last minutes of his life to the deck. He had lived only long enough to be taken below, and the command of his ship had fallen to Lieutenant Robertson, who had come with Downie from Lake Ontario. The command of the fleet had passed to Lieutenant Pring.

Despite Downie's death, the British, after a battle of two hours, appeared to be in sight of victory. Several guns on the *Linnet* were still blazing away, as were a few on the larboard side of the *Confiance*. No answer was returned by the *Saratoga*. But that ship, though silent and severely distressed, was busy. Exhorting his crew and leading the way, Macdonough let go his stern anchor, cut his bower cable, and, with the help of his men, pulled on the springs. Slowly, haltingly, the *Saratoga* came around. Robertson, knowing the purpose and probable results of Macdonough's maneuver, attempted the same. The *Confiance* never made it. Her cables were gone and would have had to be replaced under the galling fire of the *Eagle*. Punished beyond endurance and strangers to one another, the crew refused to make the attempt. Robertson and some of the other officers struggled alone, but to no avail. The *Saratoga*, her port side brought to bear, spoke anew, and the American gunboats, hesitant and of little help until then, joined their flagship for the kill. Scarcely a ship any longer, the *Confiance* struck her colors. Minutes later, Lieutenant Pring, aware of the futility of further resistance, lowered the flag of the *Linnet*. Except for the sounds of the strange war between the invalids and the *Finch*, the lake became hushed. Finally the absurd duel near Crab Island came to its end, and the bay knew peace. Then from those on the American vessels who still had voice rose a long, haunting cheer. Drifting across the water, it was heard by the troops south of the Saranac and raised by them to a roar of thanksgiving—a cry that tempered the anxiety of a nation.

North of the Saranac, it was a cheer that stopped the British army in its retarded tracks. Early that morning, before the British fleet had scaled its guns to announce its coming, Prevost had called his staff members together to repeat their assignments. Robinson and Power were to ford the river beyond the upper bridge and trounce the ever-increasing American militia who crowded the woods. The other regiments, assisted by most of the artillery, were to take Forts Moreau, Brown, and Scott and the blockhouses that crested the ridge paralleling the bay. The prospects seemed promising. It was a trained army of more than ten thousand against a regular force of less than two thousand and an unknown number—but probably less than three thousand—of militia. General Robinson, who had never served with such a disorganized army and who observed that "nothing goes right but in the commissariat," left the meeting and hurried back to his troops, for once happy in the thought that matters had improved and certain he would soon lead a march to victory.

The troops, to Robinson's annoyance, were slow to form, and not until the regiments had completed breakfast did they proceed to their places along the north bank of the river. The British fleet came into view off Cumberland Head, stalled, then sailed into the bay. To the redcoated men on shore no order was given. Only when action on water was obvious did the British cannon on land signal the start of hostilities there. Then, amid some confusion, the massive army opened fire and lumbered toward the river, "throwing bomb-shells, shrapnells, balls, and Congreve rockets. . . ."

In the American works bordering the lake the fire given and received was intense. The two blockhouses, knuckles on the fist of land that dented a northward angle into the Saranac, were belabored unmercifully. Farther up the river, at three separate locations, great contingents of British, burdened under hundreds of scaling ladders, struggled to penetrate the American lines. But their task was not easy. The four days that Prevost had delayed his attack, waiting for Downie's flotilla, had been used by the Americans to good advantage. Artillery had been positioned and anchored. Roads had been barricaded. The militia, hidden in the woods and behind breastworks, were spared the fear engendered by exposure. With few exceptions, the Americans stood their ground.

Perhaps the most serious potential threat to the American lines was posed by the troops under command of General Robinson, whose job it was to ford the river west of the concentration of militia, outflank and stampede them, and come driving down through the American lines on the forts. Eager to be on his way, Robinson cursed Prevost for waiting for the ships to engage, and when the artillery burst forth he angrily drove his men forward. And forward they went with surprising ease, led by the scouts through the river and down the road that gored the woods. Unhindered by the enemy, the column pressed ahead for half an hour, until Robinson, growing suspicious, rode to the fore. Finding the scouts in argument over whether or not they were following the correct route, the general rode alone down the sylvan path. Not a shot disturbed his ride, and, quaking with fury, he swung about, aware now that he had been trailing off toward the Adirondacks, and reversed his column. An hour afterward, he and his brigade were back at the Saranac.

Robinson's second attempt to locate the enemy was more successful. Launching forth from a spot downstream, the eight companies of the light brigade "dashed down a very steep and high bank, and forded the river like so many foxhounds, driving the Doodles in all directions." If and how badly the "Doodles" were driven was a point on which the opposing forces disagreed, but it became a matter of small consequence when Robinson was ordered to halt and await reinforcements. He reluctantly did so. He was still waiting in "full view" of the American works when Prevost's aide-de-camp arrived with news of the fleet's surrender and orders to retire across the river. "Never," recorded Robinson later, "was anything like the disappointment expressed in every countenance."

Although attempts to storm the American position were given up, a spasmodic bombardment of the fortifications continued until late afternoon, at which time it ceased so completely that Macomb was convinced it had been "silenced by the superiority of our fire." Under cover of night, the British began to withdraw and by midnight were beyond the limits of Plattsburgh, leaving their dead and wounded and much of their artillery and supplies to the Americans. What the British did not leave they destroyed, "in the most precipitate and disgraceful manner. . . ." They were in Chazy before the Americans were fully convinced of their departure from Plattsburgh, and a halfhearted pursuit was easily discouraged by a sodden downpour. In three days, through mud and cold, the remains of the once-magnificent British army retreated over a route that had required six days in their advance. On the 13th the tattered force crossed back into Canada, and on the following day Sir George Prevost was at home in Montreal, his grand invasion no more than a painful memory.

In his report to Bathurst, Prevost pointed an accusing finger at the navy, at the same time that the surviving naval officers, prisoners of Macdonough, were writing bitter denunciations of Prevost. It was the Governor-General's opinion that the fleet had not performed up to capacity and that some of its officers had been downright cowardly. When the navy failed, argued Prevost, there was no longer reason for the army to continue the assault and, considering the rabbit-like growth of the American militia, much that compelled a speedy departure. "I did not hesitate to arrest the course of the Troops advancing to the attack, because the most complete success would have been unavailing, and the possession of the Enemy's Works offered no advantage to compensate for the loss we must have sustained in acquiring Possession of them."

Although the probable truth of his statement did not fully excuse his lack of effort, Sir George was probably right in his belief that he could not long have maintained his position without having control of Lake Champlain. What he neglected to consider publicly was the help he might have given the navy. Without a doubt, he had provoked Downie into action before the flotilla, particularly the *Confiance,* was ready. Furthermore, Robertson and Pring made much of the fact that the American fleet had limped to the far side of Crab Island after its victory, away from possible interference from shore. While it is questionable whether shot from shore could have severely hurt or dislodged Macdonough's ships, it is certain that British control on land would eventually have forced Macdonough into the open lake, where Downie's fleet, when it existed, would presumably have enjoyed tactical superiority. Prevost's greatest failure was putting the burden of initial attack on the navy. It was he who should have cleared a path for them.

"The recent disgraceful business of Plattsburgh has so completely irritated the feelings of the whole army," wrote the girl in Montreal to her cousin, "that it is in a state almost amounting to mutiny." She went on to say that if there were "any man with common abilities" at the head of the Canadian government the English would "long ago have taught the Yankees submission, and been at Peace. Such is the *decided opinion of every military man* in the Province, whether his rank be high or low, so glaring are the state of affairs at this moment."

Even more sorrowful and astringent were the words of General Robinson. "I am sick at heart," he stated, "everything I see and hear is discouraging, this is no field for a military man above the rank of a colonel of riflemen. . . . This country can never again afford such an opportunity, nothing but a defensive war can or ought to be attempted here, and you will find that the expectations of his Majesty's ministers and the people of England will be utterly destroyed in this quarter."

The weakness of the American government, the disloyalty of some of her people, the usual impotence of the militia, the strategic quirks of John Armstrong—these and other impediments had been unable, for a change, to thwart an American triumph. Ignoring the odds, Thomas Macdonough, Alexander Macomb, and, in his perverse way, Sir George Prevost had prevailed. "The Almighty," reported Macdonough, ignoring his own inspired role, "has been pleased to grant us a signal victory on Lake Champlain. . . ." These were words a weary country had longed for but little expected—words that would carry to the government of the enemy, a government which anticipated them even less and would come to regret them profoundly.

A Game of Reticence

On September 11 Prevost retraced his steps northward from Plattsburgh. Two days later, the 13th, the British force that had earlier leveled Washington retreated from Baltimore, leaving the latter city largely intact. Baltimore's Fort McHenry, mocking the British assault, continued to stand; Francis Scott Key had been provoked to poetic effort; but General Ross was dead, and the British invaders were soon on their way to Halifax to mend their wounds and spirits. They were still at sea when General Drummond, proclaiming himself victorious, nevertheless withdrew his army from the perimeter of Fort Erie, abandoning that bastion to the weary Americans who remained within it. In just ten days the magnificent British offensive against the United States had collapsed—had blunted its swords against a pitiful rabble and limped away—as the summer of glorious prospects surrendered its tenure.

The dreadful, unbelievable news fluttered into London with the leaves of autumn and at first seemed so incredible that it was barely acknowledged. Even when the cabinet ceased denying the reports as premature and probably exaggerated, it refused to recognize any alteration in the relationship between the two warring countries, defensively pointing to the increasing effectiveness of the blockade and awarding to General Pakenham the task of replacing Ross and leading the expedition he was to have led against America's Gulf coast. Though wobbly, Britannia felt herself—or tried to convince herself she felt—still powerful and only momentarily obstructed in reaching her goal. At least the American commissioners had agreed to the Indian proposal, and no one at that point felt inclined to quarrel with the terms of agreement. There had been no change, wrote Bathurst to Goulburn, in the government's diplomatic plans, but, he added, "Had L.G. Prevost kept Platsburg . . . we should have had a better case of it." The reversals in America, like so many belches, were neither socially nor politically recognized, but not even the privy council was able to suppress their involuntary interruptions.

Actually, although Bathurst minimized the effects of the military disappointments, he could rightly claim that the list of areas to be kept or acquired by conquest and negotiation, while reduced, had never been precise or final and was not so then. The first step, in any case, was to obtain American acceptance of the principle of *uti possidetis*. When and not until the Americans had admitted the principle as the basis for the remainder of the negotiation would the territorial claims be presented. To the doctrine itself Bathurst did not anticipate "any serious objection," but he feared that the itemized list would invoke no small amount of opposition and argument, and again he bemoaned the news from America. "Had we continued successful, I am sure they would have at once subscribed to our terms."

Despite the fact that the detailed demands were not then to be exposed to the Americans, Bathurst revealed them to the British commissioners, requiring three letters to describe and amend them. The first point had nothing to do with possession or cession but with the old bugaboo of impressment. The British were forever convincing themselves that they had latched on to secret and veiled American instructions—usually intercepted letters of only partially informed American diplomats in Paris, Amsterdam, or Stockholm, not instructions secret or otherwise—calling for a new attempt to "press the reserve of their rights on the maritime question." Whether the reports were true or not, the cabinet prepared its agents to resist. Great Britain, pointed out Bathurst, had already been exceedingly generous in allowing the matter to "be passed over in silence." If the Americans insisted on a clause defining each country's respective rights in regard to impressment and naturalization they would get one, but it must be distinctly worded in England's favor.

Having thus at the outset of his dispatch instructed the British commissioners to remind the Americans of a cause they had put aside, Bathurst turned, in the official dispatch and in private ones, to the subjects of retention and acquisition. One of these demands, for which the British commissioners must exert themselves, was for a new boundary between Maine and New Brunswick and Quebec. Bathurst had only a rudimentary knowledge of that section of North America, and his description of the intended boundary, despite several attempts, remained confusing. It seems probable, however, that he meant for the line to cut through Passamaquoddy Bay, reserving the islands, especially Moose Island, "which was always a part of New Brunswick," to the British, and then follow the St. Croix River, eventually proceeding due west on the forty-sixth parallel. The result, however Bathurst cloudily envisioned it, would give Canada a generous slice of that northern portion of Massachusetts and a direct route from Quebec to Halifax, although it would also, as Bathurst pointed out, restore to the Americans a section east of the Penobscot which the British then held. While the proposition was important, Bathurst confessed that the British ministers could give way under pressure to the point where the British got just enough of Maine to allow for a direct communication between the two provincial capitals, and if a rupture seemed imminent they could surrender altogether. So hovered the ghost of Plattsburgh.

Of greater consequence than the creation of a new northeastern boundary was retention of Fort Niagara with a five-mile radius surrounding, and of the island and fort of Michilimackinac. "From these points I think the News must be bad, before we can be brought to relax." Not mentioned, though, and now dismissed, was hope of getting a strip of land from Fort Niagara to Buffalo. This dream, too, had died at Plattsburgh and Baltimore and Fort Erie.

An exchange of minor forts, held by the opposing parties on each other's territory, and the demand that the Americans cede Carlton Island, one of the Thousand Islands, completed the inventory of parcels to be bartered or taken. Hidden within the instructions though, were two other issues, one of which had been raised in August and then neglected, with American acquiescence presumed. The British stated that they had no objection to a clause on the usual international agreement on high-seas fishing, but the privilege the Americans had gained from the

Treaty of 1783 of drying fish on Canadian shores had, claimed
the British, been ended by the war and was not to be restored.
The final detail, "considered as already settled, by the admission of the American Plenipotentiaries," was to revise the northwestern boundary from the Lake of the Woods to the Mississippi
according to the Anglo-American arrangement of 1803, a pact
which pleased the British but had been rejected by the Americans. The American commissioners would be surprised to learn
of their "admission," and they would reflect also that the accord
of 1803 had grown no more palatable with the passage of time.

Compared to the terms which would have been inspired by a
victory at Plattsburgh, those formally sent to the British commissioners on October 18 were, by British standards, distressingly
mild, and Liverpool and Bathurst, uneasy in their unaccustomed
position of balked conquerors, impressed on the British commissioners that they should do all in their power to convince the
Americans of their unexpected good fortune. Lord Liverpool,
given a few days to meditate on Plattsburgh, was immersed in
a gloom of suppressed desire and no little malice. The British
still could, he told Goulburn, blockade all American ports, ravage
her coasts, demolish her towns, and bring a plague to her remaining commerce and agriculture. All this would cost the
British no more expenditure of men and money than they had
been bearing for some time. "If the Americans are unreasonable
in declining the moderate terms of peace which you are authorized to propose, the country at large will feel it necessary to
support a war, the worst effects of which will be the leaving them
in that state in which they had existed and prospered." The
Americans could be disabused, too, of the notion that they might
receive help from some European power. Thinking this over,
Liverpool added that if such help *were* given it would come too
late, for by then the United States might "have lost what it
would take her twenty years of peace to recover." "There is no
disposition," the Prime Minister concluded, "to exact any terms
from them inconsistent with their honour; the contest is a contest only for terms of peace."

Liverpool's letter arrived in Ghent after the British commissioners had sent their fifth note to their American counterparts.
Late also were conflicting instructions on whether or not Gambier, Adams, and Goulburn were to reveal or conceal the details

that would fulfill Britain's concept of *uti possidetis*. Bathurst, who first insisted on the Americans' accepting the principle before being told its particulars, later reminded himself that the enemy commissioners had a disposition "to resist every proposition that is made, in hopes of improving it" and that it might, therefore, be wise to outline the program in its fullest extent at the start. The British could then press one point at a time, while simultaneously convincing the Americans of British generosity.

Neither these words nor the related dispatch from Liverpool affected the actions of the British commissioners. The formal instructions, accompanied by the news from America, had arrived in Ghent late in the evening of the 20th, where the entire package had its predictable baneful influence. "Even our brilliant success at Baltimore," wrote Goulburn, indulging in some patriotic fancy, "as it did not terminate in the capture of the town, will be considered by the Americans as a victory, and not as an escape. We owed the acceptance of our Article respecting the Indians to the capture of Washington; and if we had either burnt Baltimore or held Plattsburgh, I believe we should have had peace on the terms which you have sent to us in a month at latest." Now, lamented Goulburn, things "may be very different."

As if they intended to make up for the additional time it would take to realize Britain's goals, the three commissioners hurriedly fashioned Bathurst's draft into a document fit for American eyes. Referring to the first British-American conference in August as having been a thorough exposition of Britain's basic terms, they denied the need for a formal project. Picking here and there from Bathurst's list, however, they said that notwithstanding American pretensions there was no need for a stipulation on maritime rights, nor, it having already been announced, was it necessary to discuss further the discontinuance of America's fish-drying prerogative. The only other item the British commissioners selected was the proposal on the northwestern boundary, which, they were sure, would be "admitted without objection." The bulk of the note emphasized the importance of *uti possidetis*, a principle which the Americans seemed to prefer and on which basis the British were now willing to treat. The British commissioners trusted that the American ministers would show, "by their ready acceptance of this basis, that they duly appreciate the

moderation of His Majesty's Government in so far consulting
the honor and fair pretensions of the United States as, in the
relative situation of the two countries, to authorize such a proposition."

The American reactions to the note and to the London newspapers which accompanied it were not what the British anticipated, nor what they considered proper answer to their moderation. Pausing in their extended discussion of the probable and
appropriate employment of their messenger, William Shaler, and
forgoing for a time their afterthoughts and recriminations over
their acceptance of the Indian ultimatum, the five Americans attended to both varieties of information that the British commission had sent them. As if they were reading of minor skirmishes,
the men on the Rue des Champs were remarkably unimpressed
by the subdued, vague accounts of Plattsburgh and Baltimore
which were contained in the English papers so reluctantly delivered to them. So thoroughly chilled were they by the evil apparition of British armed might, so chastened by the melancholy
pall cast by the desecration of their capital, that, although they
believed what they read, they still could not conceive that the
British reversals were anything but temporary or that these setbacks could possibly provide a salutary harvest for Americans.
The wounds dealt them by the news of Washington's devastation
were too severe to be easily healed.

The temper of the British note was equally misconstrued. To
the American commissioners this fifth communication had "the
same dilatory and insidious character as their preceding
notes. . . ." It was simply one more absurd and galling effort to
delay the negotiation—and especially exasperating as a reply
to the American request for a project. The mention of *uti possidetis* was proof to the Americans that the British had not been
stayed by the repulses at Plattsburgh and Baltimore and were
still mesmerized by their disgraceful accomplishments at Bladensburg and Washington. Clearly only one answer to the British
note was possible. It was, in whole and in part, utterly inadmissible.

Acting in rare unison and with remarkable speed, the American ministers completed in three days the briefest answer they
had yet written. Bluntly, defiantly, they refused even to consider
uti possidetis. They were not, they said, authorized to cede terri-

tory, and they had absolutely no intention of doing so. Once more, strongly intimating that the British were procrastinating, the Americans insisted on the submission of a British project or, if that were unacceptable, the simultaneous exchange of projects.

On Monday morning, October 24, the fifth American note was signed in John Quincy Adams's room and by that afternoon had begun to bear fruit within the thick, dank walls of the former monastery that housed the three Englishmen. The British were incredulous at what they read. "The case of their not accepting the basis of *uti possidetis* even for a provisional article is not provided for in the instructions which we have received," querulously noted Goulburn in his hasty letter to Bathurst, "though we have no doubt that the spirit of those instructions would warrant us in declining to proceed in the negotiation unless that basis was admitted, yet we do not like thus to break off entirely without a previous certainty that you coincide with us in opinion. . . ." That evening a special messenger was on his way to Calais and thence to London.

Had an American fleet suddenly materialized and sailed up the Thames it scarcely could have created more consternation in London than did the American note of October 24. Scrutinizing it in his study in Fife House, as if the very paper on which it was inscribed were toxic, Lord Liverpool had difficulty convincing himself that the note was the work of rational men, and, considering it further, he fumed and trembled at the thought of its implications. Taking up his pen, he began to compose a warning to Castlereagh. He thought it "very material," he wrote, that the British government should assume that the war with the United States "will probably now be of some duration." Confessing that he was "apprehensive" that some of Great Britain's allies were not "indisposed" to favor the United States, he warned Castlereagh to take care not to make enemies, especially not to further antagonize the Czar; for Walpole had reported "a most powerful party in Russia" prepared to support the Emperor if he rallied to the American cause.

On the same day, writing to Wellington of America's "extravagant doctrine . . . that they never will cede any part of their dominions, even though they shall have been conquered by their

enemies," the Prime Minister professed to believe that the United
States would find little sympathy in Europe. This contradiction
of his words to the Foreign Minister affirmed both Liverpool's
perplexity and his state of ignorance. About one thing, however,
he was sorrowfully certain. To continue the war would necessi-
tate floating a new loan, causing those who paid the property
tax to protest that they were being persecuted to secure a better
frontier for Canada. Yet Liverpool could see no other course.
All his government could do now was hope for the best and attempt "to gain a little more time before the negotiation is brought
to a close. . . ." Certainly the cabinet could not admit the American basis of "reciprocal restitution" of territory, *above all under
present circumstances.*" The reverberation of the bumbling deeds
of Prevost would not be stilled.

It was Bathurst's unenviable duty to bring the cabinet's decision to embrace indecision to the attention of the British commissioners. Praising Goulburn for not accepting the challenge to
break off, Bathurst attempted to explain the cryptic note which
the British commissioners were receiving. It had, he wrote, "two
Objects. First to gain time. We had rather that the rupture should
not form part of the King's Speech on the 8th. We shall discuss
it better afterwards—secondly we think the rupture should not,
if it can be help'd, appear to turn wholly on territorial acquisition."

So advised, the lonely and confused trio in Ghent called forth
their editorial prowess and created an uncertain something for
the members of "Bachelors' Hall." Saying they had delivered a
project in their last note (which had denied the need for a
project) and calling for an American counterproject, the British
commissioners closed their terse dispatch with the statement that
they had "no further demands to make, no other stipulations on
which they are instructed to insist, and they are empowered to
sign a treaty of peace forthwith, in conformity with those stated
in their former note." The negotiation had become a game of
reticence.

The American Project

It was on the afternoon of October 31 that the sixth British note reached its destination on the Rue des Champs, disrupting a monologue by John Quincy Adams. The document's contents, which had so pained the British ministers, scarcely caused the American commissioners to pause in their internal debate. They had been convinced by Britain's note of October 21 that the enemy had now firmly embraced delay and deceit as elements of national policy, and the new message, coming just ten days later, was but gratuitous corroboration. What the Americans did not perceive was the predicament in which the British government found itself. They saw only, and instead, an agonizing continuance of war and negotiation.

As a result of the news of Washington, Ghent was no longer comfortably isolated from the doings of the outside world. But compared to what the British cabinet knew and understood, the awareness of the American ministers was yet that of an insular tribe. Still burdened with the awful significance of Washington, the Americans failed to realize what Plattsburgh, Baltimore, and Fort Erie meant to them or, more importantly, what these repulses meant to the British. Thus, the five commissioners had no idea of the impact on the privy council of their note of October 24. *Uti possidetis* was a phrase—even if spoken *sotto voce* (and the Americans did not realize this was the way it was meant)— that to the Americans denoted cession, cruelly protracted at that. It was inconceivable to the Americans that the British might be desperate, stumbling—later, perhaps, if the Congress of Vienna resulted in a British upset and the ardor for war increased among the citizens of the United States. But at the end of October the men of "Bachelors' Hall" knew only that a compromise on the Indian demand had been followed by a British attempt to exact American territory. They suspected that one blow parried would be followed by another blow flung, in British hopes that eventually the Americans might collapse before the persistent scheming and stalling.

Except that their popularity in Ghent grew as that of the British diminished, the American commissioners found little to cheer them, and their fraternal dissension, while not as overtly acute at the end of the month as at the beginning, hovered just below the surface and ever threatened to build to a crescendo. The Shaler episode, absurd as it had been, had consumed weeks, and in the end neither note nor man was sent to either the French or Russian governments. Instead, Shaler was packed off to Paris to deliver dispatches to Crawford. In that city he prospered, a self-appointed undercover agent who gave expression to his observations and literary pretensions in long, rambling reports that were largely ignored by their recipients. Without him, Ghent was for a time quieter.

When Shaler or the latest British note was not the subject of discussion, the American commissioners, separately or as a body, were involved in a multitude of other social, political, or personal details. Crawford transmitted the offer of some French officers to enlist, for a bounty, a select corps for service in the United States. In the uncertain Anglo-American accord that followed the Indian compromise, the five men in Ghent hesitantly advised Crawford to put off the French officers for a few weeks and to do what he could in the meantime to talk them out of their desire for advances. On the matter of finances the Americans were particularly sensitive. Crawford's note on the volunteers only slightly preceded another from him, saying he could not obtain a loan for his government in Paris. Adams's and Gallatin's plea for $10,000,000 had previously been rejected by Willinks & Co. In both Amsterdam and Paris it was strongly hinted that a government that was in debt up to its ears and could not or would not defend its capital was not a very good risk. Unless, then, assistance took the form of paid volunteer troops, the United States could expect no direct help from Europe.

Throughout the month Beasley kept up a barrage of tidings from London. Usually the first American in Europe to receive news of the war, he was quick, although not always as quick as the British commissioners, to pass on the information to the Americans in Ghent. On the 11th he wrote of the British occupation of part of Maine, of the destruction of the frigate *Adams*, of the probable success of the British at Fort Erie, and, dependent as he was on London newspapers, he repeated the rumor that Plattsburgh had been abandoned to Prevost. "It is generally considered here," he concluded, "that Peace will take place very soon. The idea is that we must submit."

The following day Beasley was comforted by the news that John Bull had "swallowed his demands 'tail-foremost'" and softened the Indian *sine qua non,* although it was an uneasy comfort. Having speculated heavily in tobacco, in the belief the war would be of long duration, he had visions of peace and empty pockets. Three days later he again reported that a treaty —he did not know whether it was a good or bad one—was still expected in London. He told also, however, of the anticipation of an attack on New York City. In another three days Beasley knew the truth of Plattsburgh and was thoroughly confused. "Peace," he said, was still the word of the hour, but it was uttered as British transports filled with troops. The next day the situation was clarified, for Beasley at least, and he wielded his pen to report the prevailing opinion that the British repulse at Plattsburgh meant continued war. Given more than a week to meditate, he became sure of the fact that peace was out of the question, although he watched nervously as the market, perversely, continued to drop.

In sum total, the news from Beasley and other correspondents was generally dismal and always confusing. Only the situation in Vienna appeared to hold promise, and the American commissioners knew much less about that than was known in the principal capitals of Europe. Their ignorance, indecision, suppositions, and gloom were spelled out in the public and private letters they sent to Monroe immediately after their blunt rejection of the British proposal of *uti possidetis.*

No official word had been dispatched to the administration since young George Dallas had sailed on the *John Adams* in September—partly because the British were slow to respond to requests for passports and more recently because the *Chauncey,* a private vessel on public business, was stubbornly held in port by its agent, who hoped to return to the United States with something more profitable than messages. Consequently, the commissioners were compelled to summarize the proceedings in the negotiation since the latter part of August. They had no trouble doing so, although they were sensitive to possible criticism when explaining their acceptance of the Indian ultimatum. They were agreed that an abrupt end to the peace talks no longer seemed likely, however distant and perhaps unobtainable in the end was the goal of their bargaining. They concluded also that Great Britain was waiting and pondering, watching to see what would happen in Vienna and the United States. Vaguely aware that Talleyrand had somehow disrupted the conversations in the Austrian capital, Adams and his colleagues warned Monroe that only if France continued on her disruptive course and if Americans fought as they had never fought before would England delay in vain. Not one of the American commissioners, however, not even Clay, was optimistic about his country's chances.

It was remarkable how fully, for once, the five men concurred. They differed not so much in conviction as in degree and, at that, not appreciably. Bayard and Adams thought the war and the negotiation might last another year and that the results would depend more on what happened in the United States than in Vienna. (Both, however, wavered in this latter opinion from week to week.) Clay and Gallatin were not certain of the war's duration and gave somewhat more prominence than did Adams and Bayard—at least in October—to events in Vienna. Clay stood alone in predicting that the British would back down on *uti possidetis* just as they had on the Indians, but he shared the group's belief that peace, at that time, appeared unobtainable. Russell adopted a little here and there from the opinions of each of the others, so that his thoughts, when he put them on paper, immediately opposed one another. All that was clear was that he, too, saw scant likelihood of an end to the war. Britain did not yet appear to have peace in mind.

That this was so was proved beyond an American doubt by the packet which Anthony St. John Baker brought to the Hôtel d'Alcantara on October 31. The British had given their terms, read the dispatch. They had nothing more to say. They insisted on an American project of the treaty. This the Americans had anticipated; they had been working on their project for two days.

It was Adams who had urged the mission he formally headed to concern itself with the model of a treaty, and it was he and Gallatin who assumed the chore of drafting such a project. Actually, Adams had not so much to overcome disagreement on the necessity of the task as lethargy and distaste for beginning it. None of the five men questioned the fact—after reading the British note of October 21—that the enemy would propose no more until an American project was a reality. If the negotiation was to be preserved, the Americans knew they had better act, and in such a way that a possible resulting rupture would be to their advantage. The commissioners realized only to a limited extent that British reticence allowed for American initiative. For the first time since the negotiation began, the American commission had an opportunity to establish at least part of the agenda. No one in Ghent—or for that matter in London—appreciated the scope of this opportunity.

The American reluctance to take the first step in designing the treaty sprang from an aversion composed of ignorance of possible gain and fear of possible internal division, that might be comparable in its own way to the schism that existed between the two countries. Whatever the Americans wrought, they could not avoid mention of the subjects the British had already raised, and one of these, at least, threatened to tear the commission asunder.

Impressment, neutral rights, indemnities were no longer topics of obligatory concern, although as electives they taxed political and patriotic judgment. Incumbent upon the American commissioners, however, was some reply to Britain's repeated disavowal of the American fisheries right which had been sanctified in the Treaty of 1783, a document which simultaneously guaranteed the navigation of the Mississippi to the British. Without mentioning the Mississippi, the British made clear that the fisheries "liberty" would not be restored except for a "suitable equivalent." Did this mean, then, that both privileges had been ended by the war, or neither, or just one or the other? If one

was renewed or assumed to be immutable would the same construction hold true for the other?

To complicate matters, each right was, in the United States, a
vital sectional concern. The fisheries were important to New
England, that nest of Federalists and possible secessionists, and
important too, therefore, to John Quincy Adams, whose father
had originally wrested acknowledgment of the privilege from
the British, and important also, now and then, to Jonathan
Russell, whose allegiance, however, was more ego- than rock-
bound. The West of Henry Clay, on the other hand, the region
that had fostered and contributed most to the War of 1812, did
not and would not take kindly to Englishmen on the Mississippi,
a river that was of far more consequence to Americans in 1814
than in 1783.

Furthermore, the principal antagonists, Clay and Adams, who
by a quirk of fate had adjoining rooms, were growing ever
further apart. Not only were there extensive political differences,
but Clay gambled, enjoyed foul cigars, did much to increase
the landlord's corkage profits, and reputedly gave vain chase
to a resistant chambermaid. He emptied his room of card
players and went to bed as the sun and John Quincy Adams
rose. At five in the morning the latter began his daily study
of the Bible. He then wrote letters and read until breakfast at
nine. When the day's meetings and miscellaneous occupations
were over, he joined the others at a four o'clock dinner and
suffered through two or more hours of cigar stink, bad wine, and
desultory conversation. Most evenings he took solitary walks
about the city. He walked alone, he wrote his wife, because
no one else would go with him. He was in bed by nine.

By late October the three-storied house on the Rue des
Champs resembled an isolated boarding school during the winter
term. Its occupants, not just Clay and Adams, were tired of
one another's company, depressed by the plight of their country,
and numb from British diplomatic attacks. In this oppressive
atmosphere, on October 30, the day before the receipt of the
British note insisting on an American project, Gallatin submitted his draft of the project to the scrutiny of his colleagues.
Russell missed the meeting altogether and Clay arrived near
the end of the session, but not so late that he overlooked Gallatin's proposal that both the fisheries and the Mississippi rights

be renewed. Vehemently, the Kentuckian made known his opposition to reviving British navigation of the Mississippi and
said he saw no reason to mention the fisheries at all. Bayard
and Gallatin exerted themselves to calm him. Adams, though he
condescendingly noted Clay's intemperance, spoke not a word.
The next day Clay still showed signs of "losing his temper and
growing peevish and fractious" (Adams's report), but the arrival
of the British note and London newspapers brought a temporary
moratorium.

The truce was brief. On Tuesday Clay greeted November by
decrying the folly of swapping navigation of a great river for the
prerogative of "drying fish upon a desert." The remark was not
lost upon Adams, but that gentleman prided himself that "I
have hitherto taken no part in this discussion, and wish to postpone it as long as possible."

The limits of possibility, however, extended no further than
Friday, the 4th. The morning meeting began with a strange reversal of positions. Adams had earlier proposed and Clay had
seconded the referral of the subject of impressment to a commission which would take up its duties after peace had been
signed. Clay now balked. He wanted an article on impressment
in the treaty project, and when the vote was taken Adams
denied his own stand and joined Clay and Russell in the majority. It was a minor miracle on the Rue des Champs but an exception to the day. In minutes Clay was once more alone and
vocal in his opposition to Gallatin's fisheries-Mississippi article,
saying that all the commissioners would, if Great Britain so insisted, sign a treaty that did not provide for the fisheries.
Adams, weakly echoed by Russell, made it known that this was
not so. The test came the following morning when Adams called
for a vote. He, Gallatin, and Bayard voted for Gallatin's resolution, but Russell, putting friend before section, made common
cause with Clay, and the latter, though in the minority, brought
the proceedings to a halt. He would not sign the treaty, he
said, if Gallatin's proposition were a part of it.

The next day was Sunday, not by scripture or practice a day
for commission meetings, so the struggle was not again renewed until Monday. On the morning of that day Clay appeared with the others in Adams's room, expansive and apologetic but still refusing to accept Gallatin's draft article. His

colleagues pleaded with him and suggested compromise, but Clay would not listen. He had, he eventually revealed, his own solution. He proposed that the fisheries right be regarded as a component of American independence, requiring, therefore, no more recognition in this negotiation than did independence itself. Adams, who had originally offered this view only to have it rejected by Clay, heard this with some astonishment. He promptly announced that, while he now favored Gallatin's recommendation, he was willing to accept the Clay, nee Adams, approach. Gallatin reminded everyone that the British had served notice that the privilege was ended and that they would, consequently, regard lack of American comment as tacit surrender, but the movement to appease Clay and complete the project swept Gallatin before it. As befitted his enlarging role as commission peacemaker, Bayard called for and obtained unanimity. The card player from Kentucky had trumped an incipient article and raked in four ministers.

The next two days were spent writing and revising the remaining articles and making attempts, which foundered, to bring the entire commission together in one place at one time. Bayard arrived at the meeting of the 8th in time to apologize to the others, who were by then departing. On the 9th the commission met in the afternoon, counted noses, and sent, in vain, to the Hôtel des Pays-Bas for Russell. Postponed until 10 P.M., after the theater, the meeting of bleary-eyed commissioners was still one Rhode Island nose short and was adjourned until the following morning. "A second day belated," noted Adams humorlessly.

Tardiness and absence alone did not explain Adams's acidity, for despite the delinquency of some, each member of the commission had found time to examine Adams's draft project, with the result that three-fourths of it had been excised. Resentfully, Adams spent the evening of the 9th restoring his manuscript to nearly pristine condition and went to the meeting on the 10th prepared to fight.

For some time that morning he found scant opportunity to do so. In fact, his offerings were greeted with almost enthusiastic receptiveness—save one paragraph which finally and emphatically drew a challenge, and that was John Quincy's suggestion that the American commission tender the principle of *status quo ante bellum* as an alternative to the project. At first, Adams's only ally was Gallatin. Clay responded to the proposition with disdain. The commissioners had not been so instructed, he said; furthermore, the moment was not ripe for such an overture. It was an offer to be made only as a last resort.

Rising to heights of unusual eloquence, Adams proclaimed that he would "cheerfully give my life for a peace on this basis." Taking heed of Clay's betting instincts, the commissioner from Massachusetts predicted that the British would not accept the proposal, that it would, therefore, be excellent propaganda in the event of a rupture, and, by contrast, make the demands of the American project seem less exorbitant. Gallatin cheered Adams's every phrase. Bayard, initially hesitant, took his cue from Gallatin. And Russell, feeling the chill breeze of near-isolation, asked a final tentative question: why was the alternative of *status quo ante bellum* better than the project? "I told him," Adams later recorded in his diary, "that the project offered all the knots of the negotiation for solution now, and the proposal was to make peace first, and leave them to be solved hereafter." Clay grumbled, threatened that he might not sign the final treaty, and said that the British would find Adams's creation more mirth-provoking than a team of music hall jugglers, but he voted the party ticket nevertheless. After dinner Hughes hastened to the Chartreux, a former monastery to which the British commissioners had moved, with the sixth American answer.

The note that accompanied the project offered restoration of the *status quo*—the importance of which no American commissioner, especially Adams, underestimated ("many ill consequences are expected from it, and if they should ensue, the whole responsibility of the measure will be brought to bear directly upon me")—said nothing of the Mississippi, and assumed openly that the fisheries right could not have been abrogated by the war. The message also briefly documented the historical precedents for some of the project's articles.

The American model of the "Treaty of peace and amity between His Britannic Majesty and the United States of America" began with an article that called for immediate cessation of hostilities and the mutual restoration of prisoners, territory, and public and private property and records—so worded as to include places such as Moose Island, a legalistic construction which the British were not likely to overlook. The second article outlined the timing of the cessation of hostilities once the treaty had been ratified.

Articles three, four, five, and six broached the appointment of commissions which would, after peace had been signed, determine, respectively, the boundary running through the Maine highlands and the Passamaquoddy Islands, the exact limits of the boundary stretching north and west from the Maine highlands to the St. Lawrence, the dividing line which cut through the St. Lawrence and the Great Lakes, and the international demarcation from Lake Superior to the Lake of the Woods—all disputes dating from the Treaty of 1783. Each side would appoint one commissioner, leaving a third to be chosen by the two appointees, by lot if necessary. Article seven stipulated the powers of the commissions and set up the procedures for handling their costs. It also more precisely defined the commissioners' duties.

The eighth article established the northwestern boundary as a line drawn from the northwestern point of the Lake of the Woods "due north or south, (as the case may be)" to the forty-ninth parallel and thence westward to the "Stony Mountains." No decision was to be made in this negotiation concerning the territory which lay beyond those mountains. The article neglected to mention and effectively prohibited British access to the Mississippi, as the representatives of that country soon discovered.

The Indian proposition was delineated, much as the British and American commissioners had already agreed, in article nine. The tenth article, however, really a trailer to the ninth, insisted that both powers should "restrain the Indians living within their respective dominions from committing hostilities against the territory, citizens, or subjects of the other party" and that neither should use the Indians in any future wars between them.

From the tenth article on, in fact, were proposals almost certain to incur considerable British displeasure. Article eleven, Clay's belated bid to make true the promise of his 1812 speeches, embraced the temporary prohibition of impressment. Twelve was an attempt to restrict the British in their use of blockades.

Thirteen demanded indemnity "to the citizens of the United States for all losses and damage sustained by them during the late war between Great Britain and France, and prior to the commencement of the present war by reason of irregular or illegal captures, seizures, or condemnations of vessels and other property, under color of authority contrary to the known and established rules of the law of nations." Fourteen granted amnesty to those on either side who had aided the enemy, a proposal of sweeping proportions which, however, lost some of its benevolence when one considered the number of Americans who might be covered by it and who, because of their numbers, could not be prosecuted in any case. With article fifteen the project returned to the humdrum subject of ratifications and came to its close.

Christopher Hughes delivered the note and project as the British commissioners were heading for bed. Annoyed at being disturbed at such an unseemly hour, Henry Goulburn nevertheless sat by candlelight, reading himself into a state of even less composure. The American pretensions were, he thought, "extravagant" beyond belief. If, he later wrote Bathurst, the items of the American project were to be answered one by one volumes would be required. He suggested, instead, that the Americans be told that the treaty "must be decided entirely in favour of Great Britain." So far as the British commissioners were concerned, the Americans still could and should be firmly dealt with. It remained to be seen, however, whether a similar attitude prevailed in London.

England in Trouble

The American project crossed the Channel to a London that was shrouded, like hot coals in a cold rain, in a steaming fog of dejection, and on Sunday, November 13, Lord Liverpool sat brooding in Fife House—the American treaty draft and two letters from Wellington before him. From Ghent had come a studied insult, the product of beggars who did not know their own poverty, and from Paris, where Wellington, savior of England, was now minister to France, came an icy gust of candor. "You can get no territory;" wrote the victor of Salamanca, "indeed the state of your military operations, however creditable, does not entitle you to demand any; and you only afford the Americans a popular and creditable ground, which I believe their government are looking for, not to break off the negotiations, but to avoid to make peace." If the cabinet insisted, the Duke would, next year, go to America, where "I shall do you but little good;" for British claims rested with British sailors on the bottom of Plattsburgh Bay.

The piquant notion of involving Wellington in the American fracas had its genesis in an otherwise uninspired cabinet meeting of November 3. The day before, still angry over the American note of October 24 but sobered more and more by his nation's flourishing problems, Liverpool wrote to Castlereagh that he saw "little prospect" of the talks in Ghent "ending in peace." That he fervently wished for such a prospect, however, was not to be denied. He added up the mounting costs and the oppressive taxes, thought of the Whig reaction in Parliament when the members of that party learned more of financial matters and events in Vienna, France, the United States, and Ghent—and shuddered. Obviously the meeting on the 3rd would have to produce an antidote, at least one that would bring relief from the festering situation in and with England's former colonies.

It was Wellington himself who brought to fruition an idea that had already been conceived in the distraught minds of the members of the privy council. Patently furious over Prevost's mishandling of the proud regiments of the Peninsular campaign, the Duke released his ire in letters to Liverpool and Bathurst and more than hinted at what he might have done had he been in command. His letters told also of French ecstasy over Plattsburgh and of French sympathy for the doings of Americans in general, but of more vital import was the weight his messages added to numerous other reports saying that France was ripe for revolution. In Paris, men spat at fat Louis, yearned for Bonaparte, and took delight in the thought of Wellington dangling from a lamppost. Not insensitive to the evil that was brewing and no latecomer to the arts of self-appreciation and self-preservation, the Duke reminded the cabinet: "I *must* not be lost!" To the anguished men in London it soon seemed clear that Wellington must be adroitly and quickly removed from his post. And what better excuse than to send him to America where he could make peace or war as he saw fit?

So the cabinet reasoned in its momentous conclave of November 3, and on the next day, as Clay and Adams in Ghent were alternately joined and divided over their own problems, Liverpool transmitted the cabinet's decision to Castlereagh and Wellington. In his letter to the former, the Prime Minister's concern for Wellington's safety and his relief over the proposed Siamese solution were evident. "I feel most anxious . . . ," he wrote, "that he [Wellington] should accept the command in America." Such a step would give Britain the "best chance of peace" and "will in itself be sufficient to obviate many difficulties and much embarrassment at home." To the Duke, Liverpool had much the same to say, but he added also, with apparent consideration and respect, that England had no right to ask more than she already had of her hero—who should ignore the request if it were repugnant to him. Liverpool felt he could afford to be magnanimous. Wellington had generously tipped his hand, and at the moment Liverpool was writing to him, the Duke, referring to the attitude of the British public toward America, was penning to Bathurst: "I suspect they will never be quiet til I shall go there." He added, though, that he did not see how he could be spared until March or April.

While waiting for Wellington's reply to the overture of November 4, Liverpool had ample time to reflect on the troubles that plagued him and his nation. From every corner of the country came the rumble of complaint over excessive taxation, especially over the ruinous property tax, and, with Parliament in session, the distant thunder would shortly be transformed into clashing cymbals, expressing the annoyance and demands of Whigs and Tories alike. Yet the American war and the threat of a new European war called for ever-increasing expenditures, and even in November the budget was as stretched as a tendon in a slaughtered lamb hung to dry.

Depressing and frightening as was the news from France, the situation in Vienna was even more so. With little encouragement from the cabinet and with no support whatsoever from the British public, Castlereagh continued his attempts to wrest Poland from the Czar's grasp and to secure the balance of power in Europe. But though Castlereagh beseeched and threatened, Alexander danced, smiled, and continued to desire and occupy the territory that Castlereagh had forbidden him to possess. To the Emperor the restoration of a Polish nation, free and democratic under his restraining and autocratic hand, was the fulfillment of a dream both utopian and practical. To Castlereagh it was deceit and an immediate menace to European stability.

All else failing, the English Foreign Minister, as subtly as he could, threatened war. Barely pausing in his spin about the dance floor, the Czar reminded Castlereagh that there were 120,000 Russian troops in Poland. Nesselrode, next to be approached, outdid his master by announcing the existence of 600,000 armed Russians in and near Poland. But undaunted by Russian boasts and obstinacy, deaf to pleas from the privy council, Castlereagh persevered in his efforts. By November 4 he, Metternich, his partner in the use of the remodeled weapon of intrigue, and Metternich's mistresses, sometime shared by Alexander, had Europe trembling before a canyon of catastrophe.

Of Vienna, of Ghent, of France, of the American war the

ordinary Englishman knew little, but he sensed enough to become anxious and displeased. His concern began to show. George Milligan, Bayard's occasional secretary, fresh from a prolonged trip to Scotland and Ireland, arrived in the British capital on the evening of November 9. It took him but a few hours to gauge, somewhat incorrectly, the mood of London and to write of it to Bayard. "The ministry it is believed will not be disposed to terminate the contest before making an effort to retrieve their disgrace, but the people now began to call as loudly for peace, as six weeks ago they did for the continuance of hostilities." Milligan had no conception of how far in advance of the people was the ministry.

It was with singular impatience that the Prime Minister waited for word from both Paris and Ghent. Wellington replied to the cabinet's overture as soon as he received it, November 7, saying he had no "disinclination to undertake the American concern" but did not think the time was ripe for him to leave Europe. Liverpool did not know if the Duke had said yes or no. By Sunday, the 13th, his doubts were extinguished—as were his hopes. "You cannot," read Wellington's letter of the 9th, which had come that morning, "in my opinion, at this moment decide upon sending me to America," for if anything happened on the Continent "there is nobody but myself in whom either yourselves or the country or your Allies, would feel any confidence. . . ."

Had Wellington concluded at that point the blow to the cabinet would have been severe enough, but, confident in his political and military wisdom, the Duke went on. He again castigated Prevost, but he made clear also that even he, England's resplendent military genius, could not obtain victory in the area of the lakes without the benefit of naval control. "The question is, whether we can acquire this naval superiority on the Lakes. If we can't, I shall do you but little good in America; and I shall go there only to prove the truth of Prevost's defense, and to sign a peace which might as well be signed now." Liverpool responded immediately, feebly begging the Duke to reconsider, half-promising him naval control on *some* of the lakes. But he was not persuaded of a favorable answer. He knew, although he tried not to believe, that the privy council's splendid contrivance had been aborted. He knew, too, that a negotiated peace with the United States was all that was now possible and that it could not for long be delayed.

The American project and note and the proposed answer of the British commissioners arrived on that same Sunday. A few days after came word that Madison's administration had published its ministers' dispatches, records of the peace talks through the end of August. Accompanying notes and newspapers said Americans were enraged and united as they had not been in years. The House of Representatives had ordered ten thousand copies of the damning documents printed and circulated to the world. Liverpool, incensed, berated Madison for acting "most scandalously," but the American story of the early part of the negotiation, whether or not Liverpool thought it, too, was scandalous, was reprinted in London newspapers on Friday, the 18th. Now it was Englishmen who were appalled. The Whigs, decrying the British peace demands as absurd, leaped into the fray, aghast and delighted.

In the midst of all this, the Admiralty loosed a public blast at the Army for the latter's mistreatment and misuse of naval forces on Lakes Erie and Champlain. The distressing reports from Vienna and Paris continued to arrive. Castlereagh wrote that the future of Europe depended on the stand he was taking and he did not, therefore, intend to abandon it. The privy council, helpless to thwart the Foreign Minister's pertinacity, began to wonder, with some trepidation, how quickly it could recall its forces from America. From Paris, Wellington sent one dispatch after another concerning French unrest and the dangers he faced. He also volunteered more reasons for his refusal of the American assignment. If he went to America, he asked, wouldn't it "give ground for belief all over Europe that your affairs there are in a much worse situation than they really are?" Wouldn't it "be a triumph to the Americans and their friends here and elsewhere?"

In London, the triumph of America and her friends seemed sufficient as it was, and on Friday, the 18th, the cabinet once more assembled to devote itself to the transatlantic war. Its labors were to span most of the weekend, but after Friday afternoon its deliberations concerned only details. Britain's governing principle for the remainder of the negotiation, because of a confining lack of alternatives, was reached with depressing ease. Friday evening, a weary, harassed Robert Jenkinson, second Earl of Liverpool, relayed the privy council's intentions to the Foreign Minister, Viscount Castlereagh, in Vienna. "I think we have determined," wrote Liverpool, "if all other points can be satisfactorily settled, not to continue the war for the purpose of obtaining or securing any acquisition of territory. We have been led to this determination by the consideration of the unsatisfactory state of the negotiations at Vienna, and by that of the alarming situation of the interior of France. We have also been obliged to pay serious attention to the state of our finances. . . . Under such circumstances, it has appeared to us desirable to bring the American war if possible to a conclusion."

On Monday morning it fell to Henry Bathurst again to relay grievous news to the trio in Ghent. His repugnance for the task, the heartache he felt splotched his letter like inkblots. He began by verifying the obvious. "You will see by the Project & Instructions," he pointed out to Goulburn, "that we adopt the Status quo & do not renew the Question respecting the Fisheries." The British government, explained the Secretary, was sure the fisheries right was ended by the war, and her silence on the subject "does not necessarily abandon our right to prevent the Americans renewing this Privilege. Practically however it does, and we are all I think pretty well aware of it. We . . . are persuaded it is not an object, for which under the present circumstances we should continue the War—which we are so anxious to conclude. . . ."

As if the British commissioners might not realize it from his opening statement, Bathurst affirmed that *uti possidetis* was no longer thought to be a tenable proposition. Dizzied and sickened by the awfulness of this admission, he reached frantically for acceptable reasons, without worrying about the logic of their order. He mentioned British repulses, the American publication of the British demands, the expectation of new and "warlike" instructions to the American representatives from their government, the determination of the Admiralty to cast Plattsburgh adrift in a sea of rancor and publicity, and, almost as afterthoughts, the "very critical" conditions in France, the Czar's insatiable appetite for Poland, and the Duke of Wellington's unappealable conviction that Britain's demands exceeded her power to compel.

Finally, Bathurst attempted to cast a flicker of light into an otherwise dark and cheerless predicament. "Altho' our peace will not be very creditable compared with our Overture, yet it will be the best thing which can happen, particularly if it be soon concluded. I think it may prevent much mischief in Europe —at all Events better enable us to meet it. Next to your being able to conclude the Peace will be the breaking off, so as [to] make it clear how far we had determined to concede, while the American Pretensions as stated in their Projet shall remain unqualified." Sounding like John Quincy Adams in August, Bathurst had ended his dirge.

While the British government sought in vain for succor, their adversaries in Ghent sensed little of the forces that were working, often inadvertently, in their favor. Isolated from the mainstream, the Americans could not be sure in which direction the current flowed, but could only search the mists that rose above the current and obliterated it. In British newspapers and London rumor, so far as the residents of the Hôtel d'Alcantara were concerned, were reflected the deliberations of the privy council. On November 2, the day before the eventful meeting of the British cabinet, the London *Chronicle* predicted the announcement of a "total rupture" in the negotiation within two weeks. Reuben Beasley had already written that this belief prevailed in London. News followed that more redcoats were or soon would be traversing the Atlantic, and the Monday, the 14th, edition of the London *Courier* declared that peace seemed out of the question. Although political breezes from France and Vienna felt progressively more refreshing, they brought no real hint to Ghent of the storms that propelled them, and the thoughts and emotions of the five Americans were as confused and changeable as the November weather.

On the 15th of the month, certainly before Bathurst had risen from his bed, but on the same day, the British leader informed Goulburn that *uti possidetis* was no more. Adams, by light of candle and early dawn, inscribed glum and bitter words to Levett Harris in St. Petersburg. "Left . . . to struggle alone and friendless against the whole colossal power of Great Britain," he wrote, "fighting in reality against her for the cause of all Europe, with all Europe coldly looking on, . . . secretly wishing us success, and not doing so much as to cheer us in the strife—what could be expected from the first furies of this unequal conflict but disaster and discomfiture to us." A few minutes later he was busied with another letter to St. Petersburg, this time to his wife, with evident good humor and a show of wit that he usually hid as if it were an unseemly curse. He told Louisa that the other members of the commission, not he, rented a box at the theater.

The company is, for French players, without exception the worst I ever saw. There is but one tolerable actor, and not one actress in the whole troop. Occasionally they have had one good singer, male, but he had a figure like Sancho Panza, and one female, but she was sixty years old and had lost her teeth. Sometimes they bring out rope dancers and sometimes dancers without ropes, who are rambling about the country, and half fill the houses two or three nights; but the standards of the stage are the veriest histrionic rabble that my eyes ever beheld. . . . Some of us are very constant attendants. Mr. Gallatin and James never miss. They have become intimately acquainted with the whole troop. All our family have become in a manner domesticated behind the scenes, with a single exception. Who that is you may conjecture. I go to the theater about once a week, and have found no temptation to go oftener.

From despondence to deviltry within the space of an hour was unique even for Adams, but his November emotions, though they knew greater extremes, were not unlike those of his colleagues. Once again doomed to wait for the British to make a move, the Americans itched and idled—with more grace, however, and with, on the whole, a shade more confidence than in the past.

On Friday, November 18, as the British cabinet met in solemn session to make answer to the American note and project, the American commissioners entertained their British counterparts at dinner. It was a dull evening, in no degree brightened by the fact the Americans regarded the three Britishers as considerably less than true plenipotentiaries, a belief strengthened by the revelation that the one side knew no more of what was happening in London than did the other. The only relief was provided by Dr. Adams, who, at times, remarkably resembled the unlamented Lord Walpole. The doctor boasted that he had not been to a play in England for ten years and exposed the nature of his

cultural pleasures by describing "with ecstasies of astonishment
and delight the tricks that he had seen performed by an Indian
juggler" who balanced "straws upon his nose."

Dr. Adams and his colleagues were hardly more knowledge-
able when they met the American commissioners at a Ghent
social gathering nearly a week later. Bathurst's letters and instructions of the 21st had yet to arrive, and it was the Americans
who first informed the three Britishers of the publication of the
American dispatches in both the United States and England.
Gambier, astonished, showed unmistakable irritation for about
the first time since the peace talks had begun. Goulburn and Dr.
Adams, not ordinarily the most temperate of souls, regaled the
Americans with language that even earlier periods of duress had
failed to provoke, but the Americans were not by any means
apologetic and enjoyed giving the reasons for their government's
action. Both groups departed early from the festivities, the
Americans because word came that dispatches from America
awaited them at their house and the British because they had
nothing to celebrate. They were to have even less to celebrate
when on the following morning they, too, received a bundle
from home.

Back in their house soon after ten, the Americans eagerly inspected the contents of the packet that had come from the
United States aboard the *Fingal* to Havre, been routed through
Crawford in Paris, and sent by him in the custody of William
Shaler. In addition to personal letters to the commissioners and
messages from members of the cabinet, there were three dispatches from Monroe—the first since Washington, Plattsburgh,
Baltimore, and Fort Erie had punctuated human folly and devotion—dated October 4, 6, and 19. All three said basically the
same things, the second and third serving primarily to update
each preceding note. British depredations, Monroe assured the
American envoys and himself, had "excited nothing of alarm or
apprehension for the ultimate result of the contest." Having so
easily disposed of British threats and attacks, the Secretary went
on to cite the wonderful and surprising accomplishments of
American arms. He acknowledged signs of invasion along
America's southern coast, bearing out Gallatin's warnings of
danger to New Orleans, but he proudly related Andrew Jackson's
victories over the British-inspired Indians and affirmed his trust

in the will and ability to resist of the general and an aroused citizenry.

Turning to the commissioners, Monroe lauded them for their efforts and, remarking on the decisive effects of their published dispatches, sent them printed copies of same to "usefully" distribute throughout Europe. On the whole, Monroe was chatty and cheerful. He had, however, one alteration to make in the commissioners' instructions. Despite a revival of patriotism and military prowess in Americans, the country was unswerving, he said, in its desire for peace. And since European struggles no longer threatened America's maritime affairs, the administration was authorizing the commissioners to make the *status quo ante bellum* the basis of the treaty. "This change of our ultimatum" somewhat belied the Secretary's description of his nation's ascending position, but it answered Gallatin's plea of five months earlier, and it justified Adams for taking what he thought was his lonely stand. For once in the two and one-half years of the war's duration Madison's government had come to grips with reality. It had finally set out to obtain that which was obtainable.

Other letters in the pouch ferried by the *Fingal* brought news of changes in the cabinet. Monroe, while still remaining Secretary of State, had formally assumed his on-again, off-again role as Secretary of War. The inept Campbell had been eased out of the Treasury and replaced by A. J. Dallas, father of George, the commission's ex-messenger, and friend of Albert Gallatin, whose political enemies he shared and suffered from. As they had ousted Gallatin from the Treasury, these same opponents had, until now, kept Dallas from assuming the office. As the war appeared to be nearing its end and as the cabinet had less influence on the war itself or the negotiation that might end it, that body was allowed to become and became more competent. Thus does blind faction, thought by so many to be a necessary blessing and free expression of democracy, so often work its wonders.

That such political intransigence was not dead was borne out in private letters to the commissioners, especially those which came to John Quincy Adams. On October 17 the legislature of Massachusetts had issued a call for a convention of New England states to be held at Hartford, Connecticut, on December 15—for the purpose of reforming or rejecting the Union as it then existed. The same day on which this invitation was announced,

the first of the dispatches from Ghent, telling of British claims
to no inconsiderable portion of New England, were published
in that area's newspapers. Moderate Federalists paused, but
the irreconcilables, so abundant in state and federal legislatures,
like children in a senseless tantrum, persevered in their efforts to
destroy everything in sight, flattering themselves as they tried
to do so for their generous quantities of wisdom and patience.
The news left Adams more isolated than ever and in the position
of attempting to preserve for Massachusetts what that state and
some members of the American commission were apparently
willing to forgo.

Aside from the sad tale of Federalist New England, however, the reports from home were generally encouraging. Fired
by victory and the publication of the commissioners' dispatches
the American people, with the one exception of New England's
unknown capacity for mischief, finally seemed willing to fight.
The government, despite its whistling-in-the-dark praise of now
famous men and fortunate triumphs, appeared at last to have a
more genuine realization of its problems and possibilities. Thus
the commission had a virtually free hand to conclude its labors
as it saw fit—a welcome prerogative but one not without compli-
cating and trying responsibilities. More than ever, the commissioners would bear history's onus for their errors. Nevertheless,
the freedom to assume the diplomatic burden, which they had
previously been forced to usurp, was now granted to them and
was for that reason gladly accepted.

Spottier than the reports from home and less easy to assess
were tidings from European correspondents. Dealing without
restraint in the London rumor market, Reuben Beasley, during
the first weeks of November, swallowed and regurgitated the
same stories of rupture and continued war that filled the London
newspapers. The tone of his messages changed abruptly, though,
at the time of the London publication of the American commission's incendiary dispatches, when Beasley's more observant
informants noted the choleric condition of the highly placed
members of the British government. Beasley wrote then of the
opposition of Parliament and people to a continuance of the
income tax and gingerly ventured a guess that within six months
there might be a new cabinet.

From the opposite direction, from the city of soft shadows,

uneasy kings, and oft-removed paving stones came reports contradictory to one another in mood and portent. Shaler wrote and then carried in person excited accounts of approaching revolution and increasing French affection for the American cause. Not much of this, however, was apparent in the pages inscribed by William Harris Crawford. The minister anticipated little from Vienna. He reiterated that he could not obtain a French loan. He doubted Britain's good faith and intentions. Depressed by the prejudiced reports of Russell, he expressed fear that the American commission was retreating from its resolute stand. Having already informed the commission of his distaste for their agreement to the Indian ultimatum, he wrote in November to protest any deal that would exchange British navigation of the Mississippi for the American fisheries right. "I cannot conceive," he told Gallatin, "of one solitary reason which offers itself in favor of proposing the free navigation of the Mississippi" as an equivalent for the fisheries, and his words to Russell on the same subject were even stronger, providing that gentleman with a club to use in the debate that was fast approaching.

The dour outlook of Crawford, the nihilism of the extreme Federalists, the eternal bellicosity of the London newspapers did not in themselves obliterate the favorable signs that presented themselves to the five Americans as November grew older and its days shorter, but one letter from London, addressed to Gallatin on the 15th of the month, scattered the forces of optimism and lengthened the shadows of gloom. Writing with the same hint of inside knowledge that colored his letters on Russian mediation, Alexander Baring informed his old friend that the American account on the Baring bank was badly overdrawn. He would be happy, he said, to continue to honor all drafts of the American commissioners, but to continue to do so for the American government put him in the position of advancing money to the enemy—a position which a purist might have told Baring he had long occupied. Baring did not say he would refuse the drafts of the United States government, but he suggested only one means of ending his "anxiety." That, of course, was the signing of a peace treaty—the terms of which, the Americans felt sure, would follow hard on the heels of Baring's letter.

Gallatin answered on the 24th, advising Baring that he was both "grieved & surprised" and indirectly accusing the banker of a breach of promise. Nevertheless, Gallatin was worried and also apprehensive over the contents of Anthony St. John Baker's next delivery. The British statements normally followed seven to ten days after the receipt of each American note, yet the project had been sent fourteen days earlier, and still there was no sign of Britain's intentions. The Americans once more began to fear the worst.

The morning after Gallatin had composed his reply to Alexander Baring, Henry Goulburn received Bathurst's letters of November 21 and 22 and once more came into possession of the American draft of the treaty. Later, feeling much older than his thirty years, Goulburn slumped wearily into his desk chair and began his answer to Bathurst. "You know," he wrote bitterly, "that I was never much inclined to give way to the Americans: I am still less inclined to do so after the statement of our demands with which the negotiation opened, and which has in every point of view proved most unfortunate." He and his colleagues were directed to oppose most of the American project, to press for the navigation of the Mississippi and to stay silent on the fisheries— but *uti possidetis* was no longer possible and the ill wind from London smelled of even further compromise.

Following Bathurst's instructions, the three British commissioners worked through Friday and Saturday, the 25th and 26th. Confining their comments to the margin of the American draft, they thinned out and weeded what they and their superiors considered to be American duplicity and prolixity. The first article, which the Americans had phrased to restore "persons or places . . . taken by either party," was amended to read "places . . . belonging to either party and taken by the other," thus effectively excepting Moose Island, the original ownership of which was contested. Distrusting the motives and behavior of the American Senate, the three envoys, in the second article, specified that the end of hostilities would take place after the "exchange of ratifications," not, as the deceitful Americans wished, "after the signing of this treaty."

The third through the seventh articles were restated to obtain greater fidelity (British) in the description of the uncertain boundaries, and there was to be one commissioner from each country, with reference, if need be, to "some friendly Sovereign or State"—not two commissioners who were to choose a third, as the Americans had proposed. "The fact is," Bathurst had written, "that if the Americans got a Majority, every thing would be decided against us . . . without any regard to justice or the appearance of it. If we gained the Majority they would find some excuse to break up the Commission. The neutral Sovereign may be adverse but would probably save appearances & more probably decide by compromising the differences."

The eighth article was almost completely restated. The northwestern boundary was to be "drawn due west from the Lake of the Woods, along forty-ninth parallel of north latitude . . . so far as the territories of the United States extend in that quarter . . ."—*not* "due north or south from the most northwestern point of the Lake of the Woods, until it shall intersect the forty-ninth parallel of north latitude, and from the point of such intersection due west . . . as far as the said respective territories extend in that quarter. . . ." Furthermore, the British were to have access "to the river Mississippi, with their goods, effects, and merchandise, and . . . His Britannic Majesty's subjects shall have and enjoy the free navigation of the said river." Thus stated, this latter part of the eighth article did not specifically acknowledge its paternity in the Treaty of 1783. Consequently, it implicitly disowned its half brother, the fisheries right, about which nothing, as Bathurst had directed, was said.

The ninth or Indian article, though subtly reworded by the Americans, was endorsed by the British. In fact, from the ninth through the fourteenth articles the British commissioners reduced their editing to a one-word marginal comment opposite each article. The ninth was "Approved." But beginning with article ten the word was "Inadmissible." Restraint of the Indians, temporary but renewable prohibition of impressment, restriction of blockades, payment by the British of indemnities, and mutual granting of amnesty were summarily rejected. Bathurst had suggested that the amnesty proposal be modified so as not to include seamen and Canadian rebels, who might when they heard of the article be inspired to rebel again, but the three commissioners decided that alternatives generally induced the

Americans to argue more vehemently. If the Americans really desired an amnesty article they could resubmit it.

On two other items Gambier, Adams, and Goulburn, lacking precise instructions, decided to be firm. They would insist, unless they were otherwise informed, on the British wording of the first article and therefore on British retention of the Passamaquoddy Islands, including that one named Moose. They would not, without positive instructions to the contrary, admit the American fisheries right. But these two subjects marked the limits of their independent pugnacity. They turned at last to the privy council's remaining and most important directive and sorrowfully and defensively addressed themselves to the Americans. "The undersigned have forborne to insist upon the basis of *uti possidetis*," they wrote, "to the advantage of which they consider their country fully entitled. But should this negotiation terminate in a way contrary to their hopes and just expectations, they must protest against any claim or demand being urged by the American Government in any future negotiation, in consequence of the facilities which His Majesty's Government have now shown themselves willing to afford to the speedy restoration of peace." So read the self-assuaging bluster of His Majesty's deflated diplomatic knights. On Sunday morning, the 27th, Baker reluctantly threaded the streets of Ghent toward the Rue des Champs, carrying the British note.

When the men in the house on the Rue des Champs had finished reading the British reactions to their project even Adams thought peace was "probable." The others were sure of it, and Clay wagered his life that the British earnestly desired a speedy conclusion to the war. The doubts that had begun in Russia and spanned more than a year of delay and frustration were, with the major obstacles to peace, cautiously put aside. But the paltry differences which remained, details that accentuated the sectionalism and sometimes the pettiness of American politics, loomed large.

Gallatin, to whom Baker had delivered his trust, took the documents to Adams's room about eleven in the morning of that cold November Sunday. Within an hour the entire commission was assembled, excitedly examining what Baker had brought and, with the exception of Adams, who struggled to maintain his customary gloom, congratulating one another on the success of their efforts in rejecting *uti possidetis*. No one was surprised, particularly annoyed, or depressed at the British vetoes to the articles on impressment, blockade, amnesty, and Indian supervision. These, in their conception, had been merely gestures, dutiful and politically astute nods in the direction of Monroe's earlier instructions and expressive only of abstract reverence for America's daydreams. These articles had no further existence as serious points in the negotiation. The questions of the Mississippi, the fisheries, and the Passamaquoddy Islands formed the chasm that split the Americans and were now all that basically separated the two commissions and their countries. On Sunday afternoon Gallatin retired to his room to attempt the impossible task of bridging all gaps and healing all wounds.

Gallatin's initial comments were ready by dawn on Monday, and from six to eleven that morning, Gallatin's draft was amended by each of the other commissioners in turn, beginning with Adams. While they so edited, like so many monks one by one picking up and varying a chant, Adrian Bentzon, functionary and son-in-law to John Jacob Astor, a living reminder that "Bachelors' Hall" had once been haunted, passed from Russell to Adams to Gallatin, searching for information that would speed a waiting ship from Canton, China, to his father-in-law's northwest outpost of Astoria, listening for a hint that would lead to speculative profits. Russell told him and William Shaler, who was also inquisitive, that the commission had agreed to secrecy. Asked who had proposed secrecy, Russell answered that this was part of the secret. Shaler, deeply offended, asked to go home, but Bentzon persevered. Adams met his probes with glacial silence, and Gallatin amiably advised him to put his request in writing. Bentzon did so, but just before the mission assembled for its 11 A.M. meeting, he departed for the hopefully more productive gossip of London.

The meeting, beginning an hour before noon, was destined to last until just before dinner, and the seed of its longevity was Clay's pronounced revulsion to Gallatin's suggestion of an equivalent American article on the fisheries for the British proposal assuring her Mississippi navigation. Clay paced the room, his arms pumping and flailing in spasms of anger, his fingers, when not fanning air currents, alternately rumpling and smooth-

ing his hair. The Mississippi, a flowing avenue of vast importance, he said, was to be bargained for a fisheries privilege of
"little or no value." It was absurd.

Gallatin calmly informed him that the fisheries were important
to the East, that to surrender the right would be to play into
the hands of the Federalists. Adams not so serenely echoed
Gallatin's comments and accused Clay of speaking under the
influence of "passion," adding that he would be ashamed to go
home if he gave up either the fisheries or Moose Island. Furthermore, he noted, Britain had made little use of her right in the
past and was forced to cross an expanse of American wilderness to reach the river.

Clay snorted. To help New England, he said, was to conciliate an enemy. He threatened that the West, too, might some-
day promote its sectionalism. For the benefit of Adams he con-
jured up a frightening picture of the British crossing the border,
escaping American duties, wandering without restraint through
American territory, trading with the Indians, inciting them to
violence—all on the way, or supposedly so, to the Mississippi.

By turns and sometimes in unison, Gallatin and Adams
pleaded and reasoned. Bayard, acting the savant, polished details and grandly philosophized, providing some relief to mounting tension with his solemn inanities. Quietly guarding his corner, mutely cursing Gallatin and damning Adams, memorizing
that which might kindle his and Clay's political futures, Russell
waited for the vote. It came with the wintry twilight. A majority—Adams, Bayard, and Gallatin—adopted the latter's resolution. Clay was incensed. Russell would never forget. He would,
eight years later, attempt to use the vote and its preceding arguments to ruin Adams's political career. He would, instead, with
the crushing assistance of his intended victim, destroy his own
prospects in politics and hasten the end of his life.

The next day Clay, with more grace than evidenced by his
protégé, penned his fury, re-examined his cards, and turned to
sweet persuasion. He calmly marshaled his arguments and tried,
with no little success, to make Adams the outcast. In self-
defense, Adams volunteered to compose a corollary to the
Mississippi proposition that would severely restrict British access to that river. Written by Adams and reworked by Gallatin,
to Adams's annoyance, the limiting clause was accepted on the

30th. During the same morning meeting on that last day in November, it was decided to reduce the indemnity article to cover only the first six months of the war, when the United States had granted a moratorium on the seizure of British ships without, as it later developed, a concomitant British equivalent, and it was agreed also, over Adams's protest, to say nothing about the sale of captured Negro slaves, since proof of such capture and sale was almost nonexistent. Again contrary to Adams's stand, the commission called on the British to set a date for a meeting. The American note was sent that afternoon. By that evening it had been decided that the next joint session would be the following day, Thursday, December 1, at the British Chartreux. It would be the first since August 19.

Peace seemed close—closer than it had for two disastrous years, since the palmy days of Hull's advance on Detroit. Yet the American ministers were anxious and uncertain. Britain had delayed before, changed her ground before. Now she remained obstinate on points which primarily concerned the disaffected part of a divided nation, on "objects . . . which we cannot yield," lamented Adams, who could least afford to yield them, "which . . . are in themselves so trifling and insignificant that neither of the two nations would tolerate a war for them. We have everything," he added, "but peace in our hands."

The Final Barriers

"This you must know is the season for giving one the blue devils," wrote Beasley to Russell on December 1. "There is nothing but fog and smoke in London." As Beasley so expressed himself, the five American commissioners were filing from their house on the Rue des Champs into the overcast but less sooty atmosphere of Ghent. Entering their waiting carriages shortly before noon, they were carried off toward the outskirts of Ghent and the grey bastions of the Chartreux. Within that aged structure they were to face three Britons and the enigma of peace.

At ten thirty that morning the Americans had met to rehearse their tactics and review their note of the previous day. That note briefly and grudgingly admitted most of the British vetoes of American articles but objected strenuously to British alterations in the first and eighth articles of the original treaty draft. In the former, the British phraseology of "belonging to one party and taken by the other," in reference to restoration of territory, clearly assured their continued possession of the Passamaquoddy Islands. The amended eighth article, if left unopposed, would maintain Britain's navigational lease on the Mississippi—while America's fisheries privilege remained unstated and unclarified. Rejecting both, the American commissioners were about to insist on their prior and rightful occupation of the islands and to orally submit Gallatin's proposal—contentiously adopted and unsuccessfully striving to preserve the fiction of the immutability of the Treaty of 1783—offering exchange of restricted access to the great river for the fisheries right; or they were ready to suggest that the eighth article be expunged. The remainder of

the American note harped on indemnities for America's unilateral observance of a six-month deferment on the in-port ship
seizures after the declaration of war, suggested a time limit for
post-treaty commission deliberations, and contested the lengthy
British-proposed intervals from treaty ratification to cessation of
high seas hostilities; but these latter, in comparison to the fisheries and the Passamaquoddy Islands, were minor points, intended more for the record than for serious debate.

The American note would have occasioned little controversy
had the British commission, after receiving Bathurst's note of
November 21, not assumed responsibility exceeding the privy
council's instructions and expectations. The cabinet, as Bathurst
had written to Goulburn, had virtually if silently acknowledged
the American right to the fisheries, but the three commissioners,
hungering for vindication and a moment of honor, replied that
they would not admit the fisheries right without "positive" instructions. On the heels of this decision came another letter from
Bathurst, dated November 22, which appeared to justify the
commission's stand. "Liverpool has taken an alarm," wrote Bathurst, "lest you should consider that passage in my private letter
to you which related to the fisheries as authorizing you to consent to a declaration that we did not insist on the right we
claimed of not renewing the Privilege of curing fish & fishing on
our coasts. I do not think you are so ready to concede any thing
without a clear order to do so. I believe the American Commissioners will be satisfied with being silent on the subject &
we have determined not to renew the discussion unless provok'd
to do so." He added, however, that "we are all prepared to
think that it is better *practically* to abandon it than persist in
the War."

Afterward, when the impoverished men in London had
learned of their agents' intentions, they acquiesced by saying
nothing further and waited to see what would happen. They
responded in the same manner to the trio's decision to fight for
the Passamaquoddy Islands. In fact, the cabinet took heart from
the flare which burned brightly and belatedly in Ghent. Nevertheless, they watched Vienna, Paris, the budget, and the calen-
dar. They could not forget the flames for the flare.

At the noon conference of December 1 at the Chartreux everyone was appropriately solemn. Gambier, a caricature of himself,

elegantly arrayed in his admiral's uniform, pomposity cloth-
ing his sincerity, welcomed the Americans as if to a new negotiation—mentioning, though, that prospects seemed better in this
fourth conference than in the last, more than three months ago.
No stranger to imposing utterances, Adams replied in lengthy
kind, stopping just short of liberty and Indians. Preliminaries
finally over, the two commissions settled down to discuss the
project, article by article.

For three hours, as servants fed the fire at the far end of
the long room, the arguments, their words fluttering the small
flames of the candelabra and losing themselves in the tapestried
walls, became increasingly virulent. Fearing that their government might not support them beyond this initial conference, the
British commissioners inclined toward desperation. Sitting across
from them, the Americans, internally divided, were not sure how
far they could press their stand without risking a rupture. As a
consequence, they considerably underestimated the strength of
their position or, more properly, the limitations of their opponents.

All lawyers by profession, save Gallatin, who was one of
political necessity, the Americans fashioned the better arguments and tricked and taunted their adversaries, but lacking a
jury of uncommitted peers, they were met by unconvinced,
sometimes hysterical obstinacy. The debate over the first article
and its implication of the continued British possession of the
Passamaquoddy Islands ended inconclusively, although Goulburn thought he noted signs that the Americans would eventually give way. The three men from London did agree, without
hesitation, to reword the third article so the disputed islands
would be among those problems to be settled by a postwar commission. Until such a commission reached its decision, however,
the British intended to sit where they were—on Moose Island,
a piece of Maine which, in turn, was part of Massachusetts, the
rebellious onetime constituency of John Quincy Adams.

On the matter of the length of the periods between the exchange of ratifications and the end of hostilities, the five representatives of the United States assented, at least temporarily,
to the British version. They concurred also in the enemy proposal for the composition of the commissions—one appointee

from each side, with reference if necessary to "a friendly sovereign." Bathurst, thus, was not denied.

After these concessions by the Americans, the conferees undertook to select sites for the commission meetings. Gallatin suggested St. Andrews, New Brunswick, and Albany, New York. Agreement was unanimous. Tranquillity pervaded the darkening room, and the logs crackled comfortingly in the fireplace. There was scant movement but the rustling of papers and the stifling of yawns when John Quincy Adams, without raising his voice, began a recital of the British edition of the eighth article —that which guaranteed continued British navigation of the Mississippi. His reading completed, Adams agreed that the British had this right from the Treaty of 1783. Was he to assume, he asked, as if a positive answer were anticipated, that British silence on the fisheries indicated their consent to this concurrent 1783 right of the Americans?

The three men across the table almost chorused "yes" before they awoke and roared "no." John Quincy appeared shocked. Logically, he pointed out that there was no need of an article for either or there was need of an article for both. Furthermore, the British should realize that their approach to the river must be through one point, where duties would be collected, and by one road. Certainly, Adams stated, if the British had unlimited access to the Mississippi, the Americans would naturally expect the same right to the St. Lawrence. The Britishers were enraged but speechless, and before they could find their voices, Gallatin had assumed the burden of attack. If the British, he said, thought a northwestern boundary of the forty-ninth degree of latitude was an equivalent for the Mississippi right, they were overestimating the boundary's importance to the United States. Wouldn't it be better just to strike out the eighth article?

At this, Adams recorded later, the British became "acrimonious." After a few moments of British babel, Goulburn's voice emerged predominant. Suggesting, but not openly stating, that by their proposal of right for right the Americans had compromised their position that the Treaty of 1783 was little less than eternal, Goulburn mentioned the possible importance of the Mississippi to the British in the future and emphasized that the determination and extension of the northwestern boundary was surely an equivalent for navigation of this river. In any

case, he added, the Americans had been informed of this demand in the first British note. Dr. Adams and Lord Gambier
were still nodding and assenting to the words of the speaker of
their house when Gallatin once more interjected that the setting
of the northwestern boundary did not represent a concession
to him or his colleagues. He reminded the British also that no
mention of the Mississippi had been made by them in their
note of September 21, which supposedly contained *all* their demands. No one answered him. Silence, momentarily, and stubbornness, more enduringly, ruled the room.

Into the sullen stillness marched John Quincy Adams with
the American proposal to waive all indemnity claims except
those which resulted from his nation's initial six months of
restraint. Fretting because they had not more obviously succeeded in defending their hold on the Mississippi and in quash-
ing the American pretension to the fisheries, the threesome was
immediately irate. "Dr. Adams . . . began by an argument, as
if he had been in Doctor's Commons." When the doctor lost a
point he muttered incomprehensibly and moved to another. His
colleagues soon joined him, but by and large it was Dr. Adams's
moment to justify the cabinet's precarious judgment in appoint-
ing him to the commission.

Bayard, late in the Englishman's oration, interrupted him and
started to say something about "restoration of . . ." "No,"
thundered Dr. Adams, "as to that, we shall not refer it to our
Government—we reject it at once!"

Bayard, when he could get a word in, said he was about to
say "territory" not "ships." Sheepishly, Dr. Adams agreed that
disagreements on territorial settlements could and would be
referred, but Goulburn added that if they were forced to ask
for new instructions they could not promise that their government would not "require something else." They could, though,
Goulburn said, sign a treaty then and there on the basis of their
present instructions. Clay dryly replied that he was sure they
could, and as the uproar over this comment died, the Americans straightened their papers and began to depart.

On the surface, the joint conference of December 1 was a
forensic victory for the Americans, but one that provided no
observable change in the attitude of either side. From this
session, however, one side gained hope, and the other emerged

more divided and undecided than ever. The three Britishers, besides believing that the Americans would give in on the Passamaquoddy Islands, concluded that these gentlemen would not press the remaining indemnity claims. The trio was less optimistic about preserving the Mississippi right and extinguishing that of the fisheries.

The Americans were not certain about anything. Accustomed to regarding their opponents as no more than London's parrots, they wondered at London's motives and feared a calamitous end to the negotiation. We duel with "an adversary who, after demanding empires as an indispensable preliminary, falls to playing pushpin for straws," wrote John Quincy Adams, but he noted also that the "straws" were serious barriers to peace.

The dispatches from the British commission, reporting on the joint conference of December 1, came to the dyspeptic members of the nearly bankrupt club on Downing Street like a chocolate *torte* after the rigors of a bland diet—not very nourishing, perhaps destined to be upsetting, but something to be savored nevertheless. France was still a smoldering volcano, with Wellington sitting inscrutable within its crater—although that exalted gentleman, if he could be persuaded, was soon to replace Castlereagh in Vienna. The latter, needed at home to reply to the incessant and voluminous chirping of the government's critics, insisted on clinging to his post in a city whose waltzes were conducted ever more to the beat of a martial drum. Thus Britain, though her problems remained acute, had done better in Ghent than she had expected to do. The cabinet, belching, decided to try for one more helping.

"You have managed very well to bring the business so near to a conclusion," confided Bathurst to Goulburn. "Your answer to the Commissioners at the conference, when they press'd for an Indemnity for the Ships detained in our Ports after the declaration of War, was very triumphant." It was an opinion not necessarily shared by either commission, but the statement gave Bathurst the will to ask his country's representatives to persist, for a while at least, in their obdurate efforts.

In the first article either the American wording could be restored, providing the Passamaquoddy Islands were specifically exempted, or the British version should remain intact, with the islands to be referred to one of the boundary commissions. Any alteration was acceptable so long as the islands stayed in British possession. "We do not mean that you are to break off the Treaty, if the alteration be not admitted, but we consider it as important as to the Object propos'd, & still more in giving a better colour to the Treaty itself. You will press it therefore to the very utmost."

Bathurst professed also to be quite pleased with what had taken place on the Mississippi-fisheries controversy. In effect, at least, the Americans had been forced to admit that the rights of 1783 were no longer valid. To obtain much more from the Americans, though, would probably seriously delay the signing of the peace. They were to be offered the proposal of negotiating each right in the future for a "fair equivalent." If this failed, the British commissioners could, if their opponents suggested it, accept the renunciation of both rights. Under no circumstances were they to agree to barter the Passamaquoddy Islands for the fisheries. "The Cabinet," said Bathurst, "are becoming much more unwilling to close the Treaty without some understanding on this subject, as they foresee the greatest Inconvenience from such a termination, now that our demands have been disclos'd. You will do your utmost therefore to bring the Commissioners to an Arrangement."

Having instructed the British plenipotentiaries to do their "utmost" in respect to the first and eighth articles, the Colonial Secretary contented himself with mere words of caution on other points. In the seventh article it was to be stated that in territory that eventually changed hands the only valid land grants would be those made up to the time of the treaty's ratification. The commissioners were to be on their guard against an attempt by the Americans to write off what they "mysteriously" called the "residue" of their indemnity charges—for British absorption of the advances made to American prisoners of war. In addition, the trio was to submit an article "for the more effective Abolition of the Slave Trade—to which the American Commissioners will of course consent. You will also propose an Article for keeping open the Courts of Justice in each Country for the Claims of both Nations." Bathurst paused and examined what he had written. Afraid that it might be misinterpreted as a challenge to undo most of the havoc wrought by

Prevost, he added a brief note of caution. "You must understand that we are as anxious as ever to bring the Treaty to a conclusion. Meetings are beginning to petition against the Income Tax—& we have difficulty in keeping the Manufacturers particularly at Birmingham quiet."

Bathurst's various instructions, firmer than those the cabinet might have composed two weeks earlier but implying, nevertheless, readiness to retreat if necessary on all points, arrived in Ghent on the 9th, and that evening Baker arranged with the Americans for a meeting on the morrow at the Hôtel d'Alcantara. That conference began promptly at noon on the 10th, with the Americans playing host. Again, the two commissions proceeded article by article, but in this session, unlike the one of December 1, there was little evidence of outward hostility. Each side, though, probed carefully for signs of weakness in the other, for gaps that would admit future assault.

On that Saturday afternoon, just as on the Thursday afternoon of more than a week before, the commissioners in their discussion of the first article and valid right to the Passamaquoddy Islands wasted their energies without achieving either solution or compromise. Debate on the eighth article was, of course, the most time-consuming and the least polite. Neither group would budge. Dr. Adams finally called a halt to the discursive futility by offering the privy council's most recent alternative. The Americans said only that they would consider it. Goulburn decided that it was "hopeless" to expect the Americans ever to renounce their fisheries right.

Contrary to Bathurst's expressed opinion, the Americans did not welcome the ensuing slave trade proposal, and they replied rather belligerently to the courts article. Both propositions impressed them as being unnecessary and examples of distrust of the maturity of a nation equally as sovereign as that of His Majesty. No final answer was given to either, although Goulburn felt sure the Americans would, in time, agree to the first. In two hours the meeting was over—adjourned until Monday, the 12th.

It was after the British commissioners left that the real debate in the house on the Rue des Champs began. It meandered through the rest of Saturday afternoon, broke out afresh at noon on Sunday, and reached a peak of bitterness and despair just before Sunday dinner. It left Adams in frightful, obstinate isolation and Clay in a raving froth. At its end, only one man, Adams, seriously wished to continue to contend for the Passamaquoddy Islands and the fisheries. Gallatin and Bayard favored token efforts, and Clay was alternately for and against everything. Russell, of course, was for whatever Clay wanted, insofar as he or anyone else could understand what Clay wanted.

It was the desertion of Gallatin and Bayard that hurt Adams the most. Gallatin no longer thought that he and his colleagues occupied a tenable position on either the first or the eighth article. At one point, angered by John Quincy, Gallatin said that it was "extraordinary" that the only real barriers to peace were Moose Island and the fisheries, subjects of interest to none save Federalist Massachusetts. Bayard, though a Federalist himself, agreed. He was for giving up on the islands and trying just once more to win out on the fisheries.

But it was Clay who astounded everyone—even, for a time, Russell. He cursed the traitors of Massachusetts, who at that very moment were traveling toward their convention at Hartford; he belittled the fisheries right; he lashed out at Adams, rebuking him for the obstinacy and absurdity of his stand. Then, just a few moments later, he was for defending every American right and proposition, for fighting three more years, for establishing American honor. Pausing in his tirade, he turned and slyly asked Adams if he knew how to play brag. John Quincy most surely did not. It is, instructed Clay, the art of "holding your hand, with a solemn and confident phiz. . . ." Adams, however, could not muster his "phiz."

Although not so accomplished, Adams was not wanting in tenacity. He reminded all of their instructions; he lectured Gallatin and Bayard on their responsibilities; he asked Clay and Bayard if Moose Island were a part of Kentucky or Delaware would *they* be willing to give it up? Bayard only laughed and said Delaware couldn't afford to give up anything. Clay scowled but was heedful of the point Adams had made. No one openly conceded to Adams, but neither did he relinquish his stubborn stand, and finally Gallatin, the only one who could truly unite and lead the group, tendered what he hoped was a solution. The Americans would insist that *status quo ante bellum* be made all-inclusive, even of the Treaty of 1783. This would insure the fisheries, also unfortunately the Mississippi, and probably the American claim to Moose Island. If accepted by the British, the proposal would do away with most of the remaining differences. Adams immediately proclaimed it a splendid idea, but Clay was of a different mind.

Leaping from his chair, Clay stomped about the room and swore mightily. He would not sign a treaty on this basis, "so help [him] God!" Nor, said Russell, would he. The proposal would, bellowed Clay, make the Indian article—an ultimatum which he angrily accused Adams of inducing him to sign—a more permanent and more powerful instrument than even the British had intended. He vowed that he would not even attend a joint conference on the subject. Neither would he, said Russell. "God help him" if he would, said Clay again, as Russell peered at the ceiling. Bayard and Gallatin were silent, and Adams, fuming, knew that Clay had won once more at the game of brag. There would be no offer of general *status quo ante bellum*—although eventually it was agreed that the commission would try anew to obtain the Passamaquoddy Islands and the fisheries. Adams and Clay, each in his own way, had prevailed.

Annoyed with one another, the Americans were in anything but a friendly mood when they journeyed to the Chartreux the next morning. The British, sensing that this was their last chance to win any laurels, were hardly more cheerful. Irate outbursts greeted the American Adams's opening statement that the United States could not even temporarily cede the Passamaquoddy Islands, part of the soverign state of Massachusetts. Dr. Adams whinnied as if he were having a fit, and Goulburn, with "a sort of convulsive agitation about him," "lost all control of his temper." For an hour the two commissions traded insults, charges, and claims. Suppressing their own disagreements, the Americans stood united, and it was Henry Clay, surprisingly enough, who raised the objection that the British attempt to hold on to the islands they had recently occupied by force was a violation of the principle of *status quo ante bellum*. But the three Britishers retorted to every thrust that Adams, Bayard, Clay, and Gallatin made. Finally, when Goulburn had finished an especially vehement reply, Lord Gambier, as calmly as he could, suggested they move on to another subject. Even then, Dr. Adams sput-

tered one last thought before giving ground to John Quincy
Adams, the Mississippi, and the fisheries.

As bluntly as he had begun the turmoil over the first article,
Adams announced that his commission could not accept any of
the British proposals to negotiate the two rights that had been
permanently decided, the Americans thought, by the Treaty of
1783. Painstakingly, Adams reviewed the history of the rights,
and at the conclusion of his speech, he proposed a new American solution—to lump the fisheries-Mississippi problem, un-
specified, with all "unadjusted" differences, for negotiation after
peace had been signed. A draft article so designed was handed
to the British. They read it, noted the word "commerce" in it,
and said it would not do. Gallatin hastily scratched out the
offending word. No, said Dr. Adams and Goulburn, it still would
not do.

Dr. Adams was sure that he could draw up a suitable alternative. He promptly attempted one. The Americans denounced it.
Next it was Bayard's turn. He, too, tried and failed. Soon each
one of them was writing and rejecting. Handed one of the
scribbled efforts, Goulburn read it and grew furious—until it
dawned on him that it was his own. Exasperated, Bayard demanded to know the British "object." Goulburn and Dr. Adams
explained that they acted on instructions from London and did
not know their government's object. It was the wrong thing to
say—the admission the Americans had been waiting to hear
since August, and they launched a concerted attack. Harried
unmercifully, the British requested a temporary adjournment
and left the room. When they returned, they asked the Americans for a written ultimatum on the subject—for reference to the
cabinet. John Quincy Adams smiled wanly. He was reminded
of the caricature of Lord Malmesbury. "My Lord, I hope your
Lordship is well this morning." "Indeed, Sir, I do not know, but
I will send a courier to my Court and inquire."

After a brief and less explosive discussion on the slave trade
and courts articles, the Americans withdrew and returned
glumly to "Bachelors' Hall." Riding home, Clay and Adams
argued over whether or not there would be a rupture. Adams
thought there might. Clay was sure there would not be. Bayard
made no comment on the possibility of a rupture but said he
considered the Passamaquoddy Islands a lost issue. Russell kept

his strange thoughts to himself, and, though pressed to do so, Gallatin refused to commit himself. He said he would "sleep upon it." That evening everyone but Adams went off to the municipal ball, where for the first time the band played "Hail Columbia." Sitting alone in his room, struggling with a draft answer to the British, Adams did not hear it.

For the next two days, Tuesday and Wednesday, December 13 and 14, the American commission labored to write what it knew might be its last note from Ghent to the British government. Unaware of the extent of the difficulties which faced Great Britain, of how far and how quickly the privy council could be pushed, the five men on the Rue des Champs were obsessed with the belief that there were no longer time or opportunity to maneuver, that they must accede to the British demands or present ultimata of their own. They were tired, unsure of British motives, and, with one another, no longer even briefly polite or considerate. After so much time and effort, they still might fail to fulfill even their reduced assignment, and if they did successfully negotiate a treaty, it would be, they were sure, a bad one. At that, it might not come in time to save their country from further distress and possible ruin.

On Tuesday morning the five of them gathered in Adams's room, where for two hours they struggled, like trackers through a dismal swamp, for some solid and common ground on the Passamaquoddy Islands and the fisheries. Clay favored holding out on both but also giving in on both if finally necessary. Adams wanted to press for each right, give in on the islands if need be, but never surrender the fisheries. Russell seemed to agree with Adams, although no one doubted that he would eventually follow Clay. The resolution of the issues, therefore, clearly rested with Bayard and Gallatin, both of whom indicated opposition to further effort to secure the islands and preference for only a token attempt to keep the fisheries.

For Gallatin, particularly, these were not easy decisions to make. He thought of himself and was still considered by the others as the commissioner closest to the administration and, consequently, as the one to be held most responsible for the results of the negotiation. Though he could not warm to Adams, he sympathized with him. More important, he realized that the disposition of trifles at this stage of the negotiation would excite

more political furor at home than would the dropping of the
supposed causes for which men had fought. Yet he could not
fully credit Monroe's reports of the government's political and
military revival. He feared Britain's power, whatever her problems, and the impending British attack on America's Gulf Coast.
And he could no longer overlook the tragic state of his nation's
finances. Three times in as many weeks he had heard from Alexander Baring, whose most recent letter estimated America's
outstanding debt to his bank at more than $200,000. This, as
Gallatin knew, was only a small part of the vast sum owed by
the United States. While he recognized the unsubtle purpose of
Baring's letters, he was unable to ignore the truth of the Englishman's accounts. It was high time, Gallatin concluded, to get out
of the war. To pay for peace with a few islands and the right
to dry fish did not seem exorbitant.

The meeting which had begun at eleven ended at one without
a hint of accomplishment. Adams, leaving his room and the
smoke of Clay's cigars behind him, went for a moody walk
along the canals. While counting his paces, he was met by
Bayard, and together the two of them traipsed through Ghent,
arguing over the Passamaquoddy Islands. Bayard was the nearest Adams had to a friend among the ministers, but now even
Bayard opposed him. The two returned to the house for another
commission session at three. That, like the earlier meeting,
made no progress and was adjourned in time to allow the commissioners to keep their engagement for dinner with the British.
At dinner, Lord Gambier unburdened himself to Clay of his
opinions on the Passamaquoddy Islands. Clay listened but made
no answer, and his silence was taken by both Goulburn and John
Quincy Adams as tacit assent.

On Wednesday, soon after the morning session began, it became obvious that Adams stood completely alone. Reluctantly,
he indicated his willingness to accept the futility of further argument with the British over the Passamaquoddy Islands, but he
vowed never to change his stand on the fisheries. Badgered by
all four of his colleagues, he only became more surly in his defiance. Russell, with growing hatred, observed his every word
and gesture and later told Clay that Adams was one who "adopts
the most extravagant opinions in the hectic of the moment, and
defends them with obstinacy and vehemence while the fever

lasts, and thus reduces himself to the miserable alternative of being constantly absurd or ridiculously inconsistent. . . ."

Absurd or not, Adams, through two and a half hours of violent debate, could not be moved. At last, he told the others that they should, as they desired, give up the fisheries and complete their note to the British, but that he would sign neither the note nor the resulting treaty. Perhaps he had learned to play brag. More likely, as his colleagues believed, he was serious. Exhausted, they acquiesced. They would make one more attempt to maintain the fisheries as an inalienable right, but, whatever their success, they would sign a treaty—with or without Adams.

At three thirty that afternoon they sent their note, complete with Adams's signature, to the British. The Passamaquoddy Islands could be excepted from the article on territorial restoration, but the conflicting claims must be settled soon after the war ended. Mention of the Mississippi and the fisheries was to be omitted from the treaty. These claims, too, would be decided after the war. That evening the note was on its way to London. The result, said Clay, would be a "damned bad treaty." No one disagreed, especially John Quincy Adams.

Christmas Eve

On Thursday afternoon, December 22, Adams paced determinedly through the streets of Ghent, as was his wont, fretting over the lack of word from London. Though it was scarcely more than a week since the American note had been sent to the British capital, he counted each day without answer as a step toward hell. "I have been since our last note," he wrote to Louisa, "in a state of peculiar anxiety . . . ," for if the British reply on the fisheries were adverse, he could not, as he had told his colleagues, sign the treaty. Ruminating over the sins and sorrows of virtue, to which he was peculiarly susceptible, he crisscrossed the canals, paused in front of the cathedral, and strode down a side street as if he, and only he, had been assigned the task of ascertaining that the block had not, since yesterday, been altered in length. When he reached the corner, he looked up and saw Bayard coming toward him, waving to gain his attention. Bayard, gasping from the same burning in his lungs that had crippled him the year before in St. Petersburg, that now marked the final months of his life, approached and blurted out his message. The British had accepted. Peace was but a detail. Adams stared at him, incredulous. Then together, at a slower pace for Bayard's benefit, the two men returned to "Bachelors' Hall," each thinking his thoughts in silence.

At seven thirty that evening the five commissioners gathered in Adams's room. They had already dispatched word to Bordeaux to alert the crew of the *Transit* for that ship's voyage home with a copy of the treaty. All that remained, it seemed, was to compose minor differences among themselves and with the British commissioners and to draft and sign the final copies of the treaty. Although no one was particularly pleased with the culmination of their labors, Adams, apparently the most adamant of the group, had that afternoon assured Gallatin of his acceptance of the British note. The commission appeared to be unanimous.

Gallatin, however, had not bothered to consult Clay. Now that peace was nearly upon them, Clay vividly and desperately recalled American hopes and his promises of 1812. He shuddered to realize that two and a half years of war were to be the age of a contest without glory, victory, or even a modest award of retribution. There would be no American territory of Canada, no guarantee of neutral rights, no indemnities, perhaps no ouster of the British from the Mississippi, and, worst of all, there had already been American surrender to a British ultimatum that protected the rights of savages. As a conclusion to a great and rightful undertaking, the peace about to be made seemed intolerable. Having disclosed his "ill humor" to Adams in the afternoon, Clay came to the meeting that evening with fire in his eyes and voice. He could count on two votes, his own and Russell's. He needed but one more to change the results of the negotiation.

As evening became night, Clay thrashed about Adams's room in an unending tirade. Gallatin and Bayard, surprised and then irritated, "appeared not to know where it was that Clay's shoe pinched him." The Kentuckian unsuccessfully tried for a postponement of the meeting. He next appealed for Adams's support, to John Quincy's perverse delight, and, this failing, talked of rupture. Mocking his colleagues, abusing them, he was again, vicariously and for a time, Speaker of the House, declaring a war of vengeance and patriotism. He was still chanting his wrath when Gallatin rose from his chair, looking as no one on the commission had ever seen him look, shaking with rage. For months he had been the principal author of the commission's notes. For the same length of time, turning its acid to humor, he had kept that group from dividing irreparably into its querulous parts. He had quietly offered suggestions, teased Adams out of some of his obstinacy, coddled Russell, and joked with Clay. Now his booming fury filled the room, stunned its occupants, and in its wake left silence. Clay, astonished, sulked but said no more, and Gallatin, regaining his composure, calmly proposed a

joint meeting with the British on the morrow. Russell—"I suppose," said Adams, "to avoid voting himself"—called for a vote
on the proposal. With only Clay openly against it, the motion
carried, and Hughes hastened from the house, hoping to reach
the Chartreux before the British went to bed.

Hughes found Lord Gambier, Dr. Adams, and Mr. Goulburn
very much awake, and they readily accepted his invitation to a
meeting the next day at the American house. Their last instructions had not been equivocal. Because they had attempted their
own answer to the American note of the 14th, that note and
their draft had not reached London until the morning of the 19th.
The cabinet, anticipating the American statement, had its reply
almost ready, and Bathurst completed the instructions to the
commission on the afternoon of the 19th. Two days later the
final instructions were received in Ghent and were delivered
early the next afternoon to the Americans. Now in the late evening of the 22nd the Americans responded. The British, having
so long denied peace, suddenly sought it with greed.

The session at noon on the 23rd, at the Hôtel d'Alcantara, was
not without rancor, but from the beginning neither side seriously
doubted its outcome. Each acceded to the petty whims of the
other. Slight changes in wording went unopposed. The British
gained their slave trade proposal; the Americans rejected the
courts article. Anger flared only over the British demand that re-
payment of the debts incurred by prisoners of war, advanced in
paper, be paid in specie. Gallatin pointed out that Great Britain
would, as a result, make a profit of ten to twelve per cent. Adams,
with an even higher estimate, fumed that this was an "artifice to
filch a profit of fifteen or twenty per cent." It was Henry Clay,
on this new day a veritable dove of peace, who calmed his colleagues and allowed the British their unjust due. At three the
conference ended amicably. Each commission was to make three
copies of the treaty to be signed at the Chartreux the next afternoon.

As the two commissions parted for the day, each was numb
with weariness and something approaching disbelief. Nearly
five months had passed since the negotiation had begun. A capital had been burned, a fleet sunk, armies routed. Men had died.
Thousands of words—some harsh, some anguished, some mis-

leading—had been exchanged. In Ghent men had argued, learned more about one another than they cared to know, than perhaps was good to know. Relieved at their accomplishment, they were nevertheless not proud of it—not then, at any rate. What they had wrought was less a peace treaty than an armistice. It said nothing about impressment, which was already becoming an archaic practice, nothing about neutral rights, which would never be respected to everyone's satisfaction, nothing about indemnities, nothing about the fisheries or the navigation of the Mississippi. Boundary problems, territorial claims, including those for the Passamaquoddy Islands—all other disputes were to be settled later by joint commissions. Only the Indians appeared to emerge with a positive guarantee of their prewar rights, although the ninth or Indian article really did nothing to assure these rights beyond the day of ratification. The treaty was hardly more than an instrument that served to end the war and restore the *status quo*.

That the treaty was not more than this was most resented by the leaders of the British government. The British commissioners, having flirted briefly with the heady labors of responsibility, were at the time of the conference of December 23 once more relegated to their lowly but comfortable roles as mere messengers, but their superiors shared a liability for the outcome of the negotiation which they could not easily shirk. Pleading an uncontrollable tide of lamentable events, the members of the cabinet sought consolation where they could. "You know how anxious I was that we should get out of this war as soon as we could do so with honour," wrote Liverpool to Canning, soon after the treaty had been signed. He went on to recite the influence of the Duke of Wellington, the limitations to the probable success of British arms in America, the uproar over the property tax, and the dangerous situations in France and Vienna. He claimed some pleasure from the fact that the Americans had been forced to forgo their insistence on maritime rights, from Britain's fulfillment of its debt to the Indians, and from the nonrestoration of America's commercial advantages. At best, it was a negative and impoverished joy that Liverpool felt, but he tried to convince himself that Great Britain had done all that was in its power to do. He never quite succeeded.

Bathurst, concentrating on near insignificance, did better.

"Our Passamaquoddy Article has ended very well," he confided
to Goulburn, "& our Indian Article reads *vastly well.*" This was,
though, about all that Bathurst could find to say about the treaty,
and neither he nor the others on the privy council could escape
what was perfectly obvious to Reuben Beasley and all of London. British pride, Beasley wrote to Russell, "has received a
deep wound. . . . The continuance of the American war & the
property tax when it was understood we did not insist on a surrender of their maritime rights would have been very difficult;
and any further disasters would have driven the present ministers out of office."

If only by contrast to the discomfiture and flimsy gratification
derived by the British from the treaty, the Americans in Ghent
should have been pleased with themselves, and, in truth, their
initial feelings of emptiness and disappointment soon gave way
to more positive reactions. No one of them reached the state in
which he could kick his heels in joy, but as each received the
plaudits of the citizens of Ghent and reflected on the real and
potential disasters to his country, he came to believe that the
commission had acted with some courage and wisdom. Even
Russell, when he was not using the treaty for political purposes,
could say "I believe we have done the best, or nearly the best,
which was practicable in existing circumstances."

Gallatin, Adams, Bayard, and Clay, more responsible than
Russell (in that order) for what had resulted in Ghent, were not
unrealistic about the document's defects but neither were they
unaware of its virtues. The peace "will make us to be courted as
much as we have been neglected by foreign governments," wrote
Gallatin to Monroe. "We have," Adams reported to his mother,
"abandoned no essential right, and if we have left everything
open for future controversy, we have at least secured to our
country the power at her own option to extinguish the war."
Clay, though he disclosed something of his biases, was remarkably philosophical in his letter to Monroe. "We lose no territory,
I think no honor. If we lose a particular liberty in the Fisheries,
on the one hand, (which may be doubted) we gain, on the
other, the exemption of the Navigation of the Mississippi from
British claims. We gain also the right of exemption from the
British practice of trading with the Indians. . . . Judged by another standard, the pretensions of the enemy at the opening of

the negotiation, the conditions of the peace certainly reflect no dishonor on us."

Indeed, they did not. For a country that was internally divided, militarily impotent, and nearly bankrupt, the good fortune of the peace treaty was remarkable. It was also a credit to her commissioners. Though it settled little, it soon elevated the sometimes absurd American democracy, as Gallatin predicted, to a new level of respect in European eyes, and it brought a delicate peace between Great Britain and the United States—a peace that was eventually to become a firm partnership. Fenians, explorers, Confederates, Maine potato farmers, New Brunswick roughnecks, rumrunners, tourists—all of these would, from time to time, disturb the tranquillity of the United States-Canadian border, but that boundary, despite these disturbances, would become the longest unguarded frontier in the world. And the two belligerents of 1812 would learn, through their joint commissions, a civilized way of reconciling at least some of their differences. This was to be the legacy of the document that was signed at Ghent on December 24, 1814.

Throughout the evening of the 23rd and the morning of the 24th the two commissions, in their respective houses, transcribed the final copies of the treaty and made out instructions to their secretaries and messengers who would be going to one capital or the other. Goulburn in the Chartreux wrote to Bathurst, and Adams in the Hôtel d'Alcantara wrote to Monroe. By Saturday afternoon everyone in both houses had finished his assignment —everyone, that is, save Clay, who still struggled with his copy of the treaty. The meeting was postponed an hour, and Clay's companions waited impatiently for him, wanting to go and be done with it.

At last, Clay was ready, and the five Americans went out and got into their carriages. Though the ground was bare, the air was crisp, hinting of the snow that had already spread a mantle over Vienna, and as the horses picked up speed, the cold swept around the lap blankets of the carriages' occupants. But to the five of them it was a cold of passing consequence— not the frigid, penetrating dampness of the Russian winter of the year before or the inescapable chill of a military camp in the valley of the St. Lawrence or by the shore of Lake Champlain—and the ride, though a short one through a small Flemish city, was the end of an odyssey that had begun in London in the autumn of 1812, stumbled through St. Petersburg, Gothenburg, Stockholm, Amsterdam, London again, and finally Ghent, where it faltered, raged, slept, raged anew, and was now to fulfill itself.

At four in the afternoon of that Christmas Eve the American commission arrived at the British Chartreux. In the courtyard, Baker's carriage stood ready for the dash to Ostend, where he would take ship for London. The British greeting was almost warm, and for two hours the three Englishmen and the five Americans pored over the treaty copies and made corrections. At six, with darkness spreading over Ghent and the carillon of St. Bavon pealing its Christmas message, the eight gentlemen gathered about the long table and officially attested to a "Treaty of Peace and Amity Between His Britannic Majesty and the United States of America." When all had signed, Lord Gambier presented the British copies to the Americans and said he hoped the treaty would be permanent. Adams, in turn, handed over the American copies and replied that the Americans, too, wished that this would be the last Anglo-American treaty of peace. And at six thirty the Americans disappeared into the solemn night with peace in their pockets.

Epilogue

Although the carriage taking Anthony St. John Baker and the brother of Lord Gambier to Ostend broke a wheel on its way to the port, the messengers reached that destination by midafternoon of Christmas Day and were in London less than twenty-four hours later. The cabinet and the Prince Regent immediately approved the treaty, which received formal British ratification on the 28th. Henry Carroll, Clay's secretary, reached the British capital a few days later, and together he and Baker sailed for America aboard the British sloop of war *Favorite* on January 2. Stepping ashore in New York on Saturday evening, February 11, they got to Washington the following Friday, three days after Christopher Hughes, who had sailed directly to Annapolis. Baker, to his surprise, found that the American Senate had already unanimously ratified the document, and shortly before midnight on the day of his arrival in Washington, he and Monroe, still the acting Secretary of State, exchanged ratifications. On the next day, February 18, President Madison proclaimed the treaty in effect.

The speed with which the treaty was ratified attested to its welcome on both sides of the Atlantic but gave no real hint as to the relative warmth of the reception in the two countries. The British government and those it governed were relieved but hardly pleased, and the announcement of the Prince Regent's ratification was met by violent denunciations in the London press. "We have retired from the combat with the stripes yet bleeding on our backs," said the London *Times* of December 30, "—with the recent defeats, at Plattsburgh, and on

Lake Champlain, unavenged. To make peace at such a moment
. . . betrays a deadness to the feelings of honour, and shows a
timidity of disposition, inviting further insult. . . ." Only in
Vienna, where the news came on New Year's Day, was the treaty
greeted with unadulterated British joy. "The news of the American peace came like a shot here," wrote Lord Apsley to Bathurst. It "has made an immense sensation," echoed Cooke, Castlereagh's aide from the Foreign Office; and the Foreign Minister,
using virtually the same words, was no less ecstatic. "It has
produced the greatest possible sensation here," he told Liverpool, "and will, I have no doubt, enter largely into the calcula-
tions of our opponents. It is a most auspicious and seasonable
event. I wish you joy of being released from the millstone of an
American war."

A release from crippling economic and diplomatic burdens
it most certainly was, and most of Britain soon came to realize
that this to them was the principal merit of the treaty. Ports
were once more wide open, goods became more plentiful, and
all of England's diplomatic and most of her military energies
could be focused on the unsettled European problems. Yet hostility toward the United States, which the treaty only made
more acute, was to linger interminably, and the savage scar left
by the treaty on British pride knew no balm, save the exasperating remedy of fading memories.

For a time, the British had hope of regenerating and healing
news of triumph from New Orleans or elsewhere along America's Gulf Coast. After the discouraging events of the autumn of
1814, the British leaders did not anticipate the results from such
an invasion which postwar American historians later imputed
—especially not after the Treaty of Ghent—but the privy council
was willing to let victory serve as a bludgeon if the Americans
were slow or reticent to ratify, and the British desired, without
question, any boost to morale that General Pakenham might
help create. The setbacks at Baltimore and Plattsburgh, the delays occasioned by Ross's death and the necessity of replacing
him and many of his troops had erased grander aspirations of
ascending the Mississippi and possibly creating a barrier to
America's westward expansion. It is a figment of historical
imagination to imply that the British cabinet still clung to these
expectations in the first months of 1815. Liverpool was not even

sure in December, 1814, whether Pakenham was heading for the Gulf or the Chesapeake. He did not really care. All that mattered was "that the American war should terminate with a brilliant success on our part." It was not to be. The tidings of Pakenham's death and defeat at New Orleans reached London on March 9, just as that capital learned that Napoleon Bonaparte was again on the loose in France. News of American ratification became a looked-for blessing. It came four days later, and the English, forgetting for a time their bruises, accepted the ratification gratefully.

In the United States there was never a doubt, from the moment Anthony St. John Baker landed in New York, as to how its citizens or leaders would react to the treaty. If Americans had never before truly known desperation, they experienced it in the weeks that immediately preceded knowledge of the outcome at Ghent. The administration was woefully short of funds and, worse yet, barren of ideas of how to raise any. In the War Department, Monroe struggled, with scant success, to enlist an army, and he was forced to entrust the defense of the Gulf Coast and the Mississippi to an uncouth ruffian from Tennessee, one named Andrew Jackson, an undeniable success as a butcher of Indians but an unknown quantity against the disciplined regiments of Wellington. As if this were not enough, the emissaries of the Federalist convention at Hartford were, in February, trudging toward Washington. The message they bore was not the harsh note of secession that had been feared, but they nevertheless came demanding an end to Madison's government. Meanwhile, the elected representatives of the people rediscovered their talents for absurdity and indecision. At times, Congress appeared to be Britain's best ally. Sober men feared the end of a united and democratic government.

Then came startling news. On February 4 Washington learned of Jackson's astonishing victory at New Orleans. The news spread north and west as fast as man and horse could carry it, and the nation was still joyously bewildered when Baker, Carroll, and Hughes debarked from their ships. In New York, when Baker and Carroll stepped ashore from the *Favorite*, they were engulfed by an inquisitive throng. Within minutes the city was hysterical. Cannon boomed in the Battery; bonfires suggested a conflagration; lines of people carrying torches threaded the narrow streets. The next day, Sunday, February 12, the news came to Philadelphia, as the inhabitants streamed from the churches, and soon excited hands tugged at church bells in a travesty of the Sabbath. And to rebellious Boston the word came on Monday. In an instant, pettiness and disunion gave way to happy delirium. Schools and shops were closed; the populace spilled into the streets in frenzied celebration; and, as in New York and Philadelphia, bells were rung until they split. Yet no one in any of these cities knew the details of the treaty. No one cared. It was sufficient that there was peace.

Hardly more attention was paid to the treaty articles in Washington. Madison first saw the document on the 14th, sent it to the Senate on the 15th, and received it back, ratified without a dissenting vote, on the 16th. On February 18th, the day after Monroe and Baker had exchanged ratifications, the President told Congress that the Treaty of Ghent was "highly honorable to the nation, and terminates, with peculiar felicity, a campaign signalized by the most brilliant successes." His exaggeration was not challenged. Scarcely a soul who had survived the war or the government's incapacity to govern doubted for a moment that Britain had been driven to the wall by American arms and negotiators. From the dregs of failure and privation came a symphony of success. Even the Federalists rejoiced, save those who had delivered the message of the Hartford Convention to Washington and slunk away in terror and dismay. "Who would not be an American?" asked Niles' *Weekly Register.* "Long live the republic! All hail! last asylum of oppressed humanity!" To save the nation, to end an unpopular, frustrating, embarrassing war had come a treaty of peace more popular in the country than any before or since.

That their efforts were being so well received at home was, of course, unknown to the five American commissioners until the end of March and only partially realized then. They soon knew, however, of the discomfiture of the English, and in a few days or weeks congratulations poured in from every European capital. Amsterdam, Copenhagen, Paris, and Stockholm relaxed in their remaining efforts to hide their American sympathies. Had not David again felled Goliath? Ghent, though its fondness

for the United States and its representatives was obvious, did
its utmost to preserve a show of impartiality. Nearly every evening until the middle of January both commissions were feted
at balls, banquets, concerts, or serenades. Sitting at one head
table after another, almost always under olive branches and
the flags of both nations, the commissioners soon began to
blanch when they heard the opening notes of "God Save the
King" or "Hail Columbia." But it was an experience that the
Americans, especially, would never forget. "I left the place,"
said Adams, the day after his departure form Ghent, "with such
recollections as I never carried from any other spot in Europe."

Once the treaty had been signed, good relations were more
easily restored with the three Englishmen than among the five
Americans themselves. Two days after Christmas Clay demanded that Adams surrender the commission's papers to him,
so that he could take them aboard the *Neptune* and eventually
deliver them to the State Department. Adams refused. The
struggle lasted for nearly two weeks and equaled in acrimony
any that had accompanied the negotiation. Clay's language became vile. Adams retaliated by threatening to report the entire
incident word for word. In the end, the papers remained in
Adams's possession. Clay soon forgot the episode, but his shadow,
Russell, kept it fresh in his intriguing memory, wondering
how best to make use of it.

In January the American commissioners moved from their
house on the Rue des Champs, back to the Hôtel des Pays-Bas.
What happened soon after attested to their enormous popularity in Ghent. Every stick of furniture in "Bachelors' Hall" and
some that was imported from elsewhere was put up for auction
by the landlords at "extravagant prices." "An old inkstand, which
was used at the conference, was sold for thirty francs, though
it was not worth as many sous. Even the furniture from the
British hotel was sold at our house, for the sake of putting it in
favor. The worst part of the joke was that they put off quantities
of bad wine, as if it had been ours. We did not leave a bottle
for sale." With such unique expressions of respect and more
genuine ones, the Americans found it difficult to say farewell
to the city, but in the last two weeks of the month they departed one by one. The Gallatins, father and son, went first to
Geneva and then to Paris. The others pursued more or less

direct routes to France's exciting and excitable capital, where
in February all were once more together.

From Paris, Clay and Gallatin, and later Adams, journeyed
to London to complete their assignment of drawing up a treaty
of commerce with Great Britain. Russell, forgoing this role, proceeded directly to his post in Stockholm. Bayard, too ill to fulfill any duties, spent his Paris sojourn in bed. In May he was
removed from there to Plymouth and placed aboard the *Neptune,* which on June 18 sailed for the United States. Six days
after the vessel reached Wilmington, on July 31, Bayard, forty-
eight years of age, was dead. At least he had reached his family
and home for whom and which he had so long yearned. His
old colleagues from Ghent mourned him sincerely.

Next to leave Europe were Gallatin and Clay, who departed
together from Liverpool on July 22. Gallatin, not long after his
arrival home, faced a multitude of future possibilities. John
Jacob Astor offered him a lucrative interest in his business enter-
prises. The Democratic organization in Philadelphia wanted to
run him for Congress. Madison, who had already offered him
the position of minister to France, requested his return as
Secretary of the Treasury. After much indecision, Gallatin finally
agreed in February of 1816 to accept the assignment in Paris.
From then on, though he continued to serve his adopted country
well, he was largely beyond the reach of those political currents which sweep men to fame and glory and the often un-
knowing reverence of posterity. He served as minister to France
for eight years, as minister to Great Britain for one—separating
the two assignments with a three-year interlude at home, during
which he reluctantly allowed himself to be placed in unsuc-
cessful contention, in 1824, for the Vice-Presidency of the
United States. When he returned from London for the last time,
he became president of the National Bank of New York and
later, president of the New-York Historical Society. Always
alert, he continued to study and write and serve a number of
causes and organizations until the end of his life. That end came
in 1849, when he was more than half way through his eighty-
eighth year. "I consider him," Adams had written soon after
the Treaty of Ghent had been signed, "as having contributed
the largest and most important share to the conclusion of the

peace. . . ." Though history has failed to record the fact, Albert Gallatin was one of the greatest Americans of his day.

As Gallatin for the most part withdrew from the brawls of partisan politics, his companion on the voyage home from Europe, Henry Clay, returned to that existence with, if possible, more vigor and ambition than before. Unlike Gallatin, Clay faced no dilemma as to his immediate occupation. Already re-elected to the House of Representatives, he was again chosen Speaker of that body and served without interruption until 1821. Dissatisfied with Monroe and his administration, Clay remained out of Congress for two years, but resumed his position as head of the House from 1823 to 1825. Offered cabinet and ministerial positions by both Madison and Monroe, Clay rejected them—for reasons which were never simple but primarily because he aspired to a far greater role. He wanted to be President, and that ambition remained with him as long as life itself. Three times he ran, and as many other times he waited expectantly in the wings. Though he became Secretary of State, though he served for the better part of two decades in the United States Senate, he never achieved the real goal of his dreams. Only death, which came to him at the age of seventy-five in 1852, shortly after he had fashioned the Compromise of 1850, precluded further attempts. Though he was not of the stature of Gallatin or Adams, his talents were many, and of the five Americans who labored through the latter half of 1814 in Ghent, Clay was the best known and most popular among the common people who made him a national figure.

Least known and eventually least popular of the five Americans was he who voluntarily and not too wisely attempted to serve Clay's—and thereby his own—interests. With his colleagues, Jonathan Russell journeyed from Ghent to Paris after the peace had been signed, but, rejecting his assignment to join Adams, Gallatin, and Clay in London in pursuit of a commercial treaty, he went from Paris to his ministerial post in Stockholm, where he remained until late in 1818. Returning to the United States, he settled in Massachusetts and sought his political fortune in that state. In 1821 he began his first and—as it was to turn out—his last term in Congress.

The Ghent negotiations influenced to some extent the careers of all the remaining commissioners, but Russell's perhaps more than the others. Possessed of an incredible, perverted memory and a caustic tongue, he poured his vitriolic recollections into letters to his friends and acquaintances, including Henry Clay. John Quincy Adams was "a kind of laborious pedant, without judgement enough to be useful, or taste sufficient to be admired." Gallatin "sought for peace as a financial expedient, and appeared still to tremble at the hollow groans of the Treasury, which, in its distress, he had abandoned." Only Bayard (dead, and therefore of no political importance) escaped Russell's post-treaty wrath.

Russell's most famous letter concerning the treaty was the one he addressed privately to Monroe from Paris on February 11, 1815. It was primarily a jaundiced and distorted version of the commission debates over the Mississippi-fisheries question. The principal villain and foe of Western interests, of course, was, according to him, John Quincy Adams.

Seven years later, in 1822, Adams, Clay, and William Crawford, the ex-minister to France, were potential candidates to succeed Monroe in the election of 1824—an election in which the West and the candidates' attitudes toward that section were to be of vital concern. From the floor of the House, a friend of Russell's demanded that Adams, then Monroe's Secretary of State, produce the Ghent documents, including Russell's letter. When Adams searched the archives and could not find the letter, Russell produced a "duplicate," which ascribed to Clay and Russell an uncanny ability to predict the course history had taken. It was at this juncture that Monroe discovered the original letter in his files. A mere glance showed Adams that Russell's "duplicate" was indeed based on a copy of the original but that its most salient points had been added just a few weeks before.

Informed of the discovery, Russell lost his grip on such reason as he had and wrote and had published a "triplicate," which differed in content from both the original and the "duplicate." Adams then published all three. Russell, with the help of his fast-vanishing friends, responded with a vituperative campaign in the press. Previously restrained by Monroe, Adams now grew furious. Working throughout the steaming Washington summer, he documented the whole controversy, including a word-by-word dissection of the three versions of Russell's letter, and privately published his exhaustive findings in September. At this, Russell's friends completely deserted him—among them Clay, whom Russell next attempted to smear. But Russell was finished, so much so that a new phrase, to "jonathanrussell" someone, *i.e.*, publicly destroy him, entered the language. Russell could no longer hurt anyone but himself, and when he died ten years later, in 1832, at the age of sixty, few mourned his passing. "He is gone to his account," wrote Adams at the time of Russell's death, "and is sufficiently punished in this world for his perfidy."

In 1815 the author of this damning obituary followed his colleagues to Paris, where he lingered for some time after the others had left, witnessing Napoleon's triumphal return and brief consolidation of power. Appointed minister to Great Britain, Adams eventually joined Gallatin and Clay in London and with them negotiated the commercial convention. He remained in England until 1817, when he was recalled to become Secretary of State.

For more than seven years Adams distinguished himself as one of America's foremost heads of foreign affairs, numbering among his achievements primary responsibility for the Monroe Doctrine. For nearly the same length of time, however, he was plagued by and involved in the machinations that marked the struggle to choose a successor to Monroe—a struggle that eventually caused the disintegration of the "era of good feelings." By political prominence, by accomplishment, by political pattern, Adams was destined for the Presidency. Changing times and his own unbending personality nearly obliterated that destiny and turned its rewards to ashes.

A taste of things to come was evidenced in the Adams-Russell controversy of 1822. The election of 1824 and its aftermath brought about a strange reunion of men who had been prominent in the final chapters of the War of 1812 and produced a bitter climax. Four men fought to obtain the office that Monroe was vacating: Andrew Jackson, the hero of New Orleans and the idol of the multiplying masses; John Quincy Adams; Henry Clay; and William Crawford, minister to France during the Ghent negotiation, whose initial Vice-Presidential running mate was the embarrassed Albert Gallatin. The results of that November's balloting gave Jackson the most electors and the greatest popular vote but not a majority of either. Adams, Crawford, who had suffered a stroke, and Clay followed, in that order. The decision thus passed to the House of Representatives, wherein Clay, who could scarcely tolerate Adams but detested Jackson, threw his weight on the side of his old colleague, making Adams the sixth and one of the least popular of United States Presidents. When Clay became Adams's Secretary of State nothing was added to the popularity or political chances of either, and in 1828, in one of the vilest of American political campaigns, both fell before Jackson's massive onslaught.

At the beginning of what for him and many Americans of his day was a major political revolution and demise in American political decency, Adams left the White House in 1829. Little more than two years later he was back in Washington, this time as a member of Congress from the Plymouth district of Massachusetts; and for more than sixteen consecutive years in the House of Representatives he served as the terrible-tempered and generally puritanical conscience of the nation—opposing the annexation of Texas, attacking slavery, finally obtaining the repeal of the gag rule. It was a glorious epoch for Adams, one that fittingly ended on the floor of the House, where, on February 21, 1848, he slumped over his desk, gripped by a fatal stroke. Two days later, in his eightieth year, he was dead. It was not just the end of a man; it was the passing of an institution. Never again was America to know a figure quite like him.

The post-Ghent stories of Britain's nominal representatives at the 1814 negotiation are simpler, for, with the exception of Goulburn, the English commissioners soon returned to that obscurity from which they had been momentarily lifted. Lord Gambier and Dr. Adams departed from Ghent on January 2. Goulburn remained somewhat longer to represent his country at the rash of celebration dinners. A few months after Goulburn's return to England, he and William Adams served on the commission that in July signed the commercial convention with John Quincy Adams, Clay, and Gallatin. By that time, Gambier had returned to the Admiralty, where he soon was granted the largely honorary rank of Admiral of the Fleet, but from Ghent on, despite his awesome title, he lived in virtual retirement until his death in 1833. His niche in British history is minute. Even less imposing is the slot carved by Dr. Adams.

Returning to his law practice, he enjoyed the modest distinction of being appointed to a commission to investigate British courts. He continued in his profession until 1825, when poor health induced him to become a country gentleman, which he remained until his death in 1851.

The remainder of Goulburn's biography, if hardly more exciting, is at least more noteworthy than those of his Ghent colleagues. Re-elected to a seat in Commons, he was rewarded for hard work and party loyalty by being named to the privy council in 1821. Further honor came when, in 1828, he became Chancellor of the Exchequer in Wellington's ministry—a post he again held under Peel, whom he also served as Home Secretary. No touches of greatness marked any of his doings, but he was always dependable and devoted. Probably few Englishmen have been more faithful to their country and its government. He died in 1856, after all the other Ghent commissioners, British and American.

Although the three British commissioners made little impact on history, in the negotiation, in fact, they rose considerably above their limitations. Third-rate commissioners by choice of the British cabinet, the three plenipotentiaries turned in a better than second-rate performance—for which their government had reason to be thankful.

Nevertheless, as John Quincy Adams pointed out, the British commissioners "were little more than a medium of communication between us and the British Privy Council." It was Castlereagh who created the grand design and Liverpool and Bathurst who struggled against the odds of fortune and their own limited imaginations to carry it out. They, far more than the pedestrian threesome, were the true British negotiators at Ghent.

Henry Bathurst, like Henry Goulburn, was a model of the higher echelon civil servant—uninspired but dependable. He had, though, the wisdom to appreciate many of Britain's military needs on the Continent, and his support of Wellington during the latter stages of the Napoleonic wars and during the Frenchman's brief revival in 1815 helped to disprove the generalization that bureaucrats are eternally mired in their own dross. For his comparatively enlightened acts, Bathurst, in 1817, was made a Knight of the Garter. The rest of his public service was routine but not altogether undistinguished. He continued in his post under Liverpool, and from 1828 to 1830, in Wellington's cabinet, served as President of the Council. His bland but useful spirit ceased its mortal existence in 1834, in Bathurst's seventy-second year.

Liverpool's nature and talents were not far different from those of Bathurst. As Prime Minister he was plodding and generally lacking in acute perception, but his ministry, though often threatened, lasted for fifteen years. Bonaparte twice shivered England's foundations; the Prince Regent gained notoriety as clown prince of bedroom and salon; violent social unrest gripped the nation's vitals; and Britain was time and again threatened with economic doom—but somehow, without any real understanding of the occurrences of his time, Liverpool, his government, and the nation survived. His was a remarkable example of how effective perseverance and ignorance, in combination, can sometimes be against danger. It was a stroke, rather than enemies or political misfortunes, both of which he had in plenty, that forced his resignation in 1827. Still residing in Fife House, he died at the age of fifty-eight in December, 1828.

If genius played any part in Liverpool's cabinet it was in the person of Robert Stewart, Viscount Castlereagh, who, had the Congress of Vienna not so thoroughly distracted him, might have brought about a far different result in Ghent. As it was, he outwitted or outlasted the Czar—it is difficult to decide which—saved England and perhaps all Europe, and returned home in 1815 to stave off successfully the attacks of opposition critics. Insofar as Liverpool's government had a foreign policy it was that of Castlereagh, and it was he, too, who bore the brunt of the cabinet's shortsighted domestic policies. Because he provided what little creative impetus the government had, he was forced also to pay the penalty for his colleagues' pitiful and prejudiced actions. Liverpool, seldom overly disturbed by his problems, survived. Castlereagh, who more than any other man enabled Liverpool to survive, declined physically, emotionally, and politically. In 1815 he was, after Wellington, Britain's hero. In 1820, having lost both his popularity and his senses, he was hooted at in the streets. From the latter year on he was little more than a shadow of a man, as the virulence of his insanity increased. In August, 1822, his doctor confined him to his country home and confiscated his razor, but Castlereagh, who had secreted his penknife, slit his own throat on the 12th of that month and escaped his misery. He was but fifty-three years old. Recognizing him in death as it had failed to do in life, a grateful and remorseful populace paid its tribute to him as his body was laid to rest between those of Pitt and Fox in West-minister Abbey. For a decade he had been Great Britain's only statesman of distinction, and the nation had begun to realize what might have been without him.

The Treaty of Ghent brought peace to two nations which sorely needed it, but, except for its provisions for mixed com-missions, the treaty left unsolved most of the problems which were either causes or results of the war. It took a century of Anglo-American threat, bluster, and negotiation before these contentions were resolved. Some matters were settled with rea-sonable promptness, while other disagreements remained alive into the twentieth century.

The Passamaquoddy Islands were divided in 1817, with Britain getting the larger share but not, to John Quincy Adams's relief, Moose Island. The boundary through Passamaquoddy Bay, however, was not finally agreed upon until 1910. Several of the remaining disputes were put to rest in 1818. An outbreak of naval rearmament on the Great Lakes was stilled by the Rush-Bagot agreement, an accord initiated by Lord Castlereagh and John Quincy Adams, then minister to Great Britain. The agreement not only removed armed naval forces from the lakes but paved the way for eventual disarmament on land. The result, a common unfortified boundary of more than three thousand miles, is an example to the world. And the Rush-Bagot agree-ment was not the only accomplishment of that year. Albert Gal-latin, temporarily detached from his ministry to France, was one of the group of Britons and Americans who, in the Convention of 1818, renewed the commercial convention of 1815, settled on the forty-ninth parallel as the boundary from the Lake of the Woods to the Stony Mountains (the area west of the Rockies was to be jointly occupied for ten years), and affirmed the "liberty" of the Americans to fish and dry their fish along speci-fied Canadian coasts. This last right was not as extensive as it had been, but it was sufficient, and it was accompanied by

British renunciation of their right to navigate the Mississippi. Though the convention considerably eased the fisheries controversy it did not altogether solve it, and the question was not put to rest until arbitrated by the Hague Court in 1910.

Several issues, while partially resolved in earlier years, had to await the 1840's for further determination. It was the Webster-Ashburton Treaty of 1842 (Lord Ashburton was none other than Alexander Baring, English banker and friend of Gallatin) which finally closed the disputed eastern extreme of the United States-Canadian boundary. Employing a ruse based on some maps of doubtful origin, Webster induced Maine to reduce its claims and with Ashburton drew up a compromise line that gave the United States more than half of the disputed territory but less than the country probably had right to. The treaty also filled in some blanks in the lakes boundary, which had not been agreed upon in 1818 or 1822, but it failed to tackle the unbounded and jointly occupied area west of the Rockies. After threat of war ("Fifty-four forty or fight"), the western boundary was extended along the forty-ninth parallel to the Pacific in 1846.

The maritime questions that had been paramount in causing the War of 1812 were never satisfactorily adjusted by negotiation. Although the United States attempted several times to discuss the matter, the British clung stubbornly to the principle of impressment, but the practice itself ceased to exist, and not another American was forcibly placed aboard a British ship. This pleasant fact and subsequent agreements on related questions reduced the principle to a fiction. Other disputes over neutral maritime rights remained in all their complexity, but since World War I they have no longer disrupted Anglo-American relations. In any case, in an age when any war may bring total devastation, when radioactivity cannot distinguish between neutral and belligerent, the subject of neutral rights, maritime or otherwise, seems academic.

Both the war and the treaty that ended it meant far more to the Americans than to the British. To many Americans the war had been part two of a continuing struggle to establish their independence. To the British it was a relatively minor affair that had on occasion hampered their efforts to subdue Napoleon and bring about stable conditions on the Continent. Except for the hatred which the war had increased and for the necessity of attending to the problems which the treaty had not solved, the British soon virtually forgot the whole affair.

Even in the United States, future generations, ignorant of the lost causes of 1812, would only vaguely recall the treaty as something of a victory. The unpleasant details of the war were for the most part forgotten. The escapades of the tiny United States navy and American privateers were recollected with great exaggeration. Their deeds, to be sure, had been glorious but of minor consequence in the war, with the sweet victories usually followed by defeat and capture. Nearly every American has learned at school that a dying Captain Lawrence admonished his crew: "Don't give up the ship!" and ordered them to "blow her up!" These are rousing, courageous, and therefore well-remembered words. Not so pleasant or well-remembered is the fact that the crew of the *Chesapeake* failed to carry out either command. War is hell except in its retelling.

Also long commemorated was Jackson's postwar victory at New Orleans, a fortunate accomplishment but one that did not influence the war itself and provided limited and probably unnecessary insurance for the peace. Strangely neglected, however, has been the war's most decisive battle at Plattsburgh. If it can be said that the Americans won the war by force of arms, it was on that Sunday morning, September 11, 1814, when Macdonough accepted Lieutenant Pring's surrender and Sir George Prevost gave up his halfhearted efforts on land. Of course, the Americans, though they helped to save themselves from destruction, did not really *win* the war; the British withdrew from it.

And the British withdrew partly because of Plattsburgh but more because of troubled affairs in London, Paris, and Vienna; but none of these pressures would have found them still negotiating in the autumn of 1814 had it not been for the courage and tenacity of five Americans. It was in London, Paris, Vienna, and Ghent that the War of 1812 was finally resolved. Occurrences elsewhere were influential but not decisive.

The Treaty of Ghent, though it failed to fulfill the objectives of either side, was no small accomplishment. Besides ending a largely useless and miserable war, it established the machinery that—despite nearly a century of bitterness—has allowed for the maintenance of peace between the two nations. In 1814 the treaty was hardly more than a document of truce, but it grew in importance as its potential for peaceful negotiation was realized. Both sides may be granted credit for this, but it was the American project of November 10, 1814, more than anything else, that set the stage for the peace that was signed on Christmas Eve. Both countries eventually benefited from the exceptional caliber of the American commissioners. The Treaty of Ghent was their monument. A little known but most durable monument it has been.

A TREATY OF PEACE AND AMITY
between
HIS BRITANNIC MAJESTY
and the
UNITED STATES OF AMERICA
*signed at Ghent, December 24, 1814**

His Britannic Majesty and the United States of America, desirous of terminating the War which has unhappily subsisted between the two countries, and of restoring, upon principles of perfect reciprocity, peace, friendship, and good understanding between them, have for that purpose appointed their respective Plenipotentiaries, that is to say, His Britannic Majesty on His part has appointed the Right Honourable James Lord Gambier, late Admiral of the White, now Admiral of the Red Squadron of His Majesty's Fleet; Henry Goulburn, Esq. a Member of the Imperial Parliament, and Under Secretary of State; and William Adams, Esq. Doctor of Civil Laws—And the President of the United States, by and with the advice and consent of the Senate thereof, has appointed John Quincy Adams, James A. Bayard, Henry Clay, Jonathan Russell, and Albert Gallatin, Citizens of the United States; who after a reciprocal communication of their respective full powers, have agreed upon the following Articles:—

ARTICLE I

There shall be a firm and universal Peace between His Britannic Majesty and the United States, and between their respective countries, territories, cities, towns and people, of every degree, without exception of places or persons. All hostilities both by sea and land shall cease, as soon as this Treaty shall have been ratified by both parties as hereinafter mentioned. All territory, places, and possessions whatsoever, taken by either party from the other during the war, or which may be taken after the sign-

* Version printed in London, New York Public Library.

ing of this Treaty, excepting only the islands hereinafter mentioned, shall be restored without delay, and without causing any
destruction, or carrying away any of the artillery, or other public
property, originally captured in the said forts or places, and
which shall remain therein upon the exchange of the Ratifications of this Treaty, or any slaves or other private property. And
all archives, records, deeds, and papers, either of a public
nature, or belonging to private persons, which in the course of
the war may have fallen into the hands of the officers of either
party, shall be, as far as may be practicable, forthwith restored,
and delivered to the proper authorities and persons to whom
they respectively belong.

Such of the Islands in the Bay of Passamaquoddy as are
claimed by both parties, shall remain in the possession of the
party in whose occupation they may be at the time of the
exchange of the ratifications of this Treaty, until the decision
respecting the title to the said Islands shall have been made, in
conformity with the Fourth Article of this Treaty.

No disposition made by this Treaty, as to such possession of
the islands and territories claimed by both parties, shall in any
manner whatever be construed to affect the right of either.

ARTICLE II

Immediately after the ratifications of this Treaty by both
parties as herein after-mentioned, orders shall be sent to the
armies, squadrons, officers, subjects and citizens of the two
powers, to cease from all hostilities. And to prevent all causes
of complaint, which might arise on account of the prizes which
may be taken at sea after the said ratifications of this Treaty, it
is reciprocally agreed, that all vessels and effects which may be
taken after the space of twelve days from the said ratifications
upon all parts of the coast of North America, from the latitude
of 23 degrees north, to the latitude of 50 degrees north, and as
far eastward in the Atlantic Ocean, as the 36th degree of west
longitude from the meridian of Greenwich, shall be restored on
each side; that the time shall be thirty days in all other parts
of the Atlantic Ocean north of the equinoctial line or equator,
and the same time for the British and Irish Channels, for the
Gulf of Mexico, and all parts of the West Indies; forty days for
the North Seas, for the Baltic, and for all parts of the Mediter-

ranean; sixty days for the Atlantic Ocean, south of the equator, as far as the latitude of the Cape of Good Hope; ninety days for every other part of the world south of the equator, and one hundred and twenty days for all other parts of the world without exception.

ARTICLE III

All prisoners of war taken on either side as well by land as by sea, shall be restored as soon as practicable after the ratifications of this Treaty as herein after-mentioned, on their paying the debts which they may have contracted during their captivity. The two contracting parties respectively engage to discharge in specie the advances which may have been made by the other for the sustenance and maintenance of such prisoners.

ARTICLE IV

Whereas it was stipulated by the 2d Article in the Treaty of Peace of 1783, between His Britannic Majesty and the United States of America, that the boundary of the United States should comprehend "all Islands within twenty leagues of any part of the shores of the United States, and lying between lines to be drawn due east from the points where the aforesaid boundaries, between Nova Scotia on the one part, and East Florida on the other, shall respectively touch the Bay of Fundy and the Atlantic Ocean, excepting such Islands as now are, or heretofore have been within the limits of Nova Scotia;" And whereas the several Islands in the Bay of Passamaquoddy, which is part of the Bay of Fundy, and the Island of Grand Menan, in the said Bay of Fundy, are claimed by the United States, as being comprehended within their aforesaid boundaries, which said Islands are claimed as belonging to His Britannic Majesty, as having been at the time of, and previous to the aforesaid Treaty of 1783, within the limits of the province of Nova Scotia; in order, therefore, finally, to decide upon these claims, it is agreed that they shall be referred to two Commissioners, to be appointed in the following manner, viz.:—One Commissioner shall be appointed by His Britannic Majesty, and one by the President of the United States, by and with the advice and consent of the Senate thereof; and the said two Commissioners so appointed, shall be sworn impartially to examine and decide upon the said claims, according to such evidence as shall be laid before them on the part of His Britannic Majesty and of the United States respectively. The said Commissioners shall meet at St. Andrews, in the Province of New Brunswic, and shall have power to adjourn to such other place or places as they shall think fit. The said Commissioners shall by a declaration or report under their hands and seals, decide to which of the two Contracting Parties the several Islands aforesaid do respectively belong, in conformity with the true intent of the said Treaty of Peace of 1783: and if the said Commissioners shall agree in their decision, both parties shall consider such decision as final and conclusive.

It is further agreed, that in the event of the two Commissioners differing upon all or any of the matters so referred to them, or in the event of both or either of the said Commissioners refusing or declining, or wilfully omitting to act as such, they shall make jointly or separately, report or reports, as well to the Government of His Britannic Majesty, as to that of the United States, stating in detail the points on which they differ, and the grounds upon which their respective opinions have been formed, or the grounds upon which they, or either of them, have so refused, declined, or omitted to act. And His Britannic Majesty and the Government of the United States hereby agree to refer the report or reports of the said Commissioners to some friendly sovereign or state, to be then named for that purpose, and who shall be requested to decide on the differences which may be stated in the said report or reports, or upon the report of one commissioner, together with the grounds upon which the other Commissioner shall have refused, declined or omitted to act, as the case may be. And if the Commissioner so refusing, declining or omitting to act, shall also wilfully omit to state the grounds upon which he has so done, in such manner that the said statement may be referred to such friendly sovereign or state, together with the report of such other Commissioner, then such sovereign or state shall decide, ex parte, upon the said report alone, and His Britannic Majesty, and the Government of the United States engage to consider the decision of such friendly sovereign or state, to be final and conclusive on all the matters so referred.

ARTICLE V

Whereas neither that point of the Highlands lying due north from the source of the river St. Croix, designated in the former Treaty of Peace between the two powers as the north-west angle of Nova Scotia, nor the north-westernmost head of Connecticut River have yet been ascertained; and whereas that part of the boundary line between the dominions of the two powers, which extends from the source of the river St. Croix, directly north to the above mentioned north-west angle of Nova Scotia, thence along the said Highlands which divide those rivers, that empty themselves into the river St. Lawrence, from those which fall into the Atlantic Ocean to the north-westernmost head of Connecticut river, thence down along the middle of that river to the 45th degree of north latitude, thence by a line due west on said latitude until it strikes the river Iroquois or Cataraguy, has not yet been surveyed, it is agreed that for these several purposes, two Commissioners shall be appointed, sworn and authorized, to act exactly in the manner directed with respect to those mentioned in the next preceeding article, unless otherwise specified in the present article. The said Commissioners shall meet at St. Andrews, in the province of New Brunswic, and shall have power to adjourn to such other place or places as they shall think fit. The said commissioners shall have power to ascertain and determine the points above mentioned, in conformity with the provisions of the said Treaty of Peace of 1783; and shall cause the boundary aforesaid, from the source of the river St. Croix to the river Iroquois or Cataraguy to be surveyed and marked according to the said provisions; the said commissioners shall make a map of the said boundary, and annex to it a declaration under their hands and seals, certifying it to be the true map of the said boundary, and particularizing the latitude and longitude of the north-west angle of Nova Scotia, of the north-westernmost head of Connecticut river, and of such other points of the said boundary as they may deem proper. And both parties agree to consider such map and declaration as finally and conclusively fixing the said boundary. And in the event of the said two commissioners differing, or both, or either of them, refusing, declining or wilfully omitting to act, such reports, declarations or statements shall be made by them or either of them, and such reference to a friendly sovereign or state shall be made in all respects, as in the latter part of the fourth article is contained, and in as full a manner as if the same was herein repeated.

ARTICLE VI

Whereas by the former Treaty of Peace, that portion of the boundary of the United States from the point where the 45th degree of north latitude strikes the river Iroquois or Cataraguy, to the Lake Superior, was declared to be "along the middle of said river into Lake Ontario, through the middle of said Lake, until it strikes the communication by water between that Lake and Lake Erie, thence along the middle of said communication into Lake Erie, through the middle of said Lake, until it arrives at the water communication into the Lake Huron, thence through the middle of said Lake to the water communication between that Lake and Lake Superior;" And whereas doubts have arisen what was the middle of the said River, Lakes, and Water Communications, and whether certain Islands lying in the same were within the dominions of His Britannic Majesty or of the United States. In order therefore, finally to decide these doubts, they shall be referred to two Commissioners, to be appointed, sworn, and authorised, to act exactly in the manner directed with respect to those mentioned in the next preceding article, unless otherwise specified in this present article. The said Commissioners shall meet in the first instance, at Albany, in the state of New York, and shall have power to adjourn to such other place or places as they shall think fit. The said Commissioners shall, by a report or declaration, under their hands and seals, designate the boundary through the said river, lakes, and water communications, and decide to which of the two Contracting Parties the several Islands lying within the said rivers, lakes, and water communications, do respectively belong, in conformity with the true intent of the said Treaty of 1783. And both parties agree to consider such designation and decision as final and conclusive. And in the event of the said two Commissioners differing, or both or either of them refusing, declining, or wilfully omitting to act, such reports, declarations, or statements, shall be made by them, or either of them, and such reference to a friendly sovereign or state shall be made, in all respects, as in the latter part of the fourth article is contained, and in as full a manner as if the same was herein repeated.

ARTICLE VII

It is further agreed, that the said two last mentioned Commissioners, after they shall have executed the duties assigned to them in the preceding article, shall be, and they are hereby authorised upon their oaths, impartially to fix and determine, according to the true intent of the said Treaty of Peace of 1783, that part of the boundary between the dominions of the two Powers, which extends from the water communication between Lake Huron and Lake Superior, to the most north western point of the Lake of the Woods; to decide to which of the two Parties the several Islands lying in the lakes, water communications and rivers forming the said boundary, do respectively belong, in conformity with the true intent of the said Treaty of Peace of 1783, and to cause such parts of the said boundary as require it, to be surveyed and marked. The said commissioners shall by a report or declaration, under their hands and seals, designate the boundary aforesaid, state their decision on the points thus referred to them, and particularize the latitude and longitude of the most north-western point of the lake, of the woods, [sic] and of such other parts of the said boundary as they may deem proper. And both parties agree to consider such designation and decision as final and conclusive. And in the event of the said two Commissioners differing or both, or either of them, refusing, declining, or wilfully omitting to act, such reports, declarations, or statements, shall be made by them, or either of them, and such reference to a friendly sovereign or state shall be made in all respects as in the latter part of the fourth article is contained, and in as full a manner as if the same was herein repeated.

ARTICLE VIII

The several boards of two Commissioners mentioned in the four preceding articles shall respectively have power to appoint a secretary, and to employ such surveyors or other persons as they shall judge necessary. Duplicates of all their respective reports, declarations, statements, and decisions, and of their accounts, and of the journal of their proceedings, shall be delivered by them to the agents of His Britannic Majesty, and to the agents of the United States who may be respectively appointed and authorized to manage the business on behalf of their respective governments. The said Commissioners shall be respectively paid in such manner as shall be agreed between the two contracting parties, such agreement being to be settled at the time of the exchange of the ratifications of this Treaty. And all other expences attending the said commissions shall be defrayed equally by the two parties. And in the case of death, sickness, resignation, or necessary absence, the place of every such Commissioner respectively shall be supplied in the same manner as such Commissioner was first appointed, and the new Commissioner shall take the same oath or affirmation, and do the same duties.

It is further agreed between the two contracting parties, that in case any of the islands mentioned in any of the preceding articles which were in the possession of one of the parties prior to the commencement of the present war between the two countries, should, by the decision of any of the boards of Commissioners aforesaid, or of the sovereign or state so referred to as in the four next preceding articles contained, fall within the dominions of the other party, all grants of land made previous to the commencement of the war by the party having had such possession, shall be as valid as if such island or islands, had by such decision or decisions, been adjudged to be within the dominions of the party having had such possession.

ARTICLE IX

The United States of America engage to put an end, immediately after the ratification of the present Treaty, to hostilities with all the tribes or nations of Indians with whom they may be at war at the time of such ratification, and forthwith to restore to such tribes or nations respectively, all the possessions, rights and privileges which they may have enjoyed, or been entitled to in 1811, previous to such hostilities. Provided always, that such tribes or nations shall agree to desist from all hostilities against the United States of America, their citizens and subjects, upon the ratification of the present Treaty being notified to such tribes or nations, and shall so desist accordingly.

And His Britannic Majesty engages on His part, to put an

end immediately after the ratification of the present Treaty, to hostilities with all the tribes or nations of Indians with whom he may be at war at the time of such ratification, and forthwith to restore to such tribes or nations respectively, all the possessions, rights, and privileges, which they may have enjoyed or been entitled to in 1811, previous to such hostilities. Provided always, that such tribes or nations shall agree to desist from all hostilities against His Britannic Majesty and his subjects, upon the ratification of the present Treaty being notified to such tribes or nations, and shall so desist accordingly.

ARTICLE X

Whereas the traffic in slaves is irreconcilable with the principles of humanity and justice, and whereas both His Majesty and the United States are desirous of continuing their efforts to promote its entire abolition, it is hereby agreed that both the contracting parties shall use their best endeavours to accomplish so desirable an object.

ARTICLE XI

This Treaty, when the same shall have been ratified on both sides without alteration by either of the Contracting Parties, and the ratifications mutually exchanged, shall be binding on both parties, and the ratifications shall be exchanged at Washington, in the space of four months from this day, or sooner if practicable.

In faith whereof, we the respective Plenipotentiaries have signed this Treaty, and have thereunto affixed our seals.

Done in triplicate at Ghent, the twenty-fourth day of December, one thousand eight hundred and fourteen.

(L. S.) GAMBIER.
(L. S.) H. GOULBURN.
(L. S.) WM. ADAMS.
(L. S.) JOHN QUINCEY ADAMS.
(L. S.) J. A. BAYARD.
(L. S.) H. CLAY.
(L. S.) JON. RUSSELL.
(L. S.) ALBERT GALLATIN.

A GENERAL NOTE ON SOURCES

Some sources are of vital importance throughout the book and were used extensively in the writing of nearly every chapter. Consequently, they are described below and are not repeated under specific part and chapter headings.

The Gallatin Papers, New-York Historical Society, contain a wealth of seldom-used information, including letters to and from Albert Gallatin's wife, Hannah. The collection also contains his notebooks on the Russian mediation and the Ghent negotiation.

The Jonathan Russell Papers, the John Hay Library, Brown University, provide rich and colorful accounts of the American commission's internal doings—in addition to Russell's official and unofficial letters to Secretary of State Monroe. There are also a number of letters to and from Reuben Beasley and William Harris Crawford, among others.

In the National Archives are the State Department Records of Negotiations Connected with the Treaty of Ghent. Although the records are not catalogued, microfilm copies of them have placed in my possession most of the official documents of the Russian mediation and the Ghent negotiation. Both original and duplicate copies of the documents are contained in these records.

The British counterpart to the State Department Records is to be found in the Public Record Office, London, Foreign Office 5, vols. 88, 101, and 102. The Library of Congress allowed me to use their photostatic copies of these catalogued documents. Much that is in the State Department Records is herein duplicated, but there are also many unduplicated private and unofficial letters in this very valuable source.

John Quincy Adams's *Memoirs*, vols. 2 and 3, edited by Charles Francis Adams, and his *Writings*, vols. 4 and 5, edited by Worthington C. Ford, have been mainstays in the writing of this book. Adams kept up a voluminous correspondence, and his diary, besides being invaluable to me, is a fascinating, nearly day-by-day account of almost everything and everybody its author encountered. An examination of microfilm copies of the Adams Papers, Massachusetts Historical Society, satisfied me that nothing pertinent to this period was omitted from the published *Memoirs* and *Writings*.

Although the letters in Albert Gallatin's *Writings*, 3 vols., edited by Henry Adams, are taken largely from the Gallatin Papers, there are some items from other sources which were not so readily available to me. Also, it was a definite help to have many Gallatin papers in one place and in chronological order.

The "Papers of James A. Bayard, 1796–1815," edited by Elizabeth Donnan, in the *American Historical Association Annual Report*, 1913, contain that gentleman's diary and much of his correspondence. These documents provide interesting and unique views of the Russian sojourn and are a source for otherwise unpublished segments of Monroe's instructions.

The Papers of Henry Clay, vol. 1, edited by James F. Hopkins, was published just before the actual writing of *The Peace of Christmas Eve* was begun. The volume has filled a considerable void, for there is scant record of Clay's activities or correspondence elsewhere. The letters Clay sent and received serve as a balance to the accounts of the negotiation contained in the letters and diaries of Adams and Bayard.

For the most part, *American State Papers: Foreign Relations*, vols. 3–5, reproduces the documents found in the State Department Records and those of the Public Record Office. The documents are those which Madison and Monroe submitted to Congress.

A principal source of British documents, covering the entire span of the War of 1812, is the *Supplementary Despatches, Correspondence, and Memoranda*, vol. 9, of the Duke of Wellington. This is, in fact, a fairly complete collection of the correspondence of the British cabinet. The scope of the volume goes far beyond the immediate concerns of the Duke himself. It is in some degree a documentary history of the times.

Still the clearest, most skillfully written history of the administrations of Jefferson and Madison and of the war is Henry Adams's *History of the United States of America During the Administration of Thomas Jefferson and James Madison*. Adams allows history to live, an uncommon virtue, and his sometimes partisan leanings do not obliterate scholarly research. No twentieth-century account of the times approaches Adams's history.

The only book on the war's negotiations to precede mine is *The Diplomacy of the War of 1812* by F. A. Updyke. Though it suffers in readability from being little more than Professor Updyke's lectures in written form, it is exhaustive and generally accurate. Published in 1915, however, it was written before some important manuscript sources were made readily available.

Lastly, I have drawn heavily upon my condensed version of the Ghent negotiation, "The Peace of Christmas Eve," which appeared in *American Heritage*, December, 1960.

Part I

In addition to the principal sources of this book, those that play a key role in the first part are the Bayard Letter Book, U.S. Mission to Russia, and the James Monroe Papers. Both are manuscript collections in the possession of the New York Public Library. Other sources are:

Chapter One:

Bemis, *A Diplomatic History of the United States* and *John Quincy Adams and the Foundations of American Foreign Policy;* Bailey, *A Diplomatic History of the American People;* Mahan, *Sea Power in Its Relations to the War of 1812;* Walters, *Albert Gallatin;* and *The Federalist.*

Chapter Two:

Bemis, *John Quincy Adams.*

Chapter Three:

Webster, *British Diplomacy, 1813–1815, Select Documents* and *The Congress of Vienna, 1814–1815;* Bryant, *The Age of Elegance, 1812–1822;* Ludwig, *Napoleon;* Monroe, *Writings; Report on the Manuscripts of Earl Bathurst;* and King George IV, *Letters 1812–1830.*

Part II

Supplementing the major sources in this part of the book are the Sylvanus Bourne Papers, Library of Congress, and, again, the New York Public Library's Monroe Papers. Additional sources are:

Chapter Four:

Monroe, *Writings;* Madison, *Letters and Other Writings;* Manning, *Diplomatic Correspondence of the United States: Canadian Relations, 1784–1860;* and King, *Life and Correspondence.*

Chapter Five:

Webster, *The Congress of Vienna, 1814–1815;* Clay, *Works;* "Letters of James A. Bayard, 1802–1814," *Delaware Historical Society Papers,* 1901; and Bryant, *The Age of Elegance.*

Chapter Six:

Webster, *The Foreign Policy of Castlereagh, 1812–1815;* and Bryant, *The Age of Elegance.*

Chapter Seven:

"Negotiations at Ghent, 1812–1814," *American Historical Review,* 1914; Castlereagh, *Memoirs and Correspondence;* John Quincy Adams, "Letter from Ghent, 1814," *American Historical Review,* 1910; Webster, *The Foreign Policy of Castlereagh; The*

Dispatches of Field Marshal the Duke of Wellington; "Letters of James A. Bayard, 1802–1814"; Atcheson, "A Compressed View of the Points to Be Discussed in Treating with the United States of America," *The Pamphleteer,* 1814; and "Select British Documents of the Canadian War of 1812," a rich storehouse of letters and testimony, edited by William Wood, and one of *The Publications of the Champlain Society.*

Part III

Of inestimable importance to the writing of the last half of this book was a microfilm copy of the 1814 portion of the Henry Goulburn Papers, William L. Clements Library, University of Michigan. To the best of my knowledge, this is the first time this source has been used to shed light on the Ghent negotiations. Goulburn's private correspondence with Bathurst, Liverpool, and Castlereagh fully reveals the internal problems and decisions of the British government in the latter half of 1814.

Another much-used source in this third part of the book is Castlereagh's *Memoirs and Correspondence,* vols. 9–12, edited by Charles Vane. Also consulted were:

Chapter Eight:

Monroe, *Writings; Message from the President of the United States, Transmitting Communications from the Plenipotentiaries of the United States, Charged with Negotiating Peace with Great Britain;* Manning, *Diplomatic Correspondence of the United States;* and "Negotiations at Ghent, 1812–1814."

Chapter Nine:

Message from the President of the United States; and the William H. Crawford Papers, Library of Congress.

Chapter Ten:

The more important sources: Rees, *Battle of Bladensburg;* Gleig, *A Narrative of the Campaigns of the British Army at Washington, Baltimore, and New Orleans;* Mahan, *Sea Power in Its Relations to the War of 1812;* James Monroe Papers; Booth, "The Capture of Washington in 1814"; and Monroe, *Writings.* In addition: Madison, *Letters and Other Writings; American State Papers: Class V, Military Affairs;* King, *Life and Correspondence; Incidents in the Life of Jacob Barker;* and Smith, *The First Forty Years of Washington Society.*

Chapter Eleven:

Manning, *Diplomatic Correspondence of the United States;* Yonge, *The Life and Administration of Robert Banks, Second*

Earl of Liverpool; and *Report on the Manuscripts of Earl Bath-urst.*

Chapter Twelve:
Report on the Manuscripts of Earl Bathurst; Manning, *Diplomatic Correspondence of the United States; The Dispatches of . . . the Duke of Wellington;* and "Negotiations at Ghent, 1812–1814."

Part IV

In addition to the principal sources, those most frequently consulted for this part were the Henry Goulburn Papers, Castlereagh's *Memoirs and Correspondence,* and the *Report on the Manuscripts of Earl Bathurst.* The other sources are:

Chapter Thirteen:
Major: "Select British Documents of the Canadian War of 1812"; Lossing, *Pictorial Field Book of the War of 1812;* Folsom, "The Battle of Plattsburg"; *American State Papers: Class VI, Naval Affairs;* Skinner, *The Battle of Plattsburgh.*
Minor: James Monroe Papers; Robinson, "The Expedition to Plattsburg," *The Journal of the Royal United Service Institution,* 1916; Izard, *Official Correspondence with the Department of War;* King, *Life and Correspondence;* and Walcutt, "Anecdotes of the Battle of Plattsburg."

Chapter Fourteen:
Yonge, *The Life and Administration of Robert Banks.*

Chapter Fifteen:
"John Quincy Adams and Others on the Peace of Ghent, 1814," edited by S. E. Morison, *Old South Leaflets,* 1917; "Letters of James A. Bayard, 1802–1814"; and "Negotiations at Ghent, 1812–1814."

Chapter Sixteen:
Manning, *Diplomatic Correspondence of the United States;* Webster, *The Foreign Policy of Castlereagh* and *The Congress of Vienna, 1814–1815;* Bryant, *The Age of Elegance;* Yonge, *The Life and Administration of Robert Banks;* King George IV, *Letters 1812–1830;* Nicholson, *The Congress of Vienna;* and "Negotiations at Ghent, 1812–1814."

Chapter Seventeen:
"Letters of Jonathan Russell, 1815," *Massachusetts Historical Society Proceedings,* 1911; *The Dispatches of . . . the Duke of Wellington;* and Clay, *Works.*

Chapter Eighteen:
"Negotiations at Ghent, 1812–1814"; "Letters of Jonathan Russell, 1815"; "Letters of James A. Bayard, 1802–1814"; "The

Treaty of Ghent and Negotiations that Followed," edited by S. E.
Morison, *Old South Leaflets*, 1917; and *The Dispatches of . . .
the Duke of Wellington.*

Epilogue:

Bemis, *A Diplomatic History of the United States* and *John
Quincy Adams;* Bailey, *A Diplomatic History of the American
People;* John Quincy Adams, *The Duplicate Letters, the Fisheries
and the Mississippi;* "Letters of Jonathan Russell, 1815"; "Letters
of Jonathan Russell," *Massachusetts Historical Society Proceedings,* 1920; "Negotiations at Ghent, 1812–1814"; *State Papers
on the Negotiation and Peace with America.*

Also: Walters, *Albert Gallatin;* Yonge, *The Life and Administration of Robert Banks;* Dangerfield, *The Era of Good Feelings;*
Schlesinger, *The Age of Jackson;* Lossing, *Pictorial Field Book of
the War of 1812.*

And: *Dictionary of American Biography; Dictionary of National
Biography; Appleton's Cyclopaedia of American Biography; Biographical Dictionary; National Cyclopaedia of American Biography.*

BIBLIOGRAPHY

Manuscript Collections

Adams Papers. Massachusetts Historical Society.
Bayard Letter Book. U.S. Mission to Russia: Official Papers of Albert Gallatin, John Quincy Adams and James A. Bayard, 1813. New York Public Library.
Sylvanus Bourne Papers. Library of Congress.
William H. Crawford Papers. Library of Congress.
Gallatin Papers. New-York Historical Society.
Henry Goulburn Papers. William L. Clements Library, University of Michigan.
James Madison Papers. New York Public Library.
James Monroe Papers. New York Public Library.
Public Record Office, London. Foreign Office 5, vols. 88, 101, 102. Library of Congress.
Jonathan Russell Papers. John Hay Library, Brown University.
State Department Records of Negotiations Connected with the Treaty of Ghent. Dispatches from the American Commissioners, August 29, 1813–July 3, 1815. National Archives.

Published Documentary Material

Adams, John. *Works*, vols. 1–3, 10. Ed. Charles Francis Adams. Boston, 1856.
Adams, John Quincy. *The Duplicate Letters, the Fisheries and the Mississippi*. Washington, 1822.
——— "Letter from Ghent, 1814." *American Historical Review*, vol. 15. New York, 1910.
——— *Memoirs*, vols. 2, 3. Ed. Charles Francis Adams. Philadelphia, 1874–1877.
——— *Writings*, vols. 4, 5. Ed. Worthington C. Ford. New York, 1915.
Alexander I, Czar of Russia (Alexander Pavlovich). *Scenes of Russian Court Life: Correspondence of Alexander I with His Sister Catharine*. Trans. Henry Havelock. London, 1915.
American State Papers: Class I, Foreign Relations, vols. 3–5. Washington, 1832–1859.
American State Papers: Class V, Military Affairs, vol. 1. Washington, 1832.

American State Papers: Class VI, Naval Affairs, vol. 1. Washington, 1834.

Atcheson, Nathaniel. "A Compressed View of the Points to Be Discussed in Treating with the United States of America." *The Pamphleteer.* London, 1814.

Barclay, Thomas. *Selections from the Correspondence of Thomas Barclay.* Ed. George L. Rives. New York, 1894.

Barker, Jacob. *Incidents in the Life of Jacob Barker.* Washington, 1855.

Bathurst, Henry, 3rd Earl of. *Report on the Manuscripts of Earl Bathurst.* Historical Manuscripts Commission, Great Britain. London, 1923.

Bayard, James A. "Letters of James A. Bayard, 1802–1814." *Delaware Historical Society Papers,* vol. 31. Wilmington, 1901.

——— "Papers of James A. Bayard, 1796–1815." Ed. Elizabeth Donnan. *American Historical Association Annual Report,* 1913, vol. 2. Washington, 1915.

Booth, Mordecai. "The Capture of Washington in 1814: Letter and Communication to Commodore Thomas Tingey from Mordecai Booth, His Clerk." Ed. Ray W. Irwin. *Americana,* vol. 28. January, 1934.

Castlereagh, Viscount (Robert Stewart). *Memoirs and Correspondence,* vols. 9–12. Ed. Charles Vane. London, 1848–1853.

Clay, Henry. *Papers,* vol. 1. Ed. James F. Hopkins. Lexington, Kentucky, 1959.

——— *Works,* vols. 1–5. Ed. Calvin Colton. New York, 1896.

The Federalist.

Ford, Worthington C. "The British Ghent Commission." *Massachusetts Historical Society Proceedings,* vol. 48. Boston, 1914.

Gallatin, Albert. *Writings,* 3 vols. Ed. Henry Adams. Philadelphia, 1879.

George IV, King of Great Britain. *Letters 1812–1830,* vol. 1. Ed. A. Aspinall. Cambridge, 1938.

Gleig, George Robert. *A Narrative of the Campaigns of the British Army at Washington, Baltimore, and New Orleans.* Philadelphia, 1821.

Horseshoe Bend National Military Park Papers. (Typewritten transcript of photostats of British documents.) Ed. Thomas W. Martin.

Izard, Major General George. *Official Correspondence with the Department of War.* Philadelphia, 1816.

"John Quincy Adams and Others on the Peace of Ghent, 1814." Ed. Samuel E. Morison. *Old South Leaflets,* no. 211. Boston, 1917.

King, Rufus. *Life and Correspondence,* vol. 5. Ed. Charles R. King. New York, 1898.

A List of Pensioners of the War of 1812. Ed. Byron N. Clark. Burlington, Vermont, 1904.

Macdonough, Thomas. *Autobiography.* Ed. Rodney Macdonough. Boston, 1909.

Madison, James. *Letters and Other Writings,* vol. 2. Ed. William Cabell Rives. Philadelphia, 1865.

Manning, William R. *Diplomatic Correspondence of the United States: Canadian Relations, 1784–1860,* vol. 1. Washington, 1940.

Melish, John. *Documents Relating to the Negotiations for Peace Between the United States and Great Britain.* Philadelphia, 1814.

Message from the President of the United States, Transmitting Communications from the Plenipotentiaries of the United States, Charged with Negotiating Peace with Great Britain. Washington, October 10, 1814.

Monroe, James. *Writings,* vol. 5. Ed. Stanislaus Murray Hamilton. New York, 1901.

A Narrative of the Battle of Bladensburg. (By an officer of General Smith's staff.) Baltimore, 1814.

"Negotiations at Ghent, 1812–1814." *American Historical Review,* vol. 20. New York, 1914.

Robinson, Major-General G. W. "The Expedition to Plattsburg, Upon Lake Champlain, Canada, 1814." *The Journal of the Royal United Service Institution,* vol. 61, August, 1916.

Russell, Jonathan. "Letters of Jonathan Russell." *Massachusetts Historical Society Proceedings,* vol. 54. Boston, 1920.

———— "Letters of Jonathan Russell, 1815." *Massachusetts Historical Society Proceedings,* vol. 44. Boston, 1911.

"Select British Documents of the Canadian War of 1812." Ed. William Wood. *The Publications of the Champlain Society,* vols. 1–3. Toronto, 1926.

Skinner, St. John. *The Battle of Plattsburgh.* Plattsburgh, New York, 1835.

Smith, Margaret Bayard. *The First Forty Years of Washington Society.* Ed. Gaillard Hunt. New York, 1906.

State Papers on the Negotiation and Peace with America. London, 1815.

"The Treaty of Ghent and Negotiations that Followed." Ed. Samuel E. Morison. *Old South Leaflets,* no. 212. Boston, 1917.

Webster, C. K. *British Diplomacy, 1813–1815, Select Documents.* London, 1921.

Wellington, Arthur Wellesley, 1st Duke of. *The Dispatches of*

Field Marshal the Duke of Wellington, vols. 11, 12. Ed. Lt. Col. Gurwood. London, 1838.

—— *Supplementary Despatches, Correspondence, and Memoranda,* vol. 9. Ed. Arthur R. Wellesley, 2nd Duke of Wellington. London, 1858–1872.

General Works

Adams, Henry. *History of the United States of America During the Administration of Thomas Jefferson and James Madison,* 9 vols. New York, 1930.

—— *Life of Albert Gallatin.* Philadelphia, 1879.

Anthony, Katharine. *Dolly Madison: Her Life and Times.* New York, 1949.

Appleton's Cyclopaedia of American Biography. New York, 1898.

Bailey, Thomas A. *A Diplomatic History of the American People,* 4th ed. New York, 1950.

The Battle of Plattsburg: What Historians Say About It. New York State Plattsburg Centenary Commission. Albany, 1914.

Bemis, Samuel Flagg. *A Diplomatic History of the United States,* 3rd ed. New York, 1950.

—— *John Quincy Adams and the Foundations of American Foreign Policy.* New York, 1949.

Biographical Dictionary. Ed. Rev. Hugh James Rose. London, 1853.

Bryant, Arthur. *The Age of Elegance, 1812–1822.* New York, 1950.

Burt, A. L. *The United States, Great Britain, and British North America.* New Haven, 1940.

The Centenary of the Battle of Plattsburg. The University of the State of New York. Albany, 1914.

Cullum, General. "Narrative of the Operations Connected with the Capture of Washington in 1814." *American Historical Association Papers,* vol. 2, no. 1. Washington, 1887.

Dangerfield, George. *The Era of Good Feelings.* New York, 1952.

Davis, P. M. "The Four Principal Battles of the Late War." *The Magazine of History,* extra no. 55, 1917.

Dictionary of American Biography. New York, 1932.

The Dictionary of National Biography. London, 1921–1922.

Eaton, Clement. *Henry Clay and the Art of American Politics.* Boston, 1957.

Encyclopedia Americana. New York, 1957.

Encyclopaedia Britannica. New York, 1956.

Engelman, Fred L. "The Peace of Christmas Eve." *American Heritage,* vol. 12, no. 1, December, 1960.

Everest, Allan S. *British Objectives at the Battle of Plattsburgh.* Champlain, New York, 1960.

Folsom, William R. "The Battle of Plattsburg." *Vermont Quarterly,* October, 1952.

Gates, Charles M. "The West in American Diplomacy, 1812–1815." *The Mississippi Valley Historical Review,* vol. 26, March, 1940.

Gribble, Francis. *Emperor and Mystic: The Life of Alexander I of Russia.* New York, 1931.

Hill, Frederick Trevor. "Adventures in American Diplomacy, III, the Treaty of Ghent." *The Atlantic Monthly,* August, 1914.

Ingraham, E. D. *A Sketch of the Events Which Preceded the Capture of Washington, by the British.* Philadelphia, 1849.

Jackes, Lyman B. "Treaty of Ghent." *The Canadian Magazine,* vol. 44, November, 1914.

Lossing, Benson J. *Pictorial Field Book of the War of 1812.* New York, 1868.

Ludwig, Emil. *Napoleon.* New York, 1915.

Macdonough, Rodney. *Life of Commodore Thomas Macdonough.* Boston, 1909.

Mahan, A. T. *Sea Power in Its Relations to the War of 1812,* 2 vols. Boston, 1905.

Mayo, Bernard. *Henry Clay, Spokesman of the New West.* Boston, 1937.

Muller, Charles G. *The Proudest Day.* New York, 1960.

National Cyclopaedia of American Biography. New York, 1947.

Nicholson, Harold. *The Congress of Vienna.* New York, 1946.

Petrie, Sir Charles. *Lord Liverpool and His Times.* London, 1954.

Rees, R. I. *Battle of Bladensburg.* Department of Research, the Infantry School, Camp Benning, Georgia, 1921.

Schlesinger, Arthur M., Jr. *The Age of Jackson.* Boston, 1945.

Stschepkin, Eugen. "Russia Under Alexander I, and the Invasion of 1812." *The Cambridge Modern History,* vol. 9. New York, 1934.

Styron, Arthur. *The Last of the Cocked Hats: James Monroe and the Virginia Dynasty.* Norman, Oklahoma, 1945.

Thornton, Willis. "The Day They Burned the Capitol." *American Heritage,* vol. 6, no. 1, December, 1954.

Tucker, Glenn. *Poltroons and Patriots,* 2 vols. Indianapolis, 1954.

Updyke, F. A. *The Diplomacy of the War of 1812.* Baltimore, 1915.

Van Deusen, G. G. *The Life of Henry Clay.* Boston, 1937.

Walcutt, William. "Anecdotes of the Battle of Plattsburg." *The Republic,* May, 1913.

Walters, Raymond, Jr. *Albert Gallatin.* New York, 1957.

Webster, C. K. *The Congress of Vienna, 1814–1815.* London, 1920.
———— *The Foreign Policy of Castlereagh, 1812–1815.* London, 1934.
Williams, John S. *History of the Invasion and Capture of Washington.* New York, 1857.
Wilson, Thomas. "The Treaty of Ghent." *Magazine of American History,* vol. 20, 1888.
Yonge, Charles Duke. *The Life and Administration of Robert Banks, Second Earl of Liverpool.* London, 1868.

INDEX